A Guide to Norman Sites
in Britain

By the same authors
A GUIDE TO ANGLO-SAXON SITES
ANGLO-SAXON ARCHITECTURE

In preparation
A GUIDE TO MEDIEVAL SITES IN BRITAIN

*Opposite: The rich interlaced decoration of the
Chapter House at Much Wenlock, Shropshire.*

A Guide to Norman Sites
in Britain

Nigel and Mary Kerr

GRANADA
London Toronto Sydney New York

Granada Publishing Limited
8 Grafton Street, London W1X 3LA

Published by Granada Publishing 1984

British Library Cataloguing in Publication Data

Kerr, Nigel
  A guide to Norman sites in Britain.
  1. Normans–Great Britain   2. Great
Britain–Antiquities
  I. Title   II. Kerr, Mary
  914.1'04857   DA195

ISBN 0-246-11976-4
ISBN 0-586-08445-2 (paper covers)

Printed in Great Britain by
R J Acford, Chichester, Sussex

Contents

Introduction

This guide is concerned with the physical remains of the time during which Norman kings sat on the English throne. The period opens with the landing of William, Duke of Normandy, in Pevensey Bay on Thursday 28 September 1066. It closes less neatly with the date of 1200 which marks not the end of the Norman dynasty, for that had already occurred with the death of Stephen in 1154, but the general change in architectural styles from Romanesque to Gothic. Although it deals with an historical period, it is not a 'history book'; it aims to provide basic information and comment about the sites it contains, together with clear directions as to how they can be reached. It is a guide book, and as such is not intended as a comprehensive reference work for a whole subject, but merely to be a source of information and enlightenment for the traveller.

The 156 entries in this book – many of which are grouped entries of related sites, bringing the actual total to well over 200 – are not by any means a complete catalogue of Norman remains in Britain. If such a compendium were ever assembled, it would run to several thousand entries since hundreds of churches contain Norman workmanship in their fabrics; and when castles, monasteries, houses, planned towns and villages and other field monuments are added, the sheer weight of evidence is staggering. In less then 150 years, the Normans did much to change the face of Britain.

Many of these sites would be exceedingly unrewarding to visit, however, and are more the province of the dedicated student who wishes to see every example of a particular class of monument. What is presented here is a personal selection of the very many sites which we have visited. The basis of that selection has been that a site is a good example of a particular type of monument, or that it has strong historical or other associations, or else that it has a fine setting. Many of the sites possess all three attributes. Additionally, a few sites have not been included because although, like Rievaulx and Fountains abbeys in North Yorkshire, they were founded in the Norman period; they retained their function and developed further in the Middle Ages and so will appear in our forthcoming *Guide to Medieval Sites*. We were constantly amazed by the richness and diversity of our Norman heritage, and we hope that you too will find much to delight the eye and stimulate the mind.

Norman Britain

The prevailing view of the Normans suggests a people devoted to warfare, who were adept at building castles, and who ruthlessly sought to extend their territory at the expense of their neighbours. Coupled with these ideas is the vision of Norman society as a warrior aristocracy intent upon keeping the lower orders in check with Draconian laws and dedicated to its own survival at any price. Norman art and architecture have often been characterized as crude and unworthy and the aspirations of most Normans were not generally thought to have risen above greed and conflict.

As with most stereotypes, there is some truth in this one, although it can be argued that it obscures more than it illuminates. Certainly the way in which the Normans took control in England was by a display of military skill, and it is clear that they consolidated their hold by building many castles. Similarly, the Normans were expansionist, as their forays into Sicily and the Holy Land as well as England and Wales indicate. Again, their aristocratic model of government, the feudal system, was exclusive to a degree and every man knew his place in that hierarchy. But the laws which enforced this new structure were no more severe than those which had gone before, and many aspects of Norman lawmaking were an Anglo-Saxon inheritance in any case. Finally, appreciation of the Norman artistic achievement has been blunted by ignorance. It is hoped that this book will assist the reader to obtain a broader and more informed view of the Norman decorative arts if it achieves nothing else!

We cannot merely accept the conclusions of bygone ages; we must look to the Normans with fresh eyes and judge them for ourselves. In the first place, it is clear that William believed that his claim to the English throne was just. Furthermore, he was reinforced in that opinion by no less an authority than the Pope himself, so the conquest of England was in part at least a 'just war'. Similarly, once the Normans had gained overall political control, they had, with relatively small numbers, to establish a governmental system in detail as well. Rebellion, as the troubles with Edric the Wild in the Marches, Harold's mother at Exeter, Hereward the Wake in the Fens and the rebel earls in the north indicate, was never far over the horizon and William took firm and positive action to maintain the rule of law. For the most part, his actions appear to have been decisive and reasonable in view of what was at stake. Where he did overstep the mark, as in the infamous 'Harrying of the North', he was criticized by his contemporaries.

By the twin brilliances of the castle and the mounted knight, the Normans were able to hold down a numerically superior population with a relatively small body of professional soldiers. In the first place a castle enabled a small body of men to deny freedom of movement to a potential enemy over a wide area. In the second, medium cavalry with their superior manoeuvrability and strike power could always retain the advantage over foot soldiers. It was doubtless the effectiveness of these two military innovations which made them so unpopular with the Saxons, and it was also the reason that the castle and the knights were enshrined in the feudal code.

Once the country was secured, estates were divided unequally between the king, who retained the lion's share, the Church, which did pretty well, and the lords and commoners who had followed William to Hastings and who received rewards consonant with their lineage and worth. These men held their lands of the king who still owned the whole land in law, and they went about the job of settling the country. Each established his own 'caput' or headquarters in some convenient place, built a castle there, and arranged his lieutenants about him. Tenants swore fealty to the new lord and in many cases only gradually had to accustom themselves to new ways. For the most part, the Normans attempted to alter little; they were more interested in reward than revolution.

Of course there was change and, if you were an Anglo-Saxon nobleman or churchman, some of it would have been most unwelcome. Scarcely a handful of either of these classes was left in possession of significant estates by the time of Domesday Book in 1086. 'Domesday Book', to which constant reference will be made throughout this book, was a further manifestation of the Normans' desire to restore order out of chaos. It was decreed by the Conqueror at Gloucester during Christmastide 1085 that a great survey of his kingdom should be made both in order to establish every man's title to the land he purported to hold (for disputes were legion) and to assess its worth for taxation. No comparable survey had ever been prepared before and in the scope and detail of Domesday Book we gain a clear insight into the tremendous energy of its instigator. If William wanted to know what was what in his new realm, then his officials had better find out right speedily!

Later Norman kings lacked the personal stature of the Conqueror, although several were very able. William Rufus was detested for his partiality, personal weakness and duplicity. Henry I, called Beauclerc because of his education, acted decisively to hold the country together after the sudden death of his brother in the New Forest. Otherwise he was undramatic, more of a statesman than a soldier, a great law reformer whose life was blighted by the loss of his son and heir William in the White Ship disaster of 1120. Stephen's reign was chaotic since civil war between himself and the Empress Matilda, the rightful heiress, brought great misery on the land – 'men said openly that Christ and his saints were asleep'. Henry II was an aristocratic though faithless king who quarrelled spectacularly with Becket, introduced many administrative reforms and is generally credited with the origination of

the English Common Law, a national system of justice which is still the envy of less happy lands. Richard 'the Lionheart' and John 'Lackland' were not really Normans at all, but they did keep up the old skills of crusading and craftiness respectively.

Turning away from matters of government and state, the Church was at rather a low ebb in late Saxon times, which made it ripe for takeover by Norman clerics. The patterns of domination of Church and State proceeded in parallel; the Archbishop of Canterbury was placed at the top of a chain of command which reached down through Norman bishops, archdeacons and deans to a predominantly Saxon clergy. The Church made great strides both organizationally and structurally because it was at first virtually an arm of the State, a problem which came to a head in the confrontation between Henry II and Becket. Dioceses were arranged in order to conform to the new administrative map drawn by the Conqueror, and huge Norman cathedrals replaced earlier Saxon buildings. These major churches were as much a symbol of the conquest as were the castles and in Wales, at least, caused almost as much controversy.

Monastic orders were similarly affected. Normans replaced Saxons in the seats of power and the old Benedictine order was left behind in the wake of the new reforming orders from France such as those of Savigny and Cîteaux which merged in 1147, and the more glorious Cluniacs, who were to commission some of the noblest churches ever seen in England. Many of the new priories were staffed by monks from France who could not speak English at all. Thus, whether by accident or design, the monasteries acted as heralds of Norman culture and achievement so that even the faith of their fathers became foreign to the Anglo-Saxons.

But one of the basic questions which we can ask of this wide-ranging reorganization of English society is: 'Did it work?' The answer to that must be 'yes', at least in the materialistic terms of modern politics. The 12th century was a time of steadily expanding economic growth, notwithstanding the setback of Stephen's reign. New enterprises – be they secular such as new towns and villages, military such as the conquests of Wales and Ireland, or ecclesiastical such as the new cathedrals, the rebuilt churches and the burgeoning monasteries – got off to vigorous beginnings and saw sustained growth.

These, however, are the outward and visible signs of economic well-being. What happened inside the society? Were the spiritual and artistic needs met, and was a good standard of living generally available? Again the answer is probably yes, but it is more difficult to be sure. That the arts flourished is evident from a great mass of superb illuminated manuscripts which survives from the period, from the quality and depth of emotion discernible in the sculpture of Malmesbury, Chichester and Northampton, and by wallpaintings in Gloucestershire, Sussex and elsewhere. Similarly, a handful of houses show us that higher standards of comfort were attainable by some at least and the general absence of references to plague and pestilence suggests that the bulk of society was better nurtured than before. Again, the absence of popular rebellion after the first few years of Norman rule suggests at least a reasonable contentment. The overall impression is one of sound and surprisingly fair governance which, once nationalistic fervour was set aside, acted to the benefit of most subjects irrespective of their estate.

Finally, two 12th-century churchmen together provide a picture of their times. The first was Gerald of Wales (Giraldus Cambrensis) born at Manorbier (Dyfed) and a Cambro-Norman, for his Welsh mother and Norman father crossed the cultural divide. He fought valiantly for the independence of the Welsh Church and, though finally betrayed by his fellow clerics, he never lost the support of the common people. The second was Gilbert of Sempringham, born in Lincolnshire within 20 years of the Battle of Hastings, and like Gerald the son of mixed parentage. Gilbert was the only Englishman to found a monastic order, and he did it amongst the common people and not amongst the Norman aristocracy. Both men spoke their minds freely, and both quarrelled with their king, but their lights shine brilliantly from that period. In their different ways, Gerald and Gilbert illustrated the strengths of the Normans; they adapted themselves to the ways of their new lands and they showed the same energy and independence of spirit which had first brought the Conqueror to England with his ragbag of an army. It is surely this overwhelming sense of purpose and the success of its fulfilment which makes the Norman era such a compelling part of our history.

How to Use This Book

We have divided the mainland of Britain into six geographical regions which reflect most satisfactorily the pattern of the Norman settlement. Each region forms the basis of a separate section of the book, and each is prefaced by a brief outline of its history. A key map showing the modern county boundaries will also be found at the beginning of each section, and the numbers on it correspond with the consecutive descriptions in the text. If you wish to look up a particular site, consult the index at the end of the book in order to find its page number.

Each site is located in detail, and a six-figure Ordnance Survey grid reference is provided. An Ordnance Survey 1:50,000 metric map, which has replaced the old one-inch survey, is a valuable tool when visiting sites, but if you don't have the relevant map the directions can be followed quite easily from a good road atlas. Most of the sites lie in villages or towns, but any which are particularly difficult to find have been located by a small map showing nearest

major roads and other features as well as a verbal description. Where appropriate, nearest towns and villages are indicated, together with their distances from the site.

Some of the sites in this book are on private land, and their inclusion implies no right of access. Nevertheless, owners are generally very co-operative, and are pleased to allow genuinely interested people access to sites on their land. Many of the sites are churches, and it is hoped that visitors will behave in a suitable manner; a contribution to the fabric fund is not only courteous but also helps to ensure the survival of the very sites which the visitor sees. When in the countryside please follow the Country Code, and *never*, in any circumstances, dig into a site. This is a very complicated business which archaeologists spend a lot of time learning about!

Certain of the sites are in the guardianship of the Historic Buildings and Monuments Commission, and this is indicated under the relevant entries. Some are open at all reasonable times without charge, others have special opening hours which are indicated in the entries, while most are open during standard hours which are:

	Weekdays	*Sundays*
16 October to 14 March	09.30–16.00	14.00–16.00
15 March to 15 October	09.30–18.30	14.00–18.30

A list of the Norman kings, books to read and a glossary of unfamiliar terms will be found at the back of the book.

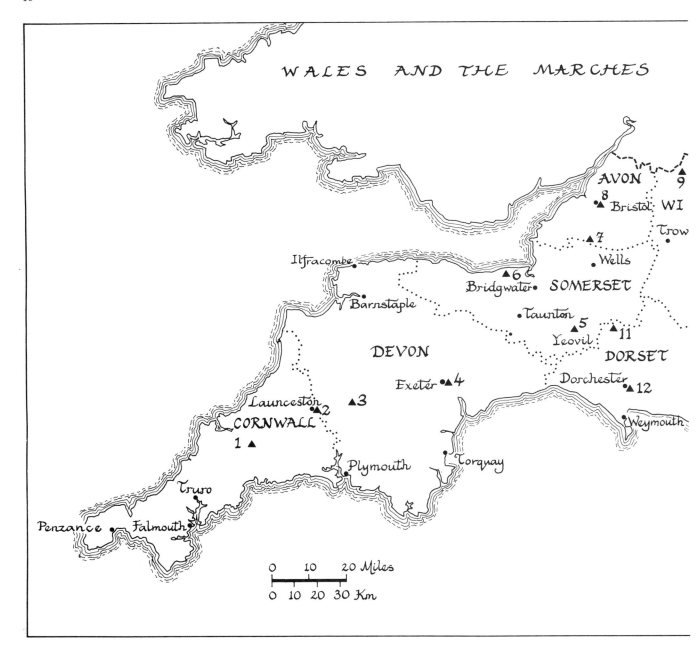

WALES AND THE MARCHES

AVON

WI

▲ 9

▲ 8 Bristol

• Trow

▲ 7

• Wells

Ilfracombe •

▲ 6 SOMERSET

Bridgwater •

✓ Barnstaple

• Taunton

▲ 5

Yeovil • ▲ 11

DORSET

DEVON

Dorchester • ▲ 12

Exeter • ▲ 4

▲ 3

Launceston • ▲ 2

CORNWALL

• Weymouth

1 ▲

Plymouth • ✓ Torquay

Truro •

Penzance • Falmouth •

0   10   20 Miles

0   10 20 30 Km

CENTRAL
ENGLAND

EAST
ANGLIA

Swindon

GREATER
LONDON
▲ 36

LTSHIRE   BERKSHIRE Reading

bridge

35 ▲

34 ▲   Canterbury ●▲ 32   31 ▲

Basingstoke

Guildford   22 ▲

Tonbridge   KENT   ▲ 30

Salisbury

HAMPSHIRE

21   SURREY

33 ▲ ▲   29 ▲

28 ▲   Dover

10

18 ▲ Winchester   Horsham

WEST SUSSEX   EAST SUSSEX   ▲ 27

20 ▲

16 ▲   17 ●▲
       Southampton

19 ▲   ▲ 23   25 ▲

● Lewes   26 ▲
Brighton

▲ 24

15 ●▲

13 ▲   Bournemouth
14 ▲

I.O.W.

southern
england

Southern England

Introduction

'Duke William crossed the sea in a great ship and came to Pevensey.' This, in the words embroidered on the Bayeux Tapestry, is the description of the very act of invasion. After landing, horses and men were disembarked and William and his nobles sat down to a great feast, the food having been blessed by Odo, Bishop of Bayeux. At Pevensey on Thursday 28 September 1066 the Norman adventure can be truly said to have started, and it was from this beach-head that William prepared his reception for King Harold on his return southwards. It is virtually certain that this banquet must have taken place within the Roman Saxon Shore fort at Pevensey, and that its 900-year-old walls afforded shelter for William's newly landed army. Had Harold been able to counter the invasion at sea, or to dispute the landing, then the course of our history could have been very different but, as we know, he was away in Yorkshire granting Harald Hardrada 'seven feet of English ground'.

After building an earth and timber castle at Hastings, William received news of the approach of Harold's army and on Saturday 14 October the issue was decided on Senlac Field near Hastings. (See our *Guide to Anglo-Saxon Sites*.) Whilst the Battle of Hastings undoubtedly broke formal resistance to the Norman invasion, local rebellions broke out later in various parts of the country. In the south, the Exeter revolt of 1067, led by Harold's mother Gytha, was the most serious. The Conqueror laid siege to Exeter, and when the defenders capitulated he built Exeter Castle, the fine gatehouse of which survives as perhaps the earliest masonry Norman building in England.

After these initial difficulties, William proceeded with the task of dividing up his new kingdom between himself, the Church and his followers. Early and important lordships were founded all over the south of England. Few 11th-century buildings survive, however, since many of the sites were altered later, but at Bramber (West Sussex), Rochester, Lydford and Old Sarum we can see traces of early Norman fortifications. It is however in the White Tower at London that we see the most dramatic manifestation of Norman military initiative. This great fortified palace was intended as the Conqueror's 'caput' for the whole kingdom.

During the 12th century, major secular buildings appeared in greater profusion. Substantial royal castles survive at Corfe, Porchester, Dover and Rochester, and in the 'prison tower' at Lydford

we see a rare example of smaller-scale royal building. Lords as well as kings built important castles. The south-western shell keeps and Christchurch motte and Constable's House bear witness to a developing taste for both security and comfort during the 12th century, a tendency also detectable in the withdrawing chambers and piped water supply in the great keep at Dover.

It is with the burgeoning power of the Church that we see the most impressive evidence of surplus wealth in the south of England in Norman times. Even during the 11th century certain churchmen such as the Conqueror's half-brother Odo, Bishop of Bayeux, and Gundulf, Bishop of Rochester, were able to exercise important political influence in the first case and to initiate large building projects in the second. At Canterbury itself Lanfranc, the first Norman archbishop, began work on the replacement of the Saxon cathedral in 1070, and building continued here for the rest of the period. The result is one of the finest Romanesque ecclesiastical complexes in Europe, with the superb proto-Gothic choir being the crowning glory. Other large-scale ecclesiastical building projects were begun at Rochester, Chichester, Christchurch, Winchester, Bristol and Exeter. The Norman impact on the Church was given physical expression in a building programme which dwarfed anything which had gone before.

The early personal power of Norman churchmen was continued in the south of England by such wealthy aristocratic bishops as Henry de Blois of Winchester and Roger, Bishop of Salisbury. De Blois built the new hospital of Winchester St Cross which continues to this very day, and provided rich furnishings for his churches as the Hampshire Tournai marble fonts indicate. Roger, on the other hand, particularly concerned himself with castles and palaces. The castle at Old Sarum with its accompanying cathedral and the remains of his lavish bishop's palace at Sherborne illustrate his personal prestige. This churchman had four castles when King Stephen humbled him in 1139, and he was not above sequestrating the revenues of Malmesbury Abbey to fund his constructions elsewhere.

If these great churchmen led the way in the matter of patronage and new building, powerful laymen were quick to follow by lavish support of religious orders. The Knights Templar enjoyed substantial popularity during the 12th century as the magnificent interior of the Temple Church in London demonstrates. Similarly, lay founders could achieve remarkable results as the atmospheric church of St Bartholomew the Great in Smithfield, also in London, reminds us. At Stogursey and Malmesbury we can see excellent carvings from the 11th and 12th centuries respectively, whilst the chapter house at Bristol is perhaps the finest late Norman interior in England, alive with intersecting arcades and zigzag patterns.

But it is in the parish churches that we find the most significant evidence of lay patronage. Fascinating sculpture may be seen at many places including Fordington, Stoke-sub-Hamdon and Compton Martin, in the works of the Kentish School and at Shoreham. Paintings can be seen in the Sussex Group and at Chaldon, whilst at Staplehurst a door with remarkable iron fittings is preserved. Among the most important categories of objects are the fonts to be seen in some southern churches. Brookland has the fine lead font with the unique scheme of the Signs of the Zodiac and the Labours of the Months. The Cornish Group's fonts have late and elaborate carving on them, as do the earlier imported Tournai marble fonts of the Hampshire Group mentioned above.

Finally, the south of England can also show us something of everyday life in Norman times. At Southampton are the merchants' houses carefully designed so as to accommodate both business and private life. At New Shoreham we see evidence of the founding zeal of the de Braose family in its attempt to continue its flourishing Continental trade in the face of adverse natural conditions, and in St Thomas's Hospital at Canterbury we see a rare example of a Norman public building in a town. Turning to the countryside, the monastic grange at Minster in Thanet reminds us of the ceaseless round of agriculture, whilst in the green vastness of the New Forest we can feel the same sense of tranquillity which Richard Fitz Neal, the Bishop of London, described late in the 12th century:

> In the forests are the secret places of kings and their great delight. To them they go for hunting, having put off their cares, so that they may enjoy a little quiet. There away from the continuous turmoil of the court, they can for a little time breathe in the grace of natural liberty.

The Norman fleet sails towards Pevensey, as depicted on the Bayeux Tapestry. The Conqueror's ship is on the right with a hornblower aft as its emblem and the cross at the top of the mast to indicate the Divine Favour (in the shape of the Pope's blessing) with which the expedition was accompanied. Immediately below the cross is a representation of the signal lamp with which this, the flagship of the fleet, gave instructions to the rest.

1

The Cornish Group of Fonts and Reliquary

There are six examples of the Cornish Group of fonts of which the finest is undoubtedly the font at Bodmin. The general form of the Cornish fonts is the 'chalice' familiar from the Aylesbury Group, but here the central shaft is augmented by four shafts at the angles of the square top. Instead of capitals, as on the Norfolk fonts, these angle shafts terminate in sombre angel heads, the wings hanging squarely down to each side. The sides of the Bodmin bowl are almost covered with deeply cut and even undercut decoration. There are flowers and twining stems, twisted and knotted serpents, and around the bottom crawl evil lizard-like creatures which are perhaps intended to be salamanders, as at Youlgreave in Derbyshire. The font at Roche is less fine, but has good knots, floral sprigs and a St Andrew's Cross. The Group must belong to the closing years of our period, and it is quite possible that the Bodmin piece could be 13th-century; this merely illustrates the time it took for ideas to travel to these remoter parts of England.

Bodmin's other Romanesque relic contradicts such suggestions of parochialism, however. It is a splendid chest decorated with ivory plates and was made in the Norman kingdom of Sicily during the 12th century. This chest is supposed to have contained the relics of St Petroc to whom the church is dedicated. The relics were stolen by a monk in 1176 and taken to France, but they were restored soon afterwards and lay undisturbed until the Reformation. Whilst the bones of St Petroc disappeared at that time, we must be grateful that their excellent container remains. This reliquary is a reminder of the far-ranging 'Norman Empire'; the distance between Bodmin and Sicily must have seemed vast indeed!

This ivory reliquary was made in the Norman kingdom of Sicily by Arab craftsmen; this one object reminds us of the breadth of the Norman 'empire'.

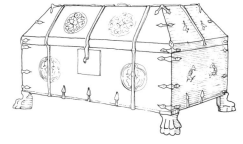

Map References: **Bodmin** SX 072671 (metric map 200. 1-inch map 185)
Roche SW 988598
St Austell SX 014525
St Stephen in Brannel SW 945533
East Newlyn SW 829563
Kea SW 810427
Nearest Town: Bodmin
Locations: All the fonts are in churches near the centres of the towns and villages. At Kea, the church of St Kea is a late-Victorian building which replaced the medieval parish church, the surviving tower of which can be seen nearby.

The superb font at Bodmin probably dates to the very end of our period, c. 1200.

2

Three Shell Keeps: Launceston and Restormel, Cornwall; and Totnes, Devon

There are three shell keeps in the south-western peninsula built after the Norman settlement of the area. The keeps are at Launceston, Restormel and Totnes; whilst the history of each is different, they all share the basic plan of a motte and bailey with the motte being crowned by a shell keep rather than a tower. These were the products of rebuilding timber defences in stone; just as the timber palisades round baileys were replaced by stone curtain walls during the 12th century, so were those around the summits of the mottes. Shell keeps are known in many parts of the country and in Scotland they carried on in use until the 13th century. Why there should be three good examples close together in the south-west is unclear; perhaps it was a local fashion.

At Launceston, which was the caput of Robert, Count of Mortain's lordship which embraced the whole of Cornwall, the first castle was built soon after the suppression of the Exeter revolt in 1067. A borough was established below the castle at that time and its plan is still evident in the street pattern. During the 12th century, the castle's defences were replaced in stone and the bailey curtain and the south gatehouse remain. On top of the motte, a low outer wall was built, probably by Reginald de Dunstan after the castle was granted to him in 1141 by Henry I, and a central round tower was added during the 13th century.

Restormel Castle was begun late in the 11th century by Baldwin Fitz Turstin after he established a bridge across the River Fowey near the site. The castle was built as a ringwork with a square stone gatehouse at this time, probably with a single wall tower or small keep. It was converted into a shell keep during the 12th century but the interior was totally rebuilt in the 13th century and the single projecting wall tower or keep was converted into a chapel.

Totnes had been an important Saxon borough; it was granted to Judhael, one of the Norman landowners in the west, who made Totnes his administrative centre. The motte here is impressive and Judhael's castle consisted of a shell keep with, at the centre, a timber tower (like those depicted on the Bayeux Tapestry), the stone foundations of which have been excavated. The bailey at least was provided with a stone curtain during the 12th century, but all the stonework on top of the motte was rebuilt during the 14th.

Map References: **Launceston** SX 330846 (metric map 201. 1-inch map 186) **Restormel** SX 104614 **Totnes** SX 800605 (metric map 202. 1-inch map 188) *Nearest Towns:* Launceston, Lostwithiel, Totnes *Locations:* All are guardianship sites and are open standard hours and Sunday mornings from 9.30, April–September. Launceston Castle is in the centre of the town. Restormel is near Lostwithiel and is well signposted off the A390. There is ample car-parking at the site. Totnes Castle is also in the town centre.

Below left: Launceston castle with its spectacular shell keep.

Below: Plan of Restormel. The early square gatehouse probably went with a timber palisade which was later replaced in stone.

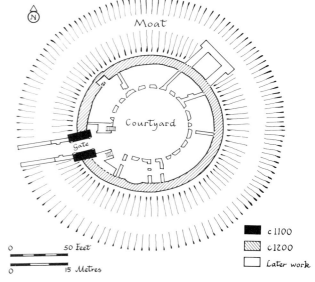

3

Lydford Prison Tower, Devon

Lydford was probably originally founded by the Saxons as an outpost against the Cornish during the 8th century. Later, it was incorporated into the chain of fortresses founded by King Alfred to combat the Danish menace. By late Saxon times Lydford was a flourishing place, its earth ramparts faced in stone and the site of a mint. By the time of Domesday Book, however, it seems that Lydford was already declining; 40 houses were described as being 'waste', though this could be due to the construction of a Norman castle here. But the site of the castle, at the extreme southern tip of the promontory on which Lydford stands, does not seem a likely place for so many houses to have occupied. Whilst there is no evidence that the economy of Lydford ever recovered its former vigour, it had been assessed on the same basis as Totnes during late Saxon times and it did become an important administrative centre.

During our period Dartmoor, on the edge of which Lydford was located, was a royal forest. This does not mean that Dartmoor was a 'forest' in the way we understand it today, but merely that it was subject to the Forest Laws, the nature of which is discussed under the entry for the New Forest. Lydford was the administrative and judicial centre from which that complex and often harsh law was applied. Also, the area was an important tin-mining centre and a series of customary and formal laws had grown up by which the industry was regulated.

This came to royal attention by virtue of the considerable profits which accrued from the industry, and hence formal regulation of the tin mining, smelting and dealing was introduced. The mining districts were divided into districts or 'stannaries' (called after the Latin *stannaria*, 'tin'), and the court at Lydford had jurisdiction over the system. The 'Tinners' Charter' was passed in 1201, but probably this did little more than formalize existing arrangements.

At Lydford there is a physical legacy of both forest and stannary laws – and, these laws being often ruthless and arbitrary, 'Lydford Law' had an ill reputation:

'I oft have heard of Lydford law
How in the morn they hang and draw
And sit in judgement after.'

Lydford 'Castle' is first heard of in 1195. This structure now appears as a small square keep-tower at the end of a sub-rectangular bailey. Despite its structural resemblance to a standard castle keep, the place was not built as a castle *per se*. Instead, it was a courtroom and prison from which 'Lydford Law' was administered. It is perhaps significant that the castle bailey was on the side of the keep away from the road; doubtless the bloody hangings and drawings were performed there. The tower as we see it today is largely a rebuilding of the 13th century: the first tower had been free-standing on flat ground, but some time early in the 13th century the tower was overthrown. Later in the century, a ditch was dug around the tower and the spoil was heaped against its base, thus making what had been the ground floor into a basement. The superstructure was rebuilt with two floors above the basement, which is what we see today.

Map Reference: SX 510848 (metric map 191. 1-inch map 175)
Nearest Town: Okehampton
Location: Lydford lies on the edge of Dartmoor 3 miles (5 km) south-east of the A30(T) about half-way between Okehampton and Launceston. It is signposted off the trunk road. The castle stands close to the church in the village; it is in guardianship and is open at any reasonable time.

Although this structure looks like an ordinary keep, it was actually built as a courthouse and prison from which the infamous 'Lydford Law' was administered.

4

Exeter Gate Tower and Cathedral, Devon

The Anglo-Saxon Chronicle tells us that in 1067, 'Then he [the Conqueror] went to Devonshire and besieged the town of Exeter for eighteen days; and there he lost many troops. But he promised them good and did evil, and they gave him the town because the thanes had betrayed them.'

This account of the first siege of Exeter relates to the rising of the townspeople against the Normans under the leadership of Gytha, King Harold's mother. The Conqueror, who had just put down 'Edric the Wild' in the Welsh Marches, and was doubtless fearing further trouble, put down the Exeter rising with some savagery. Interestingly the Norman chronicler Orderic Vitalis also records that 'after eighteen days of violent attack the walls were undermined and the city fell'. This is the earliest record of mining as a siege tactic; mining was widely used later as, for example, the surviving tunnel at Bungay indicates. The 'walls' referred to in Orderic's account were the Roman walls of Exeter, called by them Isca, which the townsmen had 'built or repaired . . . and strengthened the defences all round'.

After the rising, William determined to hold Exeter securely and to this end he built a castle in stone which utilized the north corner of the Roman defences; there was apparently no motte here, but the fine stone gatehouse survives. This structure, which probably dates from 1068, is the earliest stone castle building in England, and in its triangular-headed windows we can see Anglo-Saxon structural traditions continuing. The gatehouse was probably also the keep of the castle as at Richmond (North Yorkshire) and there are still two storeys of single rooms above the gate passage. The gate tower stands in front of the wall and has a rudimentary barbican in front of it. A stone or wooden bridge crossed the deep moat before the gate.

In 1136, during the Anarchy of Stephen's reign, Exeter was besieged by a king for the second time. Stephen sent on a 'flying column' of 200 horse with 'glittering arms and standards fluttering in the air' to prevent the rebel baron Baldwin de Redvers from supplying his garrison. The king followed on with the host and laid siege to the castle; he tried mining, and fired an 'unendurable hail' of (sling) stones, but in the end Nature came to his aid for, after three months, the weather was hot and the well went dry. The cunning defenders used wine to make loaves, boil food and quench fire arrows, but in the end the tired (and emotional?) defenders surrendered. Stephen, who was chivalrous but perhaps a ninny, allowed de Redvers a free conduct whereupon the ingrate gathered more troops and garrisoned his own newly built castle at Carisbrooke on the Isle of Wight!

In addition to the castle which inconveniently continues one of its erstwhile functions as a prison, Exeter has the fine cathedral, the transepts and particularly the transeptal towers of which are *c.* 1170, replete with spectacular blank arcading. Inside there is the fine Transitional effigy of Bishop Bartholomew who died in 1184, but which was probably not carved until *c.* 1200 in view of its advanced scrollwork.

Map References: **Castle Gate** SX 918933 (metric map 192. 1-inch map 176)
Cathedral SX 921925
Location: The cathedral is in a large close in the centre of the city. The castle is in the Rougemont North Hay Gardens, near the library off Queen Street in the city centre.

This gatehouse is probably the oldest Norman stone building in England, built after the Conqueror suppressed the Exeter Rebellion led by Harold's mother in 1067. The triangular windows in the top storey may represent a continuation of Saxon building traditions.

5

Stoke-sub-Hamdon Church, Somerset

The village is known locally as Stoke-under-Ham, the Ham being Ham Hill, source of the ochreous Ham Hill stone which had been used in Saxon times and was being transported as far as Taunton during the 12th century; Ham stone was used in the bishop's palace at Sherborne.

The little church of St Mary at Stoke has a robust tympanum over the north doorway which exhibits the same sort of mixed iconography as the font of Hook Norton. Here the Tree of Life, inhabited by three birds, perhaps symbolizing the Trinity, is flanked on the left by a centaur labelled 'SAGITARIUS' and on the right by the Agnus Dei and a crude lion. The meaning of this scheme is difficult to fathom; the placing of the Tree of Life at the centre is obscure – we would expect to see a Christ in Majesty in such a position flanked as it is by lesser subjects. Similarly the use of two signs of the Zodiac, Leo (August) and Sagittarius (December), might indicate Summer and Winter, but who can tell? The stone carver probably knew of the great decorative arches at Malmesbury and elsewhere, which employed these foreign symbols, but the feeling here is one of muddle rather than message.

But is this quite fair? There is another example of a central Tree of Life on the tympanum at Dinton in which the strange scene of beasts eating from a Tree of Life would be unexplained were it not for the presence of an interpretative inscription. Intriguingly, when we visited Stoke we found traces of a worn inscription on the lintel below the tympanum in just the same place as the one at Dinton. Did Stoke too have a written gloss on the meaning of the sculpture? We cannot tell now for the evidence is all but destroyed, but we should be wary of dismissing 'muddled' works out of hand.

The delights of Stoke church do not finish with the tympanum, however; the chancel arch matches the door and, like it, dates to 1130–40. It has a good range of decoration including scales, zigzags and lozenges. Externally, a carved corbel table and windows in the side walls of the Norman nave are visible. On the north side is a monolithic window head on which is carved a man and a dragon which look very Anglo-Saxon, as does the cable-moulded window on the south side. This occurrence of Saxon-inspired motifs here at Stoke parallels the similar work at Dinton; does the central Tree of Life motif come from a Saxon rather than a Norman milieu? Finally there is an excellent Transitional vault in the base of the tower, c. 1190, and a good font of a similar date; what a lot this beautiful and cherished church has to offer.

Map Reference: ST 473176 (metric map 193. 1-inch map 177)
Nearest Town: Yeovil
Locations: There are two sub-Hamdons, Norton and Stoke, lying either side of the A30 near Hamdon Hill. Stoke is on the north side of the road, about 4½ miles (7 km) west of Yeovil. The church is in the village street.

A primitive rendering of St George and the Dragon.

The tympanum over the south door.

6
Stogursey Sculpture, Somerset

Stoke Courcy – the modern version of the name is a corruption of the Norman French – was held by William de Falaise after the Conquest. The name came about through the marriage of his daughter to William de Courcy. Particular interest attaches to the crossing of the church at Stogursey since it appears to be a very fine and dignified example of late-11th-century architecture. The most likely date for the work would be *c*. 1080, since it is paralleled in both England and France by structures of that period. However, the documentary evidence suggests that de Falaise gave the 'priory' church to the monks of Lonlay in Normandy only some time between 1100 and 1107, which is rather late for the architecture. At present, this difficulty is unresolved.

Of the 11th-century priory church, only the crossing and parts of the tower, which contains herringbone work, have survived. Later in our period, the chancel was rebuilt in *c*. 1180 and significant parts of it remain, but the earlier work has fared less well. Despite this disadvantage, what remains of the early work at Stogursey is of the greatest interest. The capitals of the eight columns of the crossing are decorated with volutes which ultimately stem from classical Corinthian capitals. The Stogursey capitals are further ornamented with foliage, human masks, birds and beasts. They stand comparison with the contemporary but much higher-status works at Canterbury and Durham. Stogursey, set in the wilds of Somerset, is a most rewarding place to visit for those wishing to see early Norman sculpture in the west.

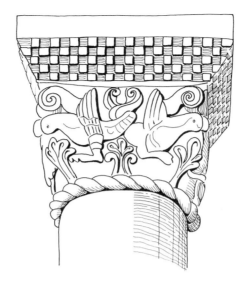

Map Reference: ST 205429 (metric map 182. 1-inch map 165)
Nearest Town: Bridgwater
Location: Stogursey lies about 2 miles (3.2 km) inland from Bridgwater Bay. It is reached by minor roads north off the A39. 7 miles (11.2 km) west of Bridgwater take the minor road to Fiddington, and Stogursey is 4 miles (6.4 km) up this road. The church is at the east end of the village.

One of the early capitals in the crossing at Stogursey showing reversed birds below a finely executed zone of chequerwork.

7
Compton Martin Small Church, Avon

Although small, the church of St Martin was designed to impress and contains the rarities of a vaulted chancel and a nave pillar decorated with a Durham-style spiral. Both nave arcades are Norman, as are the clerestory windows above, which can be seen from the exterior on the north side. Also on the north side, the carved corbel table, which has a good complement of heads and monsters, survives inside the north aisle; note the square holes below the ashlar at the top of the wall which mark the original height of the aisle roof. The chancel vault is divided into two compartments by a chevron-decorated cross rib, and the vaults of the western compartment meet in four small animal heads carved in low relief; the whole is a delightful composition of the mid-12th century.

Vaulting boss with grotesque masks in the chancel at Compton Martin.

Map Reference: ST 545570 (metric map 182. 1-inch map 165)
Nearest Town: Wells
Location: Compton Martin is at the foot of the Mendip Hills near the lakes of Chew Valley and Blagdon. It is on the main road between Bath and Weston-super-Mare, the A368, about half-way between the two. The church is just off the road on the south side up a narrow lane which runs parallel to the main road.

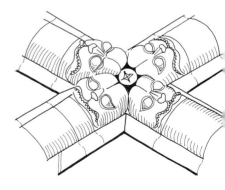

8

Bristol Chapter House and Gate Tower, Avon

The cathedral church at Bristol is a superb essay in Gothic dating from the 14th and the 19th centuries, but it is to the remains of the Norman Augustinian monastery on the site that we must turn our attention. There was probably a religious foundation here in pre-Conquest times, but it was not until 1140–2 that Robert Fitz Harding, a Bristol burgess and Lord of Berkeley, founded an Augustinian abbey here. This was during the period of the Anarchy in which Fitz Harding supported the Empress Matilda; since the times were troubled, it might explain why the church was not consecrated until 1165.

Only the south transept of the Norman church remains, and that is frankly undistinguished, but it is in the claustral ranges, built 1160–70, that we find the most interesting evidence. The first is provided by the excellent gatehouse which follows the pattern earlier established at Bury St Edmunds, though its upper parts were extensively remodelled during the 15th century. The gate passage itself has a fine ribbed vault and the external arches are enriched with spiral shafts, multiple zigzags and complex interlacements. Parts of the cloister also survive, including the small doorway into the lower cloister which continues the theme of the gatehouse portal.

The *pièce de résistance* is undoubtedly the chapter house, a superb room without peer in Norman England. Inside, the roof is a deeply groined vault, the ribs of which bear zigzag and lozenge decoration. The vestibule alone is richer than many a church elsewhere; it has composite columns, round and pointed arches and subtle hobnail motifs round the arches. In the paired columns of the lights between the vestibule and the chapter house proper we see an early use of Purbeck marble. On the walls of the chapter house are scintillating arrangements of blank arcades, zigzag patterns and pillars with twisted decoration. If the movement in the chapter house at Worcester is

grave, here instead are the same lightness and vivacity as in the Galilee chapel at Durham.

More like a wedding cake than a wall, the chapter house at Bristol marks the apogee of Norman surface decoration in the later 12th century.

Map Reference: ST 584726 (metric map 172. 1-inch map 155)
Location: The cathedral is in the centre of the city opposite the Council House. Parking is on meters or in multi-storey car-parks nearby.

9

Malmesbury Abbey, Wiltshire

The Benedictine monastery at Malmesbury was founded during the 7th century; the famous St Aldhelm was its abbot during the 8th century. Refounded in 970, the abbey was burnt down in 1042 and apparently was not rebuilt until the 12th century. The present Romanesque buildings date from around 1160–75, and were begun after the demise of Bishop Roger of Salisbury, builder of castles at Sherborne and Old Sarum, who had mis-appropriated the revenues of the abbey from 1118 onwards. This overmighty cleric attracted the wrath of King Stephen and, like his nephew Bishop Alexander of Lincoln, had to surrender his castle to the Crown in 1139. His death in the same year provided Malmesbury with the opportunity to re-establish its inde-pendence and hence work started on a new and ambitious abbey church.

The south porch has two doorways. The outer one, like the west door at Iffley, is composed of eight continuous orders without capitals and tympanum. The inner door has three orders, again continuous, but this time with a tympanum depicting Christ in Majesty in a mandorla supported by two angels. On the side walls of the porch are two further tympana, each containing six Apostles with a single angel flying above them. The work was originally painted and gilded and this portal must have formed a magnificent foretaste of the wonders within, which included the tombs of St Aldhelm and King Athelstan, 'the roof tree of the honour of the western world'; truly this was the Gate of Heaven.

Various features of the designs at Malmes-bury proclaim their French origins; the use of tympana on the side walls of the porch is unparalleled in any surviving English build-ing, but is known in south-west France. Simi-larly, the sculpture is influenced by French exemplars and in its richness it is foreign to most English compositions of the period. Yet whilst it is possible to detect strains of common

currency in the overall design, the details owe as much to England as to France. The use of the continuous orders is an English trait and the style of the figure sculpture owes more to the figures on the west front of Lincoln Cathedral than to French prototypes; it is believed that some of the Lincoln sculptures may have actually helped in the work here at Malmesbury. This seems likely enough in view of the sudden withdrawal of patronage there when Bishop Alexander, like his uncle Roger here at Malmesbury, suddenly fell from royal grace.

The outer arch has foliate or geometric orna-ment on five of its orders, but the second, fourth and sixth members have figure subjects contained in the oval openings of a delicate trellis work design. These carvings are histori-ated – that is, they tell stories which would have been familiar to 12th-century churchmen. The lower parts of the arch probably show a Psychomachia, that is, the symbolic conflict between the Virtues and the Vices discussed on p. 126. The upper parts of the three orders contain cycles of biblical history and comprise one of the most complicated iconographical sequences in England. They are arranged as type and antitype of Old and New Testament scenes from the Creation to the Death of Cain, Noah to Goliath and the Annunciation to Pentecost. The scenes are designed to be read horizontally in threes: the Creation is shown

Map Reference: ST 932873 (metric map 173. 1-inch map 157)
Location: Malmesbury is a most attractive small town on the southern edge of the Cotswolds. It is north of the M4 and can be reached from Junction 17 taking the A429 for 6 miles (9.6 km). The church is in the centre of the town.

One of the tympana from the side walls of the porch. These figures are half life size, and when they were painted and gilded they must have rivalled the very Gate of Heaven itself. As it is, they are still deeply moving and must rank as some of the greatest sculptures ever made in England.

This delicate tympanum depicting Christ in Majesty supported by angels stands above the main entrance to Malmesbury Abbey Church.

beside God and Noah and the Annunciation; an Angel gives a spade to Adam and a distaff to Eve, Moses strikes a rock and we see the Last Supper. Not all the details are comprehensible now, for later damage has been drastic, but there is no doubt that they were carefully composed. Many of the figures in the ovals are superb small-scale carvings gracefully elongated in a style quite different from that used by the second sculptor who carved the tympana on the side walls of the porch.

The tympana depict the Apostles in high relief at approximately half life size; they are perhaps the greatest sculptures to survive from the 12th century in England. There is dramatic tension in their movements and in the expressions on their faces; they are still clear and distinct personalities today after the passage of 800 years.

10
Old Sarum Castle, Cathedral and Town, Wiltshire

Elsewhere in this book we have grown quite used to the concept of deserted village sites and even, in some instances, of failed towns, but the idea of a city being removed and its site being left as a part of our silent landscape is strange indeed. Yet here at Old Sarum is a 'ghost city', a place which once bustled with life but which is now the haunt of birds and visitors. 'Old' Sarum was already ancient when its fortifications were repaired under the direction of King Alfred to resist Sweyn the Dane. The place had first been fortified during the pre-Roman Iron Age and was known to the

Map Reference: SU 138327 (metric map 184. 1-inch map 167)
Nearest Town: Salisbury
Location: This is a guardianship site which is open standard hours and Sunday mornings from 9.30, April to September. Old Sarum occupies an elevated position to the north of Salisbury about 1½ miles (2.4 km) from the city centre on the west side of the A345 road to Marlborough and Swindon.

Romans as Sorviodunum. We can also imagine that such a commanding site remained in use during the Dark Ages after the withdrawal of the legions in 410.

After the Conquest, Sarum was transformed into one of the most dramatic Norman sites in the country. A ringwork was established in the centre of the earlier fort and the great Iron Age bank and ditch was re-excavated to form a large outer bailey. Between 1075 and 1078 the bishopric of Sherborne was transferred here at William's command and Bishop Osmund was permitted to build his cathedral in the north-west quadrant of the outer bailey. The first church was consecrated in 1092, but it was largely destroyed by a storm within five years. Early in the 12th century, the church was rebuilt and a cloister constructed on the north side. The foundations of both churches are marked out on the site.

It was at the time of the rebuilding of the cathedral that Sarum came entirely under the hand of Roger, Bishop of Salisbury. Roger was an able churchman with high ambitions; at Sarum he not only rebuilt the new cathedral but also transformed the earlier earth and timber castle into an elaborate palace complex. There are similarities between Roger's work here and at his other palace at Sherborne; both are high quality structures built in an elaborate style with courtyards. Bishop Roger did not have everything his own way, however, for when in 1139 he incurred the wrath of King Stephen not only did he lose his castles at Sarum, Malmesbury, Devizes and Sherborne, but the Diocese of Salisbury also had to relinquish its false claims on the revenues of Malmesbury Abbey. Significantly, it had been in 1118 that Roger had begun to expropriate the revenues of Malmesbury – doubtless they were necessary for his ambitious buildings at Sarum and elsewhere.

There are references to a borough at Sarum from late Saxon times and it is assumed that it continued later, but little evidence of it has been found as yet. It is difficult to believe that many houses could have been fitted in after the cathedral and castle had been accommo-dated, but there is no evidence of occupation outside the earthworks either. As is well known, the site did eventually prove too small and in 1220 the present Salisbury Cathedral was begun and a fine planned town was laid out around it. Sarum was left in peace once again and it became a quarry for building stone and later a celebrated 'rotten borough' whose handful of electors returned a Member of Parliament until the Great Reform Act of 1832. Perhaps that status was the last vestige of the former glories of Bishop Roger's citadel and cathedral; within its mighty ramparts, any ambitious man could threaten a king!

Plan of Old Sarum showing the castle at the centre of the earthworks with the cathedral in the north-west quadrant. The north–south bank across the middle of the space probably divided off the ecclesiastical precinct.

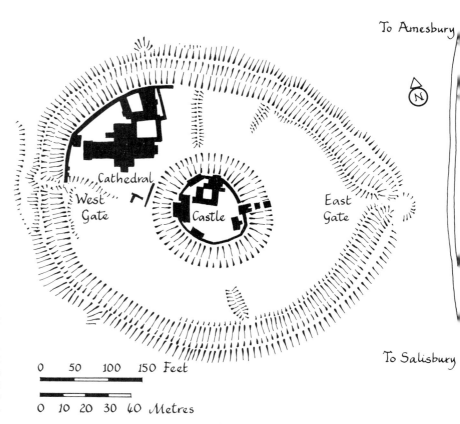

To Amesbury

N

Cathedral

West Gate

Castle

East Gate

To Salisbury

0   50   100   150 Feet

0   10 20 30 40 Metres

11

Sherborne Castle, Dorset

The see of Sherborne was founded in 705 when Ine, King of Wessex, divided the see of Winchester in half, basing the second bishopric here. St Aldhelm, Abbot of Malmesbury, was appointed as the first bishop whilst also retaining his abbacy. Later the see went through various divisions and accretions until 1075, when it was finally moved to Old Sarum. The bishops of Sarum did not immediately relinquish the abbacy of Sherborne and even after they did so in 1122 Roger, Bishop of Salisbury, retained the great manor here together with the castle east of the town.

Parts of the cathedral church built by Roger survive in the abbey church at Sherborne, and the fine south-west porch was probably built by him. A further interesting relic in the church is a fragment of the Purbeck marble tomb of Clement, one of the later Norman abbots. On the face of the canopy surrounding the head is a poetical Latin inscription which records, 'The Almighty's clemency may Clement feel, under whose sway this house advanced in weal'. Since Clement died in *c.* 1155, this stone is one of the earliest tomb portraits in the country.

The main Norman interest of Sherborne resides in the ruins of the Old Castle. The site is generally referred to as the 'old' castle in order to distinguish it from Sir Walter Raleigh's nearby residence called 'The Castle'. Raleigh actually indulged in some imaginative restoration of the earlier castle and this was accomplished with such facility that it is difficult in some cases to separate the two phases! The original quality of the place is evident from the first sight of the Norman gatehouse; it is a superb piece of fine-faced ashlar work in mellow Ham stone. The square-headed window was inserted by Raleigh and, in this later modification as in certain of its original details, the work reminds us of the gatehouse at Newark built by Roger's nephew Bishop Alexander of Lincoln. Inside the castle, the feeling

is one of roominess and grace, for this was not a 'castle' in the usual sense but a fortified palace, as was Bishop Roger's other 'castle' at Old Sarum.

Sadly, the site was partially demolished after the Civil War by General Fairfax, and hence the central buildings are greatly ruined, but sufficient remains to convey an impression of the gracious lifestyle of its builder. It consisted of a tower keep attached to the south-west corner of a large square block of buildings arranged round a central courtyard. There is much surviving structural decoration including doorways with moulded surrounds and blank arcading both inside and out. Apart from a large hall, sets of chambers and other domestic offices, there was a handsome chapel commensurate with the ecclesiastical dignity of the castle's builder. Sherborne, along with Roger's other castles, was confiscated by King Stephen in 1139.

Map References: **Castle** ST 647167 (metric map 183. 1-inch map 178)
Church ST 638165
Locations: The castle is in guardianship and is open standard hours and Sunday mornings from 9.30, April to September. It is on the south-east edge of the town, with open parkland to the south. The main railway line passes by to the north. The church is in the town centre by the school.

This elegant porch was probably built by Roger, Bishop of Salisbury, since certain of its details are paralleled in his palace nearby.

A partly reconstructed drawing of a window and blind arcading from Bishop Roger's palace.

12
Fordington: St George Tympanum, Dorset

The church of St George at Fordington is almost unrecognizable as a Norman structure since it was engulfed during the first quarter of this century by a huge new church. This late initiative in church building fortunately left the three southern bays of the small original nave intact and, even more importantly, the south doorway. As at Wentworth, a carving of the patron saint was incorporated in the Norman church and here it is preserved, doubtless in its original position, over the south door.

This splendid carving commemorates the same miracle as the star embodied in the arms of the de Veres at Castle Hedingham. During the epic Siege of Antioch by the Crusaders in 1098, St George appeared to the Christian host in the battle and led them in their attack on the Seljuks. This legend had an immediate impact and Richard I later placed his army under the saint's protection. Ultimately, the valour of St George was so celebrated that he was adopted as England's patron saint.

Here at Fordington we see St George mounted on a horse and plunging his spear into enemy soldiers who, although they look superficially like Normans, carry round shields with protruding bosses in the Saracen fashion. On the left, two knights kneel in prayer, their kite-shaped shields and spears leaning behind them. They stare in amazement at the saint's image and, like the soldiers at Mons during the Great War, take new heart from the vision. It should be noted that the gonfanon or banner which St George holds has a cross on it with three tails, probably symbolizing the Trinity. This design bears a marked similarity to the Papal Banner depicted in the Bayeux Tapestry and, in this detail as in others, the Fordington sculpture seems close to the Tapestry in style. If we are persuaded by these similarities, then the Fordington piece must date to the early 12th century, soon after the victorious Crusaders returned home bearing their wondrous tales of St George's appearance.

The miracle of St George at the Siege of Antioch in 1098. This is a powerful piece of sculpture – the Christian knights at the left offer up prayers of thanks as their enemies are put to confusion.

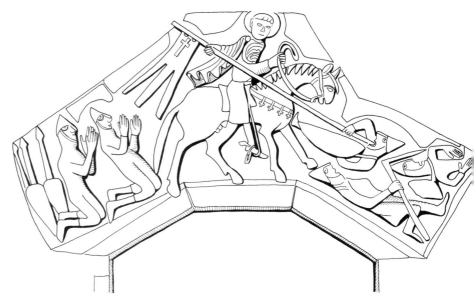

Map Reference: SX 699905 (metric map 194. 1-inch map 178)
Nearest Town: Dorchester
Location: Fordington is a suburb of Dorchester on the south-eastern side of the town. It is on the A352, called Fordington Road, to Wareham.

13
Corfe Castle, Dorset

The great keep of Corfe Castle must be one of the best-known Norman structures in England; its ruined devastation has not robbed it of its power but it must have looked superb before its deliberate demolition after the Civil War.

The first castle at Corfe was built by William I and it was to remain in royal hands until the 16th century. The inner curtain and a hall remain from the 11th-century phase, but this hilltop site which controlled traffic to and from the Isle of Purbeck was defended by the keep we see now as early as 1100. The style of the building is severe, with little internal decora-

Map Reference: SY 959824 (metric map 195. 1-inch map 179)
Nearest Town: Wareham
Location: Corfe is on the Isle of Purbeck and the castle has a commanding site above the town. An attractive though rather touristy spot, the castle has fairly recently been acquired by the National Trust and is open March–October, 10–6 every day, and November–February, Saturday and Sunday, 2–4, weather permitting.

tion and a deliberately featureless exterior. It seems that the western bailey continued in use and that a southern one may have been added at this time. The site remained as a keep and bailey castle until early in the 13th century when King John revamped and extended the defences on a lavish scale and built a suite of staterooms in the inner ward.

14
Isle of Purbeck Sites, Dorset

The 12th century saw a developing interest in this rather remote region. Doubtless the royal castle at Corfe stimulated the local economy and we know that, whilst freestone from Purbeck was used to a limited extent in Saxon times, the main exploitation of the 'marble' in particular did not begin before the 12th century, early examples of its use being the tomb of Abbot Clement at Sherborne and the Temple Church in London.

Three Norman sites in the Isle are of particular interest and two are very unusual. The first is the small church at Studland, a celebrated example of Norman work. It consists of a nave, perhaps of the late 11th century, and a tower space and square-ended chancel of *c.* 1130. Internally, the eastern parts have heavy rib-vaults and this elaboration, together with the openings to north and south under the tower suggesting transepts, indicate that the church was conceived in an ambitious style. Externally it is evident that the tower was never finished, and the elevation is rather unsatisfying. Of the carved corbel table little will be said beyond noting the dégagé couple above the south porch who seem to have anticipated the nudist beach nearby!

At Worth Matravers is a good instance of the extension of cultivation into unpromising marginal lands during the 12th century. This phenomenon, which is also reflected in drainage projects in the fens of eastern England and Romney Marsh as well as by the establishment of settlements in the inhospitable Marches of

The once strong citadel of Corfe now stands sentinel above a small market town and fields of placid horses.

Map References: **Worth Matravers** SY 975775 (metric map 195. 1-inch map 179)
St Aldhelm's Chapel SY 961755
Studland Church SZ 036826
Nearest Town: Swanage
Locations: Worth Matravers is at the end of minor roads and is reached from the B3069 between Corfe and Swanage. The field systems are explained on boards in the centre of the village in the car-park, and routes to the systems are clearly laid out. St Aldhelm's Head is a walk of about 1½ miles (2.4 km) from Worth Matravers in a southerly direction; it is by a Coast-guard station down a farm track which is unsuitable for cars.

Studland is on the north-east side of the Isle of Purbeck, at the east end of the B3351. It is possible to take a ferry from Studland to Bournemouth across the mouth of Poole Harbour.

Wales (Heath and Longtown), is dramatically manifested at Worth Matravers by strip lynchets.

Such lynchets were deliberately excavated on hill slopes in order to provide more level surfaces for ploughing. Here at Worth Matravers, they exist on both sides of a little valley leading down to the coast and they provide one of the most dramatic examples of such landscape features in the country. Lynchets are relatively common in areas like Dorset which abound in steep hillsides, and whilst they are most likely to belong to the period of 12th-century population expansion, there is hot debate as to the date at which lynchets were first developed. This problem will be resolved only by more archaeological excavation of such sites; for the present we will accept the majority view of their origins. The village itself is attractive if over-visited, but there is good Norman work in the church including a battered tympanum depicting the Crowning of the Virgin, a most unusual theme. This was the village where the ploughmen who created the lynchets lived; perhaps they needed to grow more food because of an influx of quarrymen?

The third Purbeck monument is the enigmatic structure called 'St Aldhelm's Chapel'. The 'chapel' is a small square building with a pyramidal roof. It is entered by a round-headed doorway in the north-west side and within there is a central pillar supporting four rib vaults which are probably late-12th-century. Today, the structure is used as a chapel and an altar is tucked away in one corner. There is a 13th-century reference to a chaplain but, if it was built as a chapel, there are no structural signs of it. Indeed, the square unorientated plan (i.e. not facing east–west) and the site are really quite unsuitable for such a use. What was it?

The site must hold the key; it is on a headland looking out to sea. The site is well placed for observation and commands a dangerous coastline – indeed, there is still an HM Coastguard station immediately beside the Norman building. Another factor is that the building

Above left: Studland Church; the tower was probably never finished.

Left: St Aldhelm's Chapel – was this a Norman lighthouse?

Below: Lynchets at Worth Matravers. These 'giant's steps' were probably formed during the 12th century when an increasing population required that more marginal land was brought under cultivation.

stands in a shallow square enclosure, unusual for a chapel but a common enough adjunct to Roman signal stations, e.g. at Scarborough. Was this building built as a lighthouse, with a now-vanished upper storey which contained a beacon light? Such an interpretation would fit the evidence better than the chapel theory. Whilst the structure would be unique, the Roman lighthouse at Dover must have been known to the Normans and considerable sea-borne traffic would have developed as a result of the trade in Purbeck marble. Perhaps this site at St Aldhelm's Head has been a well-known landmark to seafarers for a very long time indeed . . .

15

Christchurch Castle, House and Priory, Dorset

Christchurch is dominated by the large priory church which became so famous during the Middle Ages that it eclipsed the old name of the town, 'Twineham', referring to the confluence of the rivers Avon and Stour near the site. There had been a minster church here in Anglo-Saxon times, but it was not until the place was granted to Ranulf Flambard in 1093–7 that it came to prominence. This Flambard, who later became Bishop of Durham and built the splendid cathedral there, was a man of evil repute. He was chief minister to William Rufus and was credited with all manner of vileness. Whether or not this was true, he planned a fine new church for Twineham and began to build it. In 1100, Rufus was killed in the New Forest and Flambard fell from power. Twineham was then given to another lord of dubious renown, de Redvers, of whom we hear more in the entry for Exeter.

Parts of Flambard's church survive including three crypts beneath the choir and transepts of the priory church. Above ground, the plan was probably conceived by Flambard but most of the actual masonry belongs to the 12th century, after his fall. The transept is early 12th

century; the lower part of the nave was probably complete by 1130 but construction obviously went on long afterwards for the high altar was not finally dedicated until 1195.

Fascinating as the priory church is, the principal reason for visiting Christchurch is its castle, or rather one part of it. The castle was presumably built by Baldwin de Redvers after Henry I gave him the church and town of Twineham. Foundations of a rectangular keep with curious bevelled corners can be seen on top of a small motte, but it is the Constable's House, a fine example of Norman domestic architecture, which is most exciting. This stands beside the river, convenient for the later lavatory at the back, and is unusually built from blocks of Purbeck marble. The house has a ground floor or basement with a first-floor hall above, like Boothby Pagnell. Also like Boothby, the hall has a fireplace with a handsome circular chimney which still stands. There are some good two-light windows with restrained decoration, and it is thought that the house was built by Richard de Redvers, 2nd Earl of Devon, in c. 1160.

Map Reference: **Castle** SZ 160927 (metric map 195. 1-inch map 179)
Location: The castle and Norman house are both guardianship sites and are open standard hours. They stand in a municipal park, the house next to the bowling green on the main Broad which runs through the town. The priory is a few hundred yards south of the castle.

Right: A fine essay in surface decoration on a stair turret of the late-12th-century priory church at Christchurch.

Below: The Constable's House with its fine chimney and splendid windows.

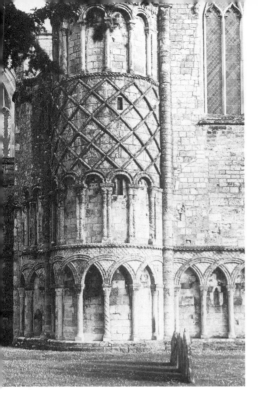

16

The New Forest and the Rufus Stone, Hampshire

One of the most familiar effects of the Norman Conquest was the widespread establishment of royal forests. The Anglo-Saxon nobility had been fond of hunting and woodland was in some cases reserved for that purpose, but the Normans promoted the idea to an unparalleled extent. The Conqueror himself 'loved the tall stags as if he were their father', and at their greatest extent, royal forests and noblemen's 'chases' covered one-fifth of England.

The word 'forest' is a term of art in this context; it did not mean what we would call a forest today. Royal forests were created by law and the term reflects their legal status, not their vegetation type; forests included large areas of arable and common pastureland as well as woodland. Nor should we imagine that Norman kings and lords spent all their time hunting; if mere sport had been the real reason for the creation of forests then they need not have been as extensive as they were. Certainly forests provided the king and his court with venison and pork as well as timber, but the principal attraction was revenue.

Royal forests provided income for the king by means of 'fines', rents and levies of various sorts. Forest Law could be strict and dwellers in the forest were not supposed to hunt the deer – the king's property – cut down trees or grub up their roots, goats found in the forest were confiscated and dogs could have a paw amputated. But whilst there were many crimes which could be committed in the royal forests, they were not all punished by cruel amputations or similar barbarities. Instead, they were resolved by fines and payments; this was how the king obtained his income. During the later 12th century, for example, it gradually became more common for villeins wishing to obtain further land to cut out 'assarts' from forests. The word comes from the Norman French *essarter*, 'to grub up', and licences to assart became an important source of revenue. Similarly, rights of pannage – the grazing of swine on acorns – and the right to take timber for house and hearth were all subject to 'fines'.

Here in the New Forest we can still see comparatively large areas of greenwood, called by the Normans 'vert' green. The word 'vert' gave rise to the term 'verderers' for some of the many officials who managed the royal forests. In the New Forest there are still verderers although they have now 'changed sides' since they represent the interests of the commoners and others whilst the privileges of the Crown have devolved on the Forestry Commission. This shadowy administration also exists in other former forests like Dean and Epping, serving to remind us that forests were not 'wild' but highly organized – the income which they generated was a weighty matter, as the court house at Lydford attests.

Map Reference: **Rufus Stone** SU 270125 (metric map 195. 1-inch map 180)
Nearest Town: Southampton
Location: The Rufus Stone is well signposted and is just north of the A31(T) about 5 miles (8 km) west of the edge of Southampton.

Forest boundaries were not normally marked on the ground, although individual woods and deer parks within a forest could be provided with banks and ditches to aid their management, as at Kincardine. The practice of planting varieties of trees in defined areas has a long history – back to the Bronze Age here in the New Forest – and this was a further important aspect of management. Few trees in the New Forest are older than the 17th century, but venerable giants like the 'Major Oak' in Sherwood Forest may well have been planted within a century of the end of our period.

Of course the most famous event to have occurred in the New Forest happened at Minstead; we will never know whether William Rufus died by pure accident, by malice or by exercise of the Black Arts as some have claimed. There is no doubt that the unfortunate king had an unpleasant reputation; the Anglo-Saxon Chronicle records his death with unconcealed glee and adds, 'He was ever agreeable to evil men's advice and through his own greed was ever vexing this nation with force and with unjust taxes.'

The memorial at Minstead where William Rufus met his end. Was he murdered or was it pure accident? We will never know.

17

Southampton Houses, Hampshire

The development of Southampton is really concerned with the stories of three towns, each of which was on a different site. The Roman town of Clausentum was on the east bank of the River Itchen; the Saxon town of Hamwih, probably the largest in Anglo-Saxon England, clustered round St Mary's church on the west bank of the river; and the medieval town, which was the first to be called 'Southampton', was located on a gravel promontory overlooking the waters of the River Test.

By the time of the Conquest, Hamwih had probably dwindled away to a few houses; the settlement had never recovered from the Danish raids of the 9th century. We learn from Domesday Book in 1086 that the Anglo-Saxon citizens were joined by 65 people of French origin and by another 31 Englishmen from elsewhere. As at Carlisle, the different communities occupied separate areas of the town. The French were in the south-west corner around French Street and the English in the eastern part near English Street, which was later renamed High Street. At that time, the town was apparently not defended and it was not until the reign of King John that stone walls were begun.

From an early stage in the town's Norman history, the French quarter was noticeably more prosperous than the English. By the 12th century, under the watchful eye of the royal castle to the north, the French merchants had

Map References: **Walls** SU 418114 (metric map 196. 1-inch map 180)
King John's House SU 418113
Canute's Palace SU 420110
Locations: 'Canute's Palace', a very run-down ruin, is down a narrow lane (Porters Lane) at the southern end of the High Street. King John's House is behind the Tudor House Museum on St Michael's Square and is reached through a delightful re-creation of a Tudor scented garden. The Norman town walls face the Western Esplanade and are marked by a stretch with flat buttresses.

begun to build themselves fine stone houses, whilst their English counterparts had to make do with wood. The merchants grew rich on the lucrative trade with Normandy and later with the wine trade from south-west France. But still the economy of the townsmen was mixed; farm animals were kept and butchered beside the houses, and in the eastern part the scene was still semi-rural.

We must therefore imagine a town which enjoyed an expanding economy and increasing disposable wealth. Something of the range of Norman trade is indicated in Fitz Stephen's account of London, in which he mentions Arabs, Scythians, Babylon, the Nile, Chinese, French, Nowegians and Russians; there is no doubt that Southampton was not far behind London in the richness of its trade. The physical legacy of this wealth is represented by the substantial remains of two large stone houses. Perhaps the more remarkable is the house called 'Canute's Palace'. It was built in about 1180 and incorporated both domestic and commercial functions under one roof. It is a markedly long house because it had at its west end a normal first-floor hall of the type seen at Christchurch, but at the east there was an additional element which consisted of a warehouse on the ground floor and a counting house above.

The second house, called 'King John's House', near the Blue Anchor postern gate in the later city wall, was sited immediately behind the 12th-century quay and its exposed position resulted in its west wall being incorporated into the city wall. As first built, it is likely that this house also had a two-cell plan, but only the western half of it survives. Here the lower floor was probably used for business whilst the upper was given over to the normal hall and chamber domestic arrangement. Both houses have some surviving architectural details including hooded fireplaces like the one at Boothby Pagnell, and two-light windows. Such houses were as fine as could be found anywhere, and they provide an eloquent tribute to the success of Southampton's early burgesses.

Norman chimney (c. 1200) re-erected behind the Tudor House Museum at Southampton.

18
Winchester: Hospital of St Cross, Hampshire

The post-Conquest history of Winchester Cathedral provides one of the most dramatic instances of the great energies of the Normans. The Saxon minster had been the crowning place of the kings of Wessex and was steeped in Anglo-Saxon tradition; perhaps no other building symbolized the English nation with such authority. It is therefore not surprising that, soon after the expulsion of the last Saxon bishop, Stigand, in 1070, work started on a new minster beside the existing one.

Work pressed on with such speed that on 8 April 1093 the monks processed from the old minster into the new and took with them the shrine of St Swithun, one of the patron saints of the minster. The very next day, workmen began to demolish the Saxon church! This single act of wholesale replacement indicates more dramatically than any other action the overwhelming desire of the Normans to break

Map Reference: **St Cross Hospital** SU 476278 (metric map 185. 1-inch map 168) *Location:* The Hospital of St Cross is close by the River Itchen, 1 mile (1.6 km) south of the city off the main road (a Roman one) to Southampton, down a short lane to the east. It is well signposted and the main road is itself called St Cross.

the Anglo-Saxon continuity. Of the new minster, only the crypt and crossing remain, the rest having been replaced later in the Gothic style.

If the remains of the cathedral at Winchester are not particularly extensive, there are other links with our period. The first of these is the fine Tournai marble font which is discussed more thoroughly in the entry on the 'Hampshire Fonts'. This was probably imported by Bishop Henry de Blois, brother to King Stephen and one of the most able of Anglo-Norman churchmen. De Blois also rebuilt the bishop's palace at Wolvesley, the ruins of which survive but are not easily accessible.

More importantly de Blois, like Rahere at St Bartholomew's, London, had a pious dream which found fulfilment and which still affects us today. When Henry was appointed bishop in 1129 he was only 28 years old, and he kept his position right through his brother's troubled reign. In 1137, two years after Stephen had mounted his precarious throne, England, its economy wrecked by civil war, faced bleak times. The Anglo-Saxon Chronicle records: 'Then corn was dear, and meat and cheese and butter, for there was none in the land. Poor men died of hunger, some went out for alms who were once powerful men, and some fled out of the land.'

Henry de Blois was a great magnate in his own right and his lavish patronage of the arts was celebrated. Yet we think that he was deeply affected by the adversity of his fellow countrymen and his religious zeal could not allow him to ignore the earthly ministry of the Church. To this end, he determined to found the Hospital of St Cross. As early as March 1137, Pope Innocent II confirmed the rights and possessions of the new hospital and we read in the foundation charter that 13 poor men were to be resident in the hospital and provided with clothing, bread, meat and drink. Additionally, a hundred other poor persons were to be received at the hour of dinner and such other benefits should be provided for the needy as the house could afford.

The new experiment worked, but it was not

free of difficulties. There were plenty of the usual gripes about greed and mismanagement and finally, in 1151, de Blois handed over the hospital to the Knights of St John of Jerusalem. All went well until his death in 1173, but then fierce quarrels broke out and the Hospitallers were ultimately expelled in 1204. Men argued for centuries over the management of the hospital and few good ideas can have provoked so much ire. As late as 1835, commissioners found discrepancies in the hospital funds, but we should perhaps be grateful that these events provided Anthony Trollope with the raw material for his 'Barchester' stories.

Winchester St Cross – one of the purest specimens of Transitional architecture in England in which chevron ornament shoots round lightly pointed arches and fully groined 'Early English' vaults.

Today, the atmosphere is more peaceful. There are still pensioners living in the hospital, though the buildings, with the notable exception of the church, are later than our period. The church is still used for worship every day and the tradition of Henry de Blois's 'hundred poor persons' being received for dinner is maintained by means of the 'Dole', which consists of a 'horn' of beer and some bread which can be obtained from the Porter's Lodge. In all these ways the hospital has remained true to the ideals of its founder; in the church we see a monument of a different kind, but it is as dramatic in its own way.

The Church of St Cross is one of the purest specimens of Transitional architecture in England. Building took a long time; it probably started in 1160 and continued into the 13th century. The result is a superb mingling of the lightest Romanesque with the simplest Gothic elements; light plays through the fine windows and the beautiful vaulting springs upwards to the sky. Anyone wanting to understand the change from Romanesque to Gothic can see at Winchester both the sombre majesty of the early Norman style in the cathedral and the exhilarating lightness which marked its passing here at St Cross. It is difficult to believe that only a century separates the two.

Portus Adurni, was put into a state of military readiness for the second time. The east and west gates, called the 'Land' and 'Water' gates respectively, were rebuilt as rectangular towers with tunnel-shaped passageways beneath them, and a great keep was raised in the north-west corner of the old fort. The keep, which dates to around 1120, oversails the line of the Roman walls and stands within a small rectangular bailey created by the simple expedient of building a new ditch and curtain wall on the south and east sides whilst retaining the Roman walls to the north and west.

The keep as first built consisted of a basement, main floor and gallery above; access was at main-floor level through a forebuilding on the east side. Whilst not as impressive as Dover or Rochester, the keep in its first phase resembled that of the other royal castle at Corfe and like it presented a severe aspect to the world. The height of the original structure is indicated by the angle and external buttresses on the north and west sides which finish a good way below the present summit of the keep. In about 1170, the keep was raised by the addition of a wholly new third floor. At the same time, the forebuilding was rebuilt in its existing form and contained a chapel and perhaps accommodation for a priest.

Map Reference: SU 625046 (metric map 196. 1-inch map 180)
Nearest Town: Portsmouth
Location: The castle is in guardianship and is open standard hours and also on Sunday mornings from 9.30, between April and September. The castle is on a promontory in Portsmouth Harbour and can be seen from the main A27 road.

Henry I's great keep; as first built it had only two storeys, but a slight kink in the right-hand side shows where the top storey was added in c. 1170.

19

Porchester Castle, Hampshire

There are few more spectacular examples of Norman military opportunism than the siting of Porchester Castle. It is tucked into one corner of a large Roman masonry fort which forms an impressive outer bailey. This fort was built late in the 3rd century as part of the 'Saxon Shore' defences, which also included the fort at Pevensey and probably at Cardiff, both of which were also reused as handy castle sites during the Norman period.

During the reign of Henry I (1100–35) the Roman fort of Porchester, originally called

An Augustinian priory was established at the instigation of Henry de Blois, Bishop of Winchester, in the south-east corner of the Roman fort in 1133. The priory did not remain here long, however, for between 1145 and 1153 the canons moved to a more spacious site at nearby Southwick. Hence the priory church can be dated with some confidence to the second quarter of the 12th century, and although the claustral ranges have gone, it stands as an interesting example of a simple and austere Norman priory church. The decorated west front is well preserved, but a second ornate doorway in the north side of the nave has largely disappeared. Inside, the church is unusually faced in ashlar and there is a fine 12th-century font which bears an elaborate scheme of decoration including intersecting arches, foliage, birds, beasts and reptiles.

The font in the priory church at Porchester has a fine band of inhabited vinescroll round the top.

20
Tournai Marble Fonts, Hampshire

Four of the eight known Tournai marble fonts imported into England during the 12th century are to be found in Hampshire. Of the four outside the county, one is represented by a fragment from the town ditch at Ipswich, and could have formed part of the ballast of a ship; and another is in St Peter's church in the same town. The others are at Lincoln Cathedral and at Thornton Curtis (Humberside). It is noteworthy that all these places were near the east coast (opposite Belgium) and were either ports in their own right or else close to the sea. Thus the occurrence of large imported fonts on the east coast is understandable.

The Hampshire distribution is more unusual, however; here they occur at St Michael's Southampton, Winchester Cathedral, St Mary Bourne and East Meon. Of these places, only Southampton is a port and, whilst

Winchester was served by the trade on the River Itchen, the other two places are well inland. This has led to the suggestion that the fonts may have been imported as the result of a personal initiative by Henry de Blois, Bishop of Winchester, rather than being the fortuitous products of trade. This theory is certainly an attractive one, and it is known that certain of the churches were within his gift. Also, we know that de Blois was 'most earnest in beautifying churches' and was wealthy enough to afford the importation of such costly and cumbersome objects into his diocese.

The fonts were made at Tournai in Belgium, where the marble is still being quarried today; in 1935, a new base was made for the font at St Mary Bourne by the successors of the early medieval craftsmen. The fonts are square blocks of marble with circular bowls in the centre lined with lead. The upper surfaces are

Map References: **East Meon** SU 681223 (metric map 185. 1-inch map 168) **Winchester Cathedral** SU 482292 **St Mary Bourne** SU 423504 **Southampton, St Michael's** SU 419113 (metric map 196. 1-inch map 180) *Nearest Towns:* Petersfield (East Meon), Andover (St Mary Bourne) *Locations:* East Meon is signposted off the A32 Fareham to Alton road; at West Meon take the main road to the east for 3 miles (5 km). The church nestles under the edge of the South Downs and has important 12th-century fabric. St Mary Bourne is on the east side of Andover about 5 miles (8 km) away. From the A303 trunk road to Basingstoke, take the B3048 to Hurstbourne Priors and then on to St Mary Bourne. St Michael's Church, Southampton, is in St Michael's Square near the Tudor House Museum (see Site 17).

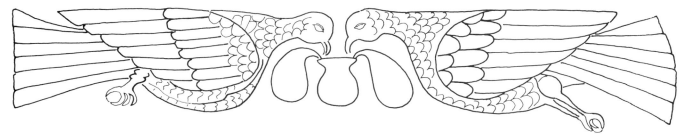

Doves drink from a vase – symbol of the sacrament of the Holy Communion – at St Mary Bourne.

The Winchester Cathedral font with its scene of the Miracle of St Nicholas in which he gave dowries to a poor nobleman which enabled his three daughters to make suitable marriages rather than being forced into prostitution! The saint stands at the right, giving a bag of money to the kneeling father, behind whom are his three daughters and, at the extreme left, a prospective suitor with a hawk, symbol of wealth.

decorated with vinescrolls, doves and other motifs whilst the sides have a variety of finely carved scenes representing such themes as the Life and Works of St Nicholas, at Winchester; the Creation and Fall, at East Meon; and Trees of Life and birds, at St Mary Bourne. Full use is made of the smooth, darkly gleaming surface of the polished stone, and the delicate details of the dress, hair and jewellery are carefully incised into the surface.

21
Compton Double Chancel, Surrey

Much of the nave of Compton church is probably Saxo-Norman, as is the lower part of the western tower. It is in the chancel that we see the most interesting Norman evidence, however, for Compton has a rare two-storeyed sanctuary which was intended to be used at both levels. The reason for this unusual configuration is unclear; it is possible either that the upper chamber was intended to hold a relic, or else that it was to be used by an

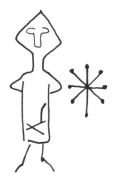

Map Reference: SU 778149 (metric map 197. 1-inch map 181)
Nearest Town: Petersfield
Location: The village is on the B2146 between Petersfield and the coast and is set in the South Downs. The church is on the east side of the road, in a lovely long churchyard, and is itself a most attractive 'vernacular' building externally.

Graffito of knight on the chancel arch at Compton.

anchorite who apparently lived in a small cell on the south side of the chancel. The double chancel was inserted within the existing walls of the sanctuary in *c.* 1180, at the time when the church was remodelled and extended.

Apart from the double chancel, Compton has a number of important individual features. The first of these is the wooden screen of the upper chancel itself; this appears from its design of simple Romanesque arches to date from the same period as the chancel. This piece of woodwork must be one of the most complete survivals of 12th-century internal fittings. The second important feature is a small fragment of late-12th-century glass depicting the Virgin and Child, now set in the east window of the sanctuary. This, like the double chancel, belongs to the refurbishing of the church and it is probable that the abstract wallpainting on the east wall of the nave similarly dates from that period.

Finally, on the south side of the chancel arch is a small graffito of a knight. This crude portrait, showing a man clad in a surcoat and wearing a conical helmet, is also 12th-century and includes an eight-armed cross. Compton is just beside the reputed line of the 'Pilgrims' Way' and doubtless many knights and others called here on their way to Canterbury. But what did they venerate in this place and why was it revamped in such an elaborate style? We will probably never know the answer to either question . . .

The 'double chancel' at Compton. Note the abstract wall painting on the east wall of the nave above the chancel arch and the wooden balustrade above the sanctuary arch in the middle distance.

22
Chaldon Wallpaintings, Surrey

It is often said that Hell is much easier to imagine than Heaven and here at Chaldon we see a grand essay in the macabre medieval imagination. On the west wall of this otherwise quiet and unassuming parish church tucked away beside the Pilgrims' Way is a vision of Damnation calculated to send a shiver down the spine. Or was it? It is frankly difficult to imagine even the most credulous

12th-century peasant taking the leering devils and cavorting imps entirely seriously. Be that as it may, the intention is clear enough – to urge the sinful man to turn from his wicked ways and look to the certain future, i.e. Death.

The composition is stolid, consisting of four sections divided up the middle by a Ladder of Salvation up which naked souls climb, and across the centre by a celestial 'floor' dividing the Horrors of Hell below from the relative tranquillity of Purgatory above. The figures are silhouettes against a background of dark red ochre. They have been repainted and are therefore rather 'sharp', but the overall effect

Map Reference: TQ 309557 (metric map 187. 1-inch map 170)
Nearest Town: Caterham
Location: Close to the Pilgrims' Way, Chaldon is amazingly rural and tranquil despite being so close to the M25. It lies on the west side of Caterham, 2 miles (3.2 km) along the B2031; turn north to Chaldon. The church is set apart from the village but there is a sign to it.

A section of the Great Doom at Chaldon showing the Horrors of Hell in which a miser is being roasted over a fire and cheating traders are uncomfortably suspended on a bridge of spikes.

must be similar to the original. The appearance of a Tree of Life in the bottom right-hand corner (a familiar 12th-century image) and the Ladder of Salvation both point to a date of *c.* 1200. The work is 'primitive' and there is no need to invoke a monastic or other high-status milieu for the painting.

Starting from the bottom left, we see devils roasting chaps in a cauldron to the right of the ladder. Two other devils hold a 'bridge of spikes' reserved for cheating traders, upon which unfortunates try vainly to carry on their earthly trades. A potter holds a pot but has no wheel, a woman has wool but no distaff, two blacksmiths have a horseshoe but no anvil: these scenes emphasize the futility of earthly preoccupations on the divine scale. Around these lower scenes can be seen the Seven Deadly Sins (or 'Vices' as they were termed at Southrop and elsewhere). On the extreme left is Sloth in which three figures walk on a beast rather than on firm ground; between the devil and the cauldron is Gluttony (drunkenness) in which a pilgrim forsakes his vocation by casting away his cloak and seizing a bottle of liquor; Pride, Anger, Lechery, Avarice and Envy all appear in their turn, but on the extreme right is the Tree of Life, indicating the true path to Salvation.

Above, there is a scene of the Archangel Michael weighing souls on the left-hand side, with a devil disobligingly attempting to hold down the scales in his favour. The Just are led away towards the Ladder of Salvation and a small roundel at the top shows Christ awaiting them. To the right, Christ appears in his 'Harrowing of Hell' role in which he closes Hell's Mouth with a spear (beneath his feet) and the Sinners supplicate Him for mercy. Nobody could feel completely confident when confronted by such a stern reminder of Judgement as this!

23
Chichester Cathedral, West Sussex

The see of Chichester was created in 1080 when the old Anglo-Saxon see of Selsey was removed here. This action was probably a part of the same deliberate Norman reorganization of the Church which resulted in the creation of the sees of Norwich, Sarum and Lincoln. Bishop Ralph de Luffa began a new church at Chichester in 1091 and the eastern part was dedicated in 1108. Building continued during the rest of the 12th century, despite various reverses, and the existing nave is basically of the 12th century although the eastern parts of the church have since been demolished. Curiously, after a damaging fire in 1187, the austere Norman interior of the nave was deco-

Map Reference: SU 859048 (metric map 197. 1-inch map 181)
Location: The cathedral is at the centre of the town on the main A259 road.

.rated *in situ* by the addition of Purbeck marble shafts and decorated string courses. This has resulted in an unusual juxtaposition of restrained Romanesque and delicate Early English elements.

Apart from the architecture of the cathedral, Chichester has another important claim to our attention. This is provided by two carved slabs now built into the south wall of the choir. Much dispute has been provoked by these slabs, with some scholars claiming them as a Saxon legacy from the earlier site at Selsey, whilst others assert that they are 12th-century. What seems most probable is that whilst the sculptures embody certain Anglo-Saxon traits such as the style of the architecture and the positioning of the figures, the overall similarities between the panels and illustrations in the St Alban's Psalter dated to 1119–45 prove that they must in fact be of the mid-12th century. If this date is accepted, then these panels are amongst the finest 12th-century sculptures in England; both were probably carved by the same man.

In the first panel, 'Christ at Mary's House', the two sisters meet Christ, who is shown taller than the other figures for dramatic emphasis. In the second panel, 'The Raising of Lazarus', there is more tension and movement. Christ is again shown somewhat larger than the rest, and it has been suggested that the careful positioning of the figures owes something to contemporary religious drama. When the original glass or metal eyes filled the now-empty sockets, the faces would have been masterpieces of Romanesque art.

Chichester nave was revamped during the late 12th century after a fire in 1187. It was then that the Purbeck marble columns were added to the austere Norman arcades.

Detail of Christ's head from the Chichester 'Lazarus' panel showing the careful tooling which lends such potency to the expression of the sculpture. The eyes would originally have been filled with paste or semi-precious stones.

24
West Sussex Wallpaintings

The three churches of Hardham, Clayton and Coombes contain important wallpaintings dated to *c.* 1100. These paintings are executed in true fresco technique and appear to be the earliest large-scale survival of such pictures in England. It was for long believed that the paintings were a demonstration of the artistic patronage of nearby Lewes Priory which, as a Cluniac house, might be expected to encourage such richness. However, more recently it has been suggested that the powerful de Braose family, founders of the new town of Shoreham, were the patrons of the painters or at any rate facilitated the introduction into England of the Continental iconography used in the pictures.

Map References: **Coombes** TQ 191082 (metric map 198. 1-inch map 182)
Clayton TQ 299140
Hardham TQ 639176
Nearest Towns: Shoreham (Coombes), Burgess Hill (Clayton), Pulborough (Hardham)

One of the fine border designs at Clayton.

Locations: Coombes is up a tiny valley road along the River Adur. Do not take the A283 to Bramber which goes up the east side of the valley, but, from the A27, take the minor road to Coombes and Bramber which goes up the west side. The tiny church is tucked into the hillside and is approached through a farmyard. Clayton is on the east side of the A273 about 3 miles (5 km) south of Burgess Hill. Hardham is 1 mile (1.6 km) south-west of Pulborough on the A29.

The paintings are coloured with red and yellow ochre, lime white and charcoal black, with green at Clayton and Coombes only. These basic hues give a wide range of tones including orange, pink, cream, grey, dark red and brown. Several painters apparently worked on the churches, but the overall quality of the paintings is very high. At Hardham there is the remnant of an inscription in a fine script. Other details such as faces, hands, the borders, architecture and vistas of the Holy City repay close examination; they are minor masterpieces in their own right.

Iconographically, the paintings depict various scenes from the Life of Christ, including a Nativity Cycle at Coombes, Lives and Works of the Saints such as St George and St Vincent, a mangled cycle of the 'Labours of the Months' and the 'Torments of Hell' at Hardham and, at Clayton, a magnificent Last Judgement. These scenes are within the standard repertoire of 12th-century church decoration elsewhere, but in these three churches they are given colour and liveliness which are difficult to parallel. The interior of Hardham church glows with reds and pale yellow with some of the haloes shining with an ethereal blue tint. At Clayton, like the scheme at Chaldon, devils frolic amongst the Damned whilst the Blessed enjoy joy unalloyed. Coombes, nestling into its hillside above the Adur Valley, is more subtle than the other two, yet here we can see snatches of the Nativity Cycle as well as a possible element of the Psychomachia, and

above the chancel arch is a fine Christ in Majesty which, like the carved examples at Elkstone (Gloucestershire) and elsewhere, is flanked by the Symbols of the Evangelists. These precious relics are a marvellous celebration of the warmth and richness of medieval faith.

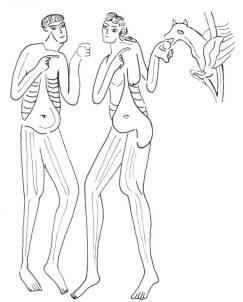

Adam and Eve at Hardham; Eve receives the apple from a griffin rather than a serpent in this version.

This figure at Coombes may represent a man struggling to support the Temple of the Soul, a theme from the 'Psychomachia' which is discussed more fully in the entry on Claverley (Site No. 89). Note the fine double-axe pattern above.

25

Shoreham Old and New, West Sussex

After the Conquest, lands including Bramber and Shoreham were given to William de Braose. The de Braose family became rich and powerful and they established their caput at Bramber, where a castle and the fine church of St Nicholas can still be seen; both of these were founded by the late 11th century. In about 1100, the old port of Shoreham on the River Adur was apparently silting up and hence was becoming impassable for merchant ships. This was a serious matter since Shoreham already had a good trade with the Continent, and so it was that the de Braoses conceived the idea of replacing 'Old' Shoreham by a new port located further south where the river was wider. This decision has resulted in an interesting legacy of monuments at the two settlements.

At Old Shoreham, the church of St Nicholas is basically of Anglo-Saxon date, with the side and west walls of the nave being of the early 11th century. Whilst the commercial importance of Old Shoreham clearly lapsed after the new town was founded in 1100, the church was provided with a fine new central tower and transepts in *c.* 1140. Only the crossing of this later Norman phase remains, but it is very handsomely decorated. There was doubtless an apsidal chancel and, on the evidence of the existing doorway in the north transept, side chapels as well. A remarkable treasure of this church is the possible Norman tie-beam at the east end of the nave. This bears characteristically Romanesque ornament and, if it is indeed of the mid-12th century, it is unique.

New Shoreham presents quite a different aspect from its predecessor. The new port was planned on a fairly lavish scale beside the mouth of the Adur and is divided into rectangular sections by a grid of streets. Little now remains of the early medieval town apart from elements of its plan, but in the High Street the house called 'Marlipins' was probably one of the original buildings of the new town. Marlipins, now used as a museum, is a two-storey house which retains vestigial traces of its early-12th-century origins. The prominent position and sound construction of this building have led to suggestions that this was the 'custom house' of the de Braoses in which they collected harbour dues from users of their port. A small 'business window' can be seen in the main façade between the two doorways.

The major relic of New Shoreham is the mighty church of St Mary de Haura, 'of the harbour' – or rather the fragment of it. Only one bay of the nave survives and the original Norman eastern parts were remodelled later in the Transitional style. But the scale of the transepts with their rather simple arches and capitals indicates the intention of the de Braoses to make Shoreham a major settlement where no town had stood before. We need only contrast the charming simplicity of the little church at Bramber with this huge edifice to see how far the de Braoses had advanced. Their confidence in their new borough was well founded; during the 12th and 13th centuries, Shoreham rose to be one of the chief ports of the south coast, and it doubtless recouped its original investment many times over!

Map References: **Old Shoreham** TQ 208060 (metric map 198. 1-inch map 182) **New Shoreham** TQ 226051 **Bramber** TQ 185107

Locations: Bramber, on the A283 north of Shoreham, is a National Trust site, well signposted and open at all reasonable times. New Shoreham church is behind the High Street in a long churchyard. Marlipins, the Norman House, is in the High Street and is now a museum. Old Shoreham church is to be found beside the A283 overlooking the River Adur and the huge interchange and crossing of the A27(T).

The motte at Bramber which is unusual since it stands at the centre of its surrounding bailey.

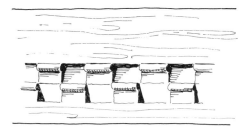

The possible Norman tie-beam in Old Shoreham church with its simple decoration.

26
Pevensey Castle, East Sussex

It was in Pevensey Bay that William the Conqueror landed on Thursday 28 September 1066, and he probably used the walls of the Roman Saxon Shore fort called Anderida as a handy shelter for his invasion force. It is possible that the 'inner bailey' in the south-east corner of the Roman fort was first demarcated at that time. Although it is now landlocked, the fort was originally sited beside Pevensey Haven, a natural anchorage with many sheltered inlets for ships – an ideal site for a landfall. Here, then, Norman England may be said to have started.

After the Conquest Pevensey was granted to William's half-brother Robert, Count of Mortain. He established a small town outside the fort and made an earth and timber castle within the Roman fort on the site of the present inner bailey. Some time around 1100, a great rectangular keep was raised, the lower parts of which are still visible. The curious D-shaped bastions which protrude from the sides of the keep were probably added later, perhaps in imitation of those on the Roman walls on the site.

In the 11th century, Pevensey saw some fighting when it was held by Odo, Bishop of Bayeux, against William Rufus (see entry on Rochester, Kent). This was not the end of

Pevensey's celebrity during our period, however, since in 1101 its castellan, William, Count of Mortain, rebelled against Henry I. Again during the Anarchy of Stephen's reign, Pevensey was besieged in 1147. These later episodes show how important Pevensey was both militarily and psychologically, for it was Pevensey rather than Dover which had shown itself to be the true 'Key to England'.

Plan of Pevensey Roman fort and Norman castle.

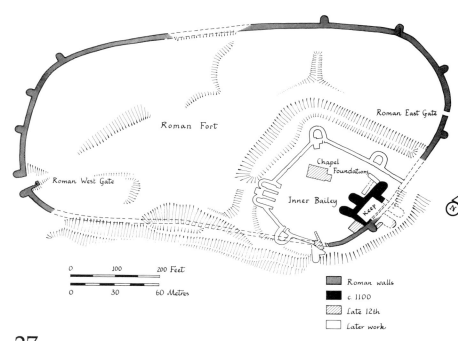

Map Reference: TQ 645048 (metric map 199. 1-inch map 183)
Nearest Town: Eastbourne
Location: The castle is just off the A27 trunk road on the north-east side of Eastbourne. It is a guardianship site and open standard hours and Sunday mornings from 9.30 April to September.

27
Brookland Lead Font, Kent

Nothing of the fabric of Brookland church is Norman, but it retains interesting links with our period. The first of these is a fine wall-painting in the south aisle of the murder of Thomas à Becket. This picture was painted

Map Reference: TQ 989258 (metric map 189. 1-inch map 184)
Nearest Town: Romney
Location: On the A259(T) between Romney and Rye about 5 miles (8 km) west of Romney. The canals are behind and to the side of the church.

during the 13th century and it shows the deep impression made by the interaction of secular and ecclesiastical politics during our period. A second, more direct, link with the Norman past is provided by the watercourse outside the west end of the church; this was dug during the 12th century as part of the reclamation of Romney Marsh, an activity paralleled in the Fens of eastern England (see the entry on the Fenland Abbeys, site No 58).

The greatest Norman treasure at Brookland is, however, its fine lead font which is richly decorated with Signs of the Zodiac and the Labours of the Months. These themes occur separately at several sites, including Burnham Deepdale, but their occurrence together as a single scheme is more difficult to match; the doorway at Barfreston has some of the same elements. The combination of the two themes finds parallels in contemporary manuscripts, however, and more particularly in calendars which were attached to psalters for liturgical purposes. The layout here, with the Zodiac above the Labours, makes it virtually certain that this was the source of the motif.

The font is very probably a French import, for three reasons. First, the closest calendrical parallels are French rather than English. Secondly, whilst the names of the Signs of the Zodiac are rendered in Latin, the names of the months are in Norman French. Thirdly, an almost exactly similar font is known at Saint-Evroult-de-Montfort in Normandy. These factors, together with Brookland's proximity to the coast, suggest that the font was imported during the 1160s. This links in turn with the suspected importation of Tournai marble fonts during the same period by Henry de Blois, Bishop of Winchester.

The font is a cylindrical tub with a strongly modelled rim. Plates for locks or catches can be seen at the top of the sides of the bowl and this reminds us of the ordinances that were passed during the Middle Ages designed to secure the holy water, which was kept in fonts, from the attentions of sorcerers and witches. Below the rim are strongly moulded bands of cable ornament which resemble the similar work on the

East Yorkshire fonts, with a band of chevron moulding beneath. Below, the scenes are arranged in two tiers of architectural arcades which were apparently cast two to a mould, the moulds being laid side by side to form a continuous scheme. There are actually 20 separate arches, the months from March onwards being repeated to fill the circumference of the sides. The Labours of the Months are important since they are an early instance of scenes taken from real life being used in a Norman decorative composition. One rather Continental detail is that for October, which shows a man treading grapes in a huge vat; we know that there were vineyards in England at the time, notably at Ely, but such an image would doubtless have been more familiar to a French rather than an English congregation!

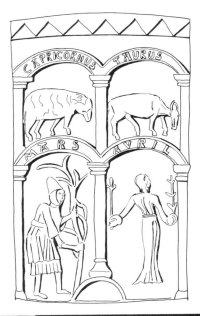

The Brookland lead font. Note the point near the rim on the left where the lid was locked down to prevent misappropriation of the holy water for Black Magic.

*Left: One of the double panels from the font.
'Capricornus' should actually be 'Aries'; perhaps the
craftsman mixed up the ram and the goat. Below,
March is represented by a man pruning a vine and
for April there is a figure of Venus, Goddess of
Fertility; an interesting example of mixed pagan and
Christian themes!*

The Labours in order are:

MARS A man in a hooded cloak pruning a
vine

AVRIL Figure of Venus, the Goddess of
Fertility; an indication of the currency
of classical themes during the 12th
century

MAI A man hawking on horseback

JUIN A man mowing with a scythe

JUILLET A haymaker in a broad-brimmed
hat

AUOUT A man harvesting with a sickle

SEPTEMBRE Threshing with a flail; the man
is stripped to the waist indicating his
exertions!

VITOVRE (A known Norman French form)
The man treading grapes

NOVEMBRE A man knocking down acorns
for a pig to eat

DECEMBRE A man braining the same pig
before winter

JANVIER A two-faced Janus (marking the
'turn' of the year) drinking heartily

FEVRIER A man in a hooded cloak keeping
house by the fire; this in fulfilment of
the excellent advice of Thomas Tusser
(d.1580):

> Feb, fill the dyke
> With what thou dost like.

Note the excellent hooded fireplace beside
which the man sits, as at Boothby Pagnell.

28
Brabourne Church Fittings, Kent

The church of St Mary at Brabourne was
rebuilt *c.* 1180, probably at the time that it was
given to Horton Priory. The church was conceived on a fairly ambitious scale, and important traces of its furnishings survive. Before
considering these detailed matters, the fine
sculpted imposts of the chancel arch and the
elaborate priest's door in the north wall of the
chancel must be mentioned. The doorway
bears an exceptional wealth of ornament
which shows some links with Barfreston, a
product of the Kentish group of sculptors.

High up in the north wall of the chancel is a
single-splayed   round-headed   window,
remarkable because it retains its original
stained glass. This is arranged in a formal
pattern of four tiers of semicircles set back to
back, each of which contains simple petalled
flowers. This design, which closely resembles
the contemporary tile patterns at Byland
Abbey, is of a piece with the rest of the
12th-century church. The pattern made by the
leading, which was accurately renewed during
the last century, complements the design of
the string course beneath, and the balance of
the colours – golden yellow, emerald green,
pale purple and deep red – remind us of
Norman wallpaintings elsewhere. This is the
only 12th-century glass which we know to be
in situ in an English parish church and it
provides a fleeting impression of the beauty of
such an interior. It is, in quite a different way,
as satisfying as the more complex stained glass
at Canterbury.

The second surprise at Brabourne is the
tower stair. This is of simple, even primitive,
construction made from two halves of a 30-
foot-long oak with adzed triangular oak treads
fixed with treenails. The stair is supported by a
forked branch. Since the tower is basically
Norman, though with a 15th-century capping,
there seems no reason to believe that this
crude stair has not provided access to the first
floor ever since it was first built 800 years ago.

Map Reference: TR 103416 (metric map 189.
1-inch map 173)
Nearest Town: Ashford
Location: This lovely village can be reached
from the M20. From the third junction
eastwards take the B2068 northwards for
2½ miles (4 km) and then turn west on
minor roads to Brabourne for about 2
miles (3.2 km). Do not confuse with Brabourne Lees, a larger village to the south-
west.

The 12th-century window at Brabourne.

29
Dover Castle, Kent

Dover Castle, predictably known as the 'Key to England', got off to rather a late start. Until Henry II decided to build his great keep there in 1168, there is no record of a Norman castle on the site. Interestingly however, Harold had promised to William in 1064 that he would give him his 'castle' at Dover, and hence we imagine that some sort of fortification existed there although no other record of it exists. If there was an early motte and bailey on the site, then it is hardly surprising that no trace of it has been found. Even Henry's mighty keep is now just one element in a massive complex of defence works which was still being extended during the Second World War.

The first reference to Dover keep occurs in 1181–2 and it was in use by 1185. Despite Henry's experiment with a near-circular plan at Orford, he fell back on the tried and tested square plan here at Dover with size making up for what it lacked in imagination. Internally there were a basement, middle floor and main floor with a gallery above; a complicated fore-building provided access at main-floor level rather than the more normal first-floor entrance. There is a surprising amount of space inside the keep because many rooms were built into its thick walls. New standards of comfort are evidenced by a piped water supply inside the keep as at Hamelin Plantagenet's castle at Conisbrough and by excellent latrines.

Whilst the keep looks backwards in its design, the outer defences were much more up to date. A substantial curtain wall was laid around the keep and, like Framlingham, it was provided with a regular series of wall towers as well as two double-towered gatehouses and barbicans. These developments, again familiar from Conisbrough, show a growing tendency to regard perimeter defence as being more important than the keep itself. Here at Dover we see an early stage in the process whereby both options are pursued simultaneously. That this over-provision was unattractive is proved

by the great cost of the enterprise, reckoned at around £7,000 by 1190 – a prodigious sum! But even more innovatory was the commencement of an outer curtain wall during Henry's reign. This was begun on the west side of the castle and marked a movement towards the more easily defensible 'concentric' plan. Also on the west wall is the famous Avranches Tower which is multangular rather than square in plan and which contains arrow loops at two levels. In these refinements, both domestic and military, Dover pointed the way forward.

Map Reference: TR 326416 (metric map 179. 1-inch map 173)
Location: The castle, at the top of a very steep hill, is in guardianship and is open standard hours and on Sunday mornings from 9.30, between April and September.

Artist's impression of what the castle might have looked like at the time of Henry II's death in 1189. It was left to later kings to continue the line of the outer curtain along the line indicated by the dots. (View from north-west).

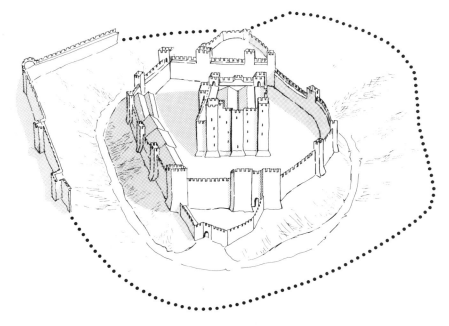

30
The Kentish Sculpture Group

During the 12th century we can trace the development of a school of sculptors in Kent who relied for their inspiration upon the works of western France. The earliest work by the school is at St Margaret's at Cliffe dated to

Right: A jolly frieze from Barfreston featuring creatures from the Bestiary – a wyvern, a mantichora and probably a lion.

c. 1150. The church was almost entirely rebuilt at that time on a grand scale and it is in the western doorway that the purest French influence is to be seen. The doorway, like the church itself, is large and profusely decorated and has carved voussoirs; above are carvings of figures which resemble those in the gable of the south door at Adel (West Yorkshire). This doorway is ambitious but indifferently carved – the sculptors knew the decorative effect they wanted, but were unable to do it justice.

The next stage in the development is marked by the later doorway inserted into the west front of Rochester Cathedral. The outer orders of the doorway are of *c.* 1130, but some time in the second half of the 12th century a tympanum was inserted above the doorway and the inner shafts were modified to take standing figures, perhaps representing Solomon and the Queen of Sheba rather then Henry I and Matilda, as has been suggested. The tympanum itself has a Christ in Majesty with thin standing angels which are better paralleled in Burgundy than in England. The lintel beneath bears carvings of the Twelve Apostles and on the innermost voussoirs are unusual backward-looking birds which are precisely similar to work at Poitiers and which were taken up by the school elsewhere.

That the Rochester masons exercised an influence over the surrounding area is evidenced by the two remarkable churches at Patrixbourne and Barfreston. At Patrixbourne, the inner order of the south door has human heads outlined with coils of foliage, a motif which occurs on the third order of the Rochester arch, and the use of birds and leaf scrolls further attests the work of the Rochester masons. It is at Barfreston that we see the most

spectacular product, however, a small two-cell church which boasts an incredible richness of decoration, a phenomenon commented upon in the entry for Tickencote. The church dates to the 1180s and the extensive use of Caen stone imported from France illustrates a French connection in an economic as well as an artistic sense.

Apart from the Caen stone, Barfreston also shows direct western French influence in the occurrence on the east end of a figure of a mounted knight set in a niche – a well-known French motif. There is so much decoration at Barfreston that it is perhaps inevitable that many theories have been advanced about its various inspirations. Basically, most of the elements can be found originally in France, then at Rochester and finally here as well. However, the extensive use of fabulous and humorous subjects at Barfreston has led to suggestions of influences from Canterbury

Map References: **St Margaret's at Cliffe** TR 359448 (metric map 179. 1-inch map 173)
Barfreston TR 189552
Patrixbourne TR 264501
Rochester TQ 743685
Nearest Towns: Dover (St Margaret's at Cliffe and Barfreston), Canterbury (Patrixbourne)
Locations: St Margaret's at Cliffe is up the coast from Dover (approx. 5 miles/8 km) and is reached by B roads from the A258 between Deal and Dover. Barfreston, a tiny picturesque village among small Kentish lanes, is situated between the A2 and the A256. From the A256 turn west to Eythorne and then on to Barfreston, which is signposted from there. Patrixbourne is to the north-east of the A2, 3 miles (5 km) south of Canterbury. It is reached by following the signs from the A2.

Above: Doorway at Barfreston; a stylish product of the Kentish School at the height of its powers. Note the 'scratch dials' on the jambs of the doorway.

where, during the first half of the 12th century, grotesque and amusing subjects were carved on the capitals of Lanfranc's crypt. Whilst this may be true, there was by the later 12th century such a widespread currency of ideas that it seems unnecessary to invoke yet another source of inspiration for this Kentish group. The occurrence on the south door of Signs of the Zodiac as well as the Labours of the Months equally illustrates a knowledge of the same psalters as the maker of the (French) Brookland font had seen. By this time, books and manuscripts must have assured a wide dispersal of artistic ideas and Barfreston appears to have been the last baroque flourish of this highly distinctive Kentish group of sculptors.

31
Minster in Thanet Monastic Grange, Kent

Monastic granges were the agricultural outposts of monasteries and their produce was a vital source of income both in cash and kind. The Cistercians were to develop the idea of the grange estate during the 13th century, but already by the 12th the Benedictines were alive to the advantages of the system. Where a monastery owned a single large estate or had several scattered properties, the granges either acted as farms *per se* or else as collecting centres for produce. Either way, a permanent staff was required to administer the transactions, and it was to meet these needs that the grange was developed. Later, granges were to become highly specialized, with some concentrating on cereals, others on livestock and even some on horses, but in the 12th century such specialization was still rare, although Byland Abbey's Bentley Grange was given over to the production of iron.

Small granges were probably arranged like the Templars' estate at South Witham described in the entry on Cressing Temple, in a single great court containing barns and other buildings as well as an area set aside for occupation by the grange stewards. A monastic grange of any size was designed with two courts, however, with one containing the agricultural activities and the other the domestic offices with a chapel, if any. Only the most important granges were supplied with a hall, chambers and chapel; most would have had simpler buildings on a smaller scale.

Here at Minster we can see the remains of the ranges of buildings in the domestic court of a grange. There is some uncertainty about the date of some elements of the structures; parts may be late Saxon since we know there were monastic buildings here as well as beside the parish church during the 11th century. The structures are laid out round three sides of a square. The west range, which contained the chambers in which the residents lived, is probably early 12th century, as indicated by the herringbone work within its walls. The hall to the north was added in the mid-12th century, at the same time as the apsidal chapel was built. What remain above ground today are the altered remains of the north and west ranges and part of the west tower of the chapel. The buildings were never large or extensive – they did not need to be. Whilst the grange farm here controlled a large acreage either directly or indirectly, the administration could have

Map Reference: TR 313645 (metric map 179. 1-inch map 173)
Nearest Town: Ramsgate
Location: The grange is part of the St Mildred's Abbey buildings belonging to the Benedictine nuns. Opening hours, from Easter to 30 September, are: weekdays 11–12 and 2–4.30, Saturday 3.30–5.

The monastic grange at Minster in Thanet is now a small Benedictine nunnery with a delightfully peaceful atmosphere. On the left are the remains of the west tower of the Norman chapel and the round-headed windows of the mid-12th-century hall can be seen on the right.

been undertaken by quite a small staff, and most of the farmhands probably lived in the village, as at South Witham.

Confusingly, the buildings of the grange are used today by Benedictine nuns, but this monastic use of the site dates only from 1930. Originally the grange was a possession of the great abbey of St Augustine at Canterbury, and was reckoned to be one of the most valuable of their estates.

32
Canterbury Cathedral and St Thomas's Hospital, Kent

Canterbury, the shrine of English Christianity, already had a long history of religious life behind it before the Normans came; this is discussed in our *Guide to Anglo-Saxon Sites*. On the site of St Augustine's original abbey, the Saxon buildings were borne away by Abbot Scotland who built a fine new abbey church in 1073–91. This was the abbey to which the grange at Minster was attached. The Saxon cathedral was similarly replaced during a building campaign which started under Archbishop Lanfranc in 1070. The choir of this building was in turn replaced by Anselm in 1096–1130 and yet again after the fire in 1174. This last occasion provided the opportunity for the importation of the French mason William of Sens, who brought with him the new Gothic style. Masons who worked on this great project probably also went to Oakham to build the Castle Hall there.

There is so much Norman work to be seen at Canterbury Cathedral that it is impossible to do it justice here. Of Lanfranc's work, the crypt is the most dramatic survival; it is the largest Norman crypt in Britain and the capitals, decorated *in situ* in 1120, are amongst the finest Romanesque sculpture in England. Also in the crypt are fine wallpaintings of *c.* 1150; the Christ in Majesty on the ceiling of St Gabriel's Chapel is a superb work which puts the provincial renderings of the same subject

at Copford (Essex) and Kempley (Gloucestershire) firmly in their place. Above ground, the stained glass depicting Adam and Jareth belongs to the revamped choir after the 1174 fire. The choir itself is perhaps the most impressive work of all; built as a magnificent setting for Becket's tomb after his martyrdom in 1170, it was one of the wonders of its age and the first truly Gothic construction in England.

Apart from being a cathedral, Christ Church, Canterbury was also a very large Benedictine monastery. The Cathedral Priory was famous as an artistic centre and the manuscripts produced in its scriptorium were amongst the finest Romanesque work. The treasury of *c.* 1150 beside the east end of the cathedral is finely decorated with zigzag arches and retains its original strongly barred windows. Fine vaulting abounds, in the undercroft of the lavatorium tower and in that of Lanfranc's dormitory dated to around 1120. In the midst of so much that claims our attention, the complete North Hall, built for poorer pilgrims visiting Becket's shrine, has the finest Norman staircase in England; it could almost have come from the Doges' Venice.

The city of Canterbury as well as the cathedral itself thrived on the pilgrim trade and many townspeople must then have provided goods

The 12th-century North Hall at Canterbury with its finely vaulted undercroft, elegant windows and, in the building on the right, a stately staircase.

Map References: **Cathedral** TR 151579 (metric map 179. 1-inch map 173)
Hospital TR 148579
Locations: The cathedral is in the centre of the city. Eastbridge Hospital is on the main High Street of Canterbury, by the bridge just past the library.

and services for travellers just as they do today. One subsidiary Norman building which survives is the Eastbridge Hospital. This, as its name suggests, was sited beside the east bridge over the river in about 1180. The front has been rebuilt later, but the ground-floor undercroft in which the pilgrims slept is extant and the modified first-floor hall can still be seen. Also on the upper floor is a small chapel appropriately dedicated to St Thomas à Becket. There is a fine though damaged Christ in Majesty wallpainting on the surviving chapel wall. Such hospitals were not necessarily for the sick but were intended to provide accommodation for pilgrims to the shrine of Canterbury.

33
Staplehurst Iron Door Fittings, Kent

The south door of Staplehurst church is one of the curiosities of Norman England. There are various examples of more or less spectacular metalwork in Norman parish churches, including the doors at Castle Hedingham and Sempringham, but the most bizarre is here at Staplehurst. The door is reset in its present position since it occupies a pointed-arched opening, but the semicircular iron band near the top of the door shows that it was built to fit a round-headed opening.

The decoration of the door comprises a collection of iron appliqués in a variety of

Three of the jolly capitals in Archbishop Lanfranc's crypt, c. 1120. The animal musicians were copied elsewhere and notably in the castle hall at Oakham (site No. 76).

Ironwork on the north door at Staplehurst church; what was the inspiration for all these bizarre creatures of the deep?

Map Reference: TQ 785430 (metric map 188. 1-inch map 172)
Nearest Town: Maidstone
Location: Staplehurst is 9 miles (14.5 km) due south of Maidstone on the A229. The church is on the main road on the east side.

fantastical shapes, of which the flying fish with toothed mouth, a wriggling eel, a shoal of smaller fish and a boat are amongst the more distinguishable elements. Large curved hinge pieces can also be recognized, but they may be reset.

One of the most interesting motifs is the square containing a twisted lozenge shape which is set centrally on the door. This shape is similar to that on the font at Stone, which is also remarkable for the diversity of its decoration. The Stone font, apart from the square and lozenge motif, also has a large 'fishy' element in its scheme, including all manner of things that swim, both probable and improbable. In view of the similarities between these designs, we should perhaps look for some common linking theme; at present, there is no obvious explanation of this correspondence of designs.

34
West Malling: St Leonard's Tower, Kent

Gundulf, first Norman bishop of Rochester, founded an abbey at Malling in 1090 and parts of the monastic buildings survive. Both abbey and town were burnt in 1190 and there was substantial rebuilding after that time. Since an Anglican Benedictine community now uses the site of the abbey, public access is impossible; we should thank Henry VIII that our study of Romanesque abbeys was to some extent facilitated by the Dissolution!

There is another accessible structure at West Malling which, in its way, is as fascinating. It is called St Leonard's Tower and dates to *c.* 1100. The tower stands on a commanding site back from the road on a shelf of rock. There are two storeys, marked by windows on the exterior, and there are shallow clasping buttresses on the angles, one of which contains a turning stair.

The tower was probably built by Gundulf since the style resembles that of his tower at Rochester. But what is it? There is a reference to 'St Leonard's cemetery' late in the 12th

century and there are later references to a chapel; this has led to suggestions that this was a church tower. But we feel that this is unlikely in view of the situation of the tower and the nature of its construction. St Leonard's Tower is effectively a small keep and its prominent situation beside the road must mean that it was intended to control its traffic. Perhaps it could only have been built by Gundulf, a man who combined a flair for both ecclesiatical and military architecture!

Map Reference: TQ 675570 (metric map 188. 1-inch map 171)
Nearest Town: Maidstone
Location: St Leonard's Tower is on St Leonard's Street on the south-west side of West Malling, on the A228 to Tonbridge about half a mile (0.8 km) outside the town. The site is in guardianship and open at any reasonable time.

St Leonard's Tower has a commanding site beside the road and looks remarkably like a more than usually ornate keep, yet opinions are still sharply divided about its function.

35

Rochester Cathedral and Castle, Kent

Rochester had been an important town in Roman times as it stood at the point where Watling Street crosses the Medway on its way from London to Canterbury and Dover. Roman roads were important arterial routes in the early medieval period, and hence Rochester retained its importance as both an ecclesiastical and military centre. Dramatic confirmation of these two roles is provided by the superb early-12th-century keep and the impressive Cathedral Church of Christ and the Blessed Virgin Mary beside it. This juxtaposition of civil and religious architecture is paralleled only at Durham.

Bishop Gundulf of Rochester was a friend and confidant of Lanfranc, first Norman Archbishop of Canterbury. Gundulf was appointed to the vacant see of Rochester in 1077 and began to build his new cathedral church almost at once; it was completed within 'a few years'. Gundulf was a great builder and is credited, amongst other things, with the supervision of the construction of the White Tower at London and the keep at Colchester, the curious keep at West Malling and the abbey there. Here at Rochester we can see the unornamented crypt of his original church together with his tower, apparently built for defence, which stands to the north of the cathedral church.

The western parts of the nave are probably basically Gundulf's work as well, but it was cased in Caen stone by Bishop Ernulf in 1114–30 and there was later embellishment as well. Ernulf was also responsible for the cloister range, parts of which can still be seen on the south side of the cathedral. Externally, the west front of the cathedral is a well-balanced composition of mid-12th-century date, marking the end of Bishop John of Canterbury's building programme. It is a remarkably successful essay in Romanesque decoration with much blank arcading and surface patterning, all finished off by turrets at the outer angles.

The west door is of two periods, the lower parts including the jamb shafts being of the same date as the rest of the front, whilst the standing figures to each side and the tympanum and voussoirs were all inserted some time later (see entry on the Kentish Sculpture Group).

To turn to the secular history of Rochester, we find that after the Conquest the town and a newly built castle were placed in the hands of Odo, Bishop of Bayeux and the Conqueror's half-brother. The first motte and bailey castle was sited outside the walls of the Roman town on the place called Boley Hill. Notwithstanding his religious office, Odo took an active part in the politics of the period and he actually appears in the Bayeux Tapestry waving a club and 'cheering on the young men'! His politickings resulted in his undoing, however, for he fell from grace in 1082.

But Odo was not finished yet. After the death of the Conqueror, his two sons Robert and William Rufus inherited the Duchy of

Map Reference: **Castle** TQ 742686 (metric map 178. 1-inch map 172)
Cathedral TQ 743685
Locations: The castle has a fine site on the Medway and is a guardianship site open standard hours and on Sunday mornings from 9.30 between April and September. The cathedral is behind the castle.

Rochester Keep raised during the reign of Henry I.

Normandy and the Kingdom of England respectively. This division of Norman interests did not find general favour, and Odo was prominent in his opposition to William Rufus. In 1088, Odo and his friends held Rochester against Rufus, and it was only after a prolonged siege that they surrendered. Odo went back to Normandy in disgrace and died fighting in the First Crusade soon afterwards.

It is assumed that this siege took place on the site of the first castle at Rochester on Boley Hill but, some time before 1089, Bishop Gundulf began a new stone castle for William Rufus on the site of the present great keep. This move probably followed the earlier siege which had underlined the importance of Rochester. In keeping with Gundulf's sparkling reputation as a builder, he carefully sited the new castle in one corner of the Roman town defences. The new castle was a strongly defended enclosure of the same shape and size as the later one and substantial parts of his curtain wall are incorporated in the later work.

The castle remained a royal possession, but in 1127 Henry I issued a charter which made the Archbishops of Canterbury constables of the castle in perpetuity. The archbishop of the time, William de Corbeil, was further enabled to make 'a fortification or tower within the castle'. It is almost certain that the great keep is the tower licensed by this charter. Thus the Castle of Rochester consisted of Gundulf's wall and Corbeil's keep for the rest of our period.

This keep resembles that at Castle Hedingham and fortunately is fairly well preserved. Many of the internal features, such as the combining of two storeys to form a lavish great hall with upper gallery, are paralleled at Hedingham and both keeps make concessions to gracious living as well as defence. Interestingly, the only significant damage suffered by the keep was during the siege of 1215 when King John's miners brought down the south-east corner by means of a gallery very like that at Bungay.

Rochester cathedral from the south-west showing the west front which is a smaller and more ornate version of that at Southwell (site No. 82)

36

London: The Tower, Westminster Hall, St Batholomew's Hospital and Temple Church

William the Conqueror was crowned King of England on Christmas Day 1066 at Westminster Abbey. He appointed Geoffrey de Mandeville I as 'portreeve' or chief officer of the city, and hastened to reassure its inhabitants, who probably numbered some 10–12,000: 'I will not allow any man to do you any wrong. God keep you.' Nor did he intend that the citizens should do him any harm either, and to this end he rapidly established the strongpoints of Baynard's Castle and the Tower of Montfichet which controlled the road between the royal palace of Westminster and St Paul's, symbolic centre of the city. Probably also at this time, he began work on another site in the south-east corner of the city which was, after 1080, to become the great fortified palace called the 'White Tower'.

The Tower of London must have astounded the inhabitants of the city to whom the concept

Map References: **Tower of London** TQ 334806 (metric map 177. 1-inch map 166) **Westminster Hall** TL 304796 **St Bartholomew's** TQ 323817 **Temple Church** TQ 315811

Locations: The Tower of London is on the north bank of the Thames, close to Tower Bridge. Nearest tube is Tower Hill. Opening hours:
Weekdays Mar–Oct 9.30–5
           Nov–Feb 9.30–4
Sundays Mar–Oct 2–5
The priory church of St Bart's is off Smithfield Market, close to St Bartholomew's Hospital. Nearest tube is Barbican. Temple church is off Fleet Street, on the south side, on Inner Temple Lane. Nearest tube is Temple.

of any 'castle' would have been unfamiliar, let alone such a prodigious structure as this was to be. This important work was entrusted to Gundulf, Bishop of Rochester, who was described as being 'very competent and skilful at building in stone'. The kernel of the defences was the White Tower itself, which was a hall-keep of four storeys with a main hall and many lesser rooms and galleries. On the first floor on the east side is the majestic Chapel of St John, *c.* 1090, which appears as an apsidal projection in the external wall. Little remains above ground of the outer works of the castle, but on the river side they used the standing Roman river-wall and the rest of the circuit probably consisted of a deep ditch with a palisaded bank inside.

Westminster had been established by Edward the Confessor as the regal centre of London and his dual arrangement there of a great abbey church and a king's hall was continued by William. This separation of London itself and Westminster foreshadowed the later division of the mercantile and administrative functions of the capital. William Rufus was not content with the older arrangement and he demolished Edward's old hall and built another in its place in 1097–9. It was very large, 240 feet (73 metres) long with stone walls and a wooden roof; with a new, more elaborate roof added in the 1390s, it survives to this day. Despite its size, Rufus thought it 'not big enough by half'!

Religious foundations grew up outside the city, doubtless because there was more room for expansion beyond its crowded purlieus. One of these was the Priory and Hospital of St Bartholomew which stood in what had been called 'Smoothfield' in Anglo-Saxon times but which we know as Smithfield. This foundation was made by Rahere, traditionally King Henry I's jester, who supposedly contracted plague when in Rome and vowed that, should he recover, he would establish a hospital for poor men. Rahere did recover and received permission in 1122 to build the priory and hospital on part of the king's market at Smithfield. The king himself was still reeling under the shock

of the loss of his heir in the White Ship disaster in 1120, and we must imagine that his jester's new-found piety would have matched his mood.

Building was apparently completed in 1127 and much of the present highly atmospheric building dates from that time. What remains is actually only the eastern part of the priory church, but it makes a superb setting for worship with its majestic pillars, curving apse and tunnel-like ambulatory. But it is not the only architectural legacy that we can thank Rahere for; all round the church are the modern buildings of 'Bart's' Hospital, still bustling with doctors and nurses, albeit in 20th-century uniforms. How many 'poor men' still give thanks in Rahere's church for the hospital he founded over 800 years ago?

South of the road leading from the City to Westminster, beside the Thames, the Knights Templar were established. This place, still called 'Temple' but now a nest of lawyers, was the headquarters of the order in England and here the Master of the Temple presided over a

The Great Seal of William the Conqueror, King of England.

The majestic apsidal chapel of St John replete with miniature ambulatory and massive drum pillars.

flourishing organization which included preceptories like Cressing Temple. In fact this was the 'New Temple', founded during the second half of the 12th century; the earlier site had been in Holborn.

All that remains of this once great complex of buildings is the Temple Church which, like others associated with the order at Cambridge and Bristol, was circular in plan in imitation of the Church of the Holy Sepulchre in Jerusalem. This church was consecrated on 10 February 1185 in honour of the Blessed Mary by Heraclius, Patriarch of Jerusalem. This was doubtless a glittering occasion graced by Henry II and his court.

The architecture of the church is Transitional; the main west door is developed late Norman with, interestingly, the same 'double cone' motif used by the 'Broadlands School' in Norfolk. Internally, however, the vaults are all pointed and the extensive use of Purbeck marble shafts prefigures the Gothic glories of the Angel Choir at Lincoln.

It is fitting that this shrine of chivalry preserves the mortal remains of William Marshall, Earl of Pembroke. Before he died in 1219, William was admitted to the Order of the Knights Templar. At his funeral service, the Master said, 'In the world you have had more honour than any other knight for prowess, wisdom and loyalty,' and Archbishop Stephen Langton said, 'Behold, all that remains of the best knight who ever lived.' We can still see the effigy of William Marshal, battered by the blitz, in the floor of the Temple Church.

To turn once more to the City of London itself, we are fortunate that a man called William Fitz Stephen wrote an account of London during the 1180s, the time at which the Temple Church was built. Stephen was, like his master, a Londoner; his master was Thomas à Becket, and Stephen was an eyewitness of Becket's murder. The description of London occurs as a preface to his account of the saint's life. It is highly evocative and conveys something of the bustle of this his native city; one small passage must suffice here: 'Among the noble cities of the world which Fame cele-

brates, the city of London, seat of the monarchy of England, is the one which spreads its fame more widely, distributes its goods and merchandise further and holds its head higher.'

Amen to that!

Temple Church, battered by the blitz, still guards the mortal remains of the knights whose effigies clutter the floor. They include amongst their number the incomparable William Marshall, 'the best knight who ever lived'.

east anglia

East Anglia

Introduction

The Norman conquest of East Anglia was fairly uneventful at first, with no major disturbances being recorded before 1069. The relatively high population density of the region meant that the Conqueror took early steps to secure the territory; royal castles were established at Norwich, Cambridge, Colchester and less certainly at Thetford. The keep at Colchester was a fine building constructed on a particularly large scale in stone from the first, probably because of Danish raids in the area during 1071. It was an amalgamation of these same Danish raiders and Anglo-Saxon dissidents which led to the East Anglian revolt.

Hereward the Wake, traditionally a dispossessed Anglo-Saxon nobleman, retreated to his fenland fastness at Ely. After the suppression of the northern rebellion in 1069, the Danish army took ship in the Humber and sailed to join Hereward. Together, the Saxons and the Danes burnt Peterborough Abbey in 1070, the Danes afterwards retiring to Denmark and Hereward to Ely. William, determined to put an end to this threat, besieged the Isle of Ely in 1071, took it after various difficulties, and broke Hereward's power. 'The Wake' himself disappeared into obscurity, never again to resist the Norman domination.

After this initial difficulty, the Norman settlement proceeded more quietly and by the time of Domesday Book in 1086 we see a picture of lords, some of them like the de Mandevilles at Pleshey, the de Veres at Hedingham and the de Warennes at Castle Acre, being very powerful, settling down to enjoy the fruits of conquest. But East Anglia was rich and relatively secure, and these same lordly families were to prove very troublesome to later Norman kings. During the difficult days of Stephen's reign and even, in the case of the Bigods of Framlingham and Bungay, into that of Henry II, revolt and opportunism were to become second nature. Geoffrey de Mandeville, who held the intriguing site at Pleshey amongst others, became a brigand during the Anarchy of Stephen's reign and was hunted down like a common criminal at Burwell in Cambridgeshire.

It was Hugh Bigod, made Earl of the East Angles by King Stephen, who exalted the art of treachery to its greatest heights, however. During the reign of Stephen, Bigod changed sides twice, and in the early years of his reign Henry II took steps against him. Bigod's castles were seized in 1157, and in 1165 Henry began his great keep at Orford as a counter to further trouble in East Anglia.

In the event, it was only just finished in time, for Bigod besieged it in 1173. But after this final revolt, Bigod's power was utterly broken and he died a disappointed man. In East Anglia, then, we find a dramatic legacy of impressive castles which were built by these proud and turbulent lords.

If that was the negative side of the Norman settlement, there were more positive aspects. Those same powerful lords left a series of fascinating sites like that at New Buckenham where the outlines of a 12th-century new town can still be traced on the ground. Additionally, the wealth at the disposal of those Norman lords resulted in important monastic foundations being made in the region. An early start was made at St Botolph's Priory at Colchester late in the 11th century and substantial fragments can be seen of the huge Benedictine abbey of Bury St Edmunds. Other Benedictine houses at Ramsey, Thorney and Peterborough, apart from the great church at Ely, attest the flourishing of the 'Black Monks' in the east. Later, Cluniac monasteries were founded at Castle Acre and Thetford by the de Warennes and the Bigods, and at Cambridge we see the Temple Church which was apparently built by the military order of the Knights Templar. Some of these sites, notably Peterborough and Castle Acre, are spectacular examples of Romanesque architecture and in the 'Broadlands School', at Castor and at Wentworth in the Isle of Ely, we see the influence of the monastic schools of sculpture reaching out into the surrounding countryside.

Other lesser churches also have important Norman evidence. At Copford are the fine if heavily restored wallpaintings probably commissioned by the bishops of London who held the manor. Waltham Holy Cross and Orford have important Durham-influenced drum pillars with characteristic mass and spiral decoration, whilst in the church of St Nicholas at Castle Rising we see the high quality of workmanship which a man as powerful as William de Albini could lavish even on a parish church. Also at Castle Rising is one of the Norfolk Fonts, which were a remarkable product of the admixture of Saxon and Norman styles during the later 12th century.

It is with the more secular side of life, though, that we end this brief account of Norman East Anglia. The sturdy font at Burnham Deepdale shows us the 'Labours of the Months' which were so important to these rural communities. In the large timber barn at

Cressing Temple we have an even more compelling link with this endless round of husbandry. It is fitting that the fertile eastern lands should have two such agricultural reminders of their Norman heritage.

We must however return to Norwich for the most spectacular manifestation of the Norman urban achievement: the biggest town in East Anglia and one of the largest in England. Here are a royal castle with a huge 12th-century hall-keep proudly standing upon a large motte, a cathedral church of undoubted elegance and splendour built from its foundations by the Normans, and finally the house of a merchant whose family were amongst the most prominent financiers in the land. At Norwich, with its representatives of royal and ecclesiastical prestige, we reach the highpoint of the Norman achievement in East Anglia.

The delicate decoration on the side walls of the nave at Waltham Abbey contrasts with the massive scale of the openings and the drum pillars beneath.

37

Waltham Holy Cross Abbey, Essex

The first foundation here was during the reign of Canute in the first half of the 11th century. It was engendered by the miraculous discovery of a buried stone cross at Montacute (Somerset) which was subsequently brought here by Tovi le Prude, Standardbearer to Canute, who owned both estates. Later, in 1061, Harold Godwinson, Earl of Wessex and later King of England, founded a college of secular canons here; nothing remains of his building. In 1177, Henry II refounded Waltham as an Augustinian priory which became an abbey in 1184.

The parish church at Waltham is actually the nave of the Norman collegiate church minus its apsidal presbytery and transepts. When the Augustinian church was built after 1177, its west end butted up to the east end of this earlier nave, but all trace of the later church has gone. What remains is a fine example of Durham-influenced work with bold round drum pillars arranged in double bays. The nave was originally vaulted and had a gallery and clerestory; it is a fine building and probably dates to around 1120. We know that Henry I's consort Matilda took an interest in Waltham, and it might be that she financed the building of the nave.

Apart from its architecture, Waltham is of particular interest because it is the traditional burial place of King Harold whose corpse was eventually brought here to his own foundation. A plaque on the site of the high altar records the claimed site of the grave. It is ironical that the burial place of the last of the Saxon kings should now be chiefly celebrated for a fine example of Norman architecture.

38

Pleshey Castle and Town, Essex

After the Conquest, the site of Pleshey was granted to one Geoffrey de Mandeville, father of the notorious Geoffrey of that name whose career is dealt with more fully under the entry for Burwell. Opinions vary as to what, if anything, was here before the de Mandevilles decided to make it the caput of their Essex estates. The placename Pleshey is Norman French – *plessis*, which has a similar meaning to 'pleached', as in a woven hedge round an enclosure or forest. So we have a Norman name and a Norman motte and bailey castle, but more difficult is the 'village enclosure'; is this too a product of Norman planning, or was it an earlier Saxon feature which they adopted?

After Geoffrey de Mandeville II's fall from grace in 1143, we are told that his two most important castles were seized at (Saffron) Wal-

Map Reference: **Waltham Abbey** TL 381007 (metric map 166. 1-inch map 161)
Location: Waltham Abbey, although on the north side of London, is a separate town set in open countryside. The abbey is in the centre of the town.

Map Reference: **Pleshey** TL 665145 (Metric map 167. 1-inch map 148)
Nearest Town: Chelmsford
Location: The town is north of Chelmsford. Take the A130 towards Great Dunmow for 5 miles (8 km). At Howe Street, turn west down minor roads to Pleshey which is 2 miles (3.2 km) from the main road.

Plan of Pleshey castle and town; there was possibly a second bailey to the north of the motte, now marked by a triangle of streets.

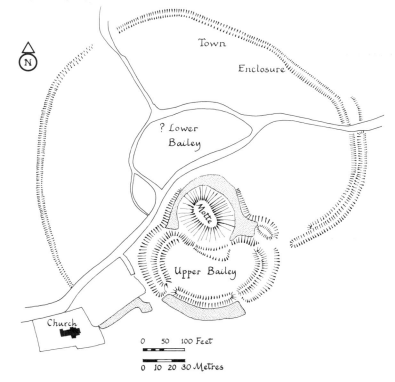

den and Pleshey. We do not know what form of castle there was here at the time, but it was presumably a motte and bailey of some sort. Later, in 1174, William de Mandeville received permission from Henry II to build a castle here and the foundations of a rectangular masonry keep, presumably of his period, are known to exist on top of the motte. Most scholars suggest that the defences of the village also belong to this later 12th-century period, and that William intended to found a town as well as a castle here. But this need not preclude some earlier activity on the site and the shape and size of the village enclosure might well suggest some earlier influence on the plan.

39

Cressing Temple Barn, Essex

The 'temple' element in the placename gives the game away at once; as with the Temple Church in London, we are dealing here with the famous military order of the Knights Templar. The Templars were founded by Hugh de Pays and seven other French knights in 1119, and were officially called the 'Order of the Poor Knights of the Temple'. This title indicates the high ideals which were attendant upon the foundation of the order. Its members, who followed the Benedictine Rule, did sterling service in protecting pilgrims to the Holy Land and guarding the Holy Sepulchre at Jerusalem. Sadly, after the passing of the Crusades, the original function of the order was lost and they became subject to envy and greed.

The basis of the order's economy was the preceptory or 'grange farm' as we would call the monastic equivalent (see entry on Minster). The term 'preceptory' stems from the fact that such an establishment was in the charge of a preceptor (commander) who was responsible to the Master of the Temple in London. At South Witham (Lincolnshire) one of these preceptories was totally excavated in advance of destruction, revealing a plan of

farm buildings contained in a courtyard on one side of which was a small hall and chapel used by the resident Templars. The farmworkers apparently lived in the village nearby.

Lands at Cressing were granted to the Templars in 1136 by Matilda and were later confirmed by her husband Stephen. When the order was suppressed, the Essex lands, which would have been administered by the preceptor at Cressing Temple, yielded a profit of £70 annually, which was handsome indeed. It is likely that the Cressing community was always small, however, and for most of the time it may not have exceeded the three chaplains who served the chapel here.

When we visit the site today, it appears as a small group of farm buildings standing in the rich cereal lands of Essex, as prized during the 12th century as they are today. Notice the slight traces of a ditch around the site which marks the extent of the courtyard as at South Witham, but the real reason for visiting the site is the incomparable Barley Barn. Recent research on this barn suggests that it probably dated to the latter part of the 12th century and as such it is one of the oldest farm buildings in

Map Reference: TL 799187 (Metric map 167. 1-inch map 149)
Nearest Town: Braintree
Location: Take the B1018 between Braintree and Witham. The barns are visible from the road on the east side by a turning to Silver End. They are on private property; the entrance is 100 yards from the junction of a minor road and the B1018. Permission should be sought to look inside the barns. The Barley Barn is the first to be reached.

Interior of the Barley Barn. The passing braces are the long angled members in the lower part of the roof structure.

Britain. It is a secular cathedral, a superb essay in carpentry which reminds us of all the great Norman timber buildings and roofs which we have lost.

The Barley Barn has an aisled plan with opposed doorways in the centre of each long side. This central bay was used as a threshing floor and we must imagine the threshers working at the corn sheaves with flails of the sort depicted on the font at Burnham Deepdale. Here came the crops not only from the Cressing estate itself but also from the Templars' other local possessions at Witham and Kirsting. How many harvest homes must this great barn have seen? But already by the 12th century such great barns, with their 'passing brace' roof construction which was very demanding of good quality timber, were becoming a thing of the past and could only be built by rich and powerful owners. The next stage in the development of barns will be illustrated in our *Guide to Medieval Sites*. Next door is the Wheat Barn, itself probably of the early 13th century; these two great barns together make one of the most satisfying views of medieval England and are a welcome change from castles and churches!

40
Castle Hedingham Castle and Church, Essex

The keep at Castle Hedingham was probably built by Aubrey de Vere, Earl of Oxford, in about 1141. The first de Vere, also called Aubrey, was granted lands in eastern England by the Conqueror and probably built a motte and bailey castle here at Hedingham. His son, the second Aubrey, supported Matilda during the Anarchy of Stephen's reign, and it was she who made him Earl of Oxford; he may have built the keep to demonstrate his new prominence.

Standing on the site of the earlier motte, the keep is one of the best preserved in England; it has four storeys and was originally about 100 feet (30 metres) high. Only the base of the

forebuilding survives on the west side but the handsome first-floor doorway still provides access to the keep from a modern stair. A rectangular chamber at the head of the stairs has a turning stair in one corner which gives access to the other floors and rises to battlement level. Above the chamber is the Great Hall which has the unusual feature of a gallery cut into the thickness of the wall 12½ feet (3.8 metres) above floor level. This hall-space is so large that it had to be supported above and below by wide arches which are amongst the largest Norman arches in the country. This hall would have been a generous place in which to feast and plan further triumphs, a fitting backdrop to a highly successful man.

The church in Castle Hedingham village was also rebuilt on spectacular lines during the 12th century. Apart from the scale of the building, evidence of lavish patronage is provided by the (much restored) sedilia with their mass of carving, the fine cross in the churchyard and by the good ironwork which still survives on the south door. Church and castle together provide a convincing demonstration that Aubrey de Vere had come out on top of the uncertain political situation existing during the mid-12th century.

Map References: **Castle** TL 787358 (metric map 155. 1-inch map 149)
Church TL 785355
Nearest Town: Halstead
Locations: The castle is on private property and is open at the following times:
May–Sept: Tues, Thurs, Sat, 2–6
Bank holidays, 2–5.30
Castle Hedingham is 4 miles (6.4 km) north-west of Halstead. Take the A604 Halstead to Haverhill road. At Sible Hedingham take the B1058 east to Castle Hedingham. The castle is on the north-east side of the town.

Motif from the fine 12th-century cross in the churchyard.

The keep showing the ruined forebuilding before it. The roof of the forebuilding fitted into the horizontal chases above the first floor archway entrance.

41
Copford Wallpaintings, Essex

The church at Copford, called St Michael and All Angels since a thoroughgoing restoration in 1880, contains some remarkable wallpaintings of mid-12th century date. Unfortunately, the restorers' zeal was such that they did not stay their hands when it came to the paintings and what now survives at Copford is part-original and part-pastiche. Before considering the paintings in more detail, the church must be briefly described since it is of great interest in its own right.

The manor of Copford was held by the bishops of London, and it seems that they built the first church here in *c*. 1130. This patronage may account for the fact that the church belongs to a small and select group of vaulted parish churches with the further distinctive feature that the chancel and nave were structurally undivided. Thus the plan of Copford was a simple rectangle with an apse at the east end; nave and chancel were presumably separated originally by a now-vanished wooden screen.

The interior would have been remarkable with a tunnel-vaulted nave and a semi-spherical vault over the apse which still survives. Furthermore, Copford was a two-storeyed structure since there was a priest's attic over the vaulted nave lit by two existing circular lights high up in the west wall of the nave. This attic chamber was entered through a door set high up in the second buttress in the north wall. The nave was remodelled in about 1190 when the Transitional arch in the south side was inserted and later, during the 13th century, a south aisle was built and the nave vault removed. Enough of the springing of the nave vault remains to see the original arrangement, however, and we must be grateful that much early painting was left intact during this drastic replanning.

The paintings in the apse were not so much restored during the 19th century as repainted. However, the layout of the decoration prob-

ably follows the original pretty closely and we see a figure of Christ in Majesty in the vault which matches the later work at Kempley. Here there are angels, symbolic representations of the Holy City and figures of the Apostles. Whilst the style is Victorian rather than Romanesque, the bright colours probably capture something of the original impact of the work. On the soffit of the chancel arch are the Signs of the Zodiac and again they probably reflect the generality though not the detail of the Norman composition. We also encounter the familiar theme of the Virtues and Vices in the reveals of the nave and chancel windows.

Pride of place must go to the painting of the Miracle of the Raising of Jairus's Daughter on the north wall of the nave. This is both an unusual subject and the best-preserved scene in the church. The scene is divided into two halves, the left-hand one showing Jairus's daughter lying on a couch and covered by a dark red coverlet, with a sorrowing female figure standing beside her, presumably the girl's mother. The right-hand panel depicts Jairus 'the ruler of the Synagogue' entreating a benimbed Christ to help his daughter, while behind stands an Apostle with his hand raised

Map Reference: TL 935227 (metric map 168. 1-inch map 149)
Nearest Town: Colchester
Location: From Colchester, follow the signs to Lexden and then Stanway. On the B1408 at Copford, turn left down School Lane, opposite a garage on the right. This is signposted on a fingerpost to Copford Green. Carry on down this road, past the Alma pub for about three-quarters of a mile (1.2 km). At the end of the green turn left down Church Road, signposted to Copford church. At the T-junction, turn right. At the next T-junction, turn left through white gates and park in the church car-park on the right opposite the Cricket Club.

View into the chancel showing the lower part of the Christ in Majesty on the vault and figures of angels and saints beneath.

in astonishment at the miracle. This is a fine Romanesque composition and here we can also appreciate some of the original colours – yellow, black, green and blue – as well as the details of contemporary dress.

42
Colchester Castle and Priory, Essex

It has long been known that the great fortress-keep at Colchester was built on the foundations of the Roman temple of Claudius, and this dramatic link between the Roman and Norman periods provides the key to Colchester's past. When the Normans came to Colchester they found a flourishing Saxon town still contained within the walls of Camulodunum, as the Roman city had been called. The town had been refounded by Edward the Elder in 917, and by the time of Domesday Book in 1086 there were probably 2,000 people living here. In 1071, the town was sacked by the Danes and it was probably the fear of further seaborne attacks which led the Conqueror to build such a massive keep here.

For Colchester Castle was a huge undertaking and had originally been intended to be even larger than the Tower of London. An interesting feature of the foundation of the castle is that, despite its urban situation, there is no mention of houses having been destroyed by its construction, as at Lincoln and Norwich. Recent excavations have located a finely built and decorated late Saxon chapel on the site and this, together with other evidence, has led to the suggestion that the area occupied by the castle had already been in royal hands before the Conquest. If there had been a royal hall on the site, then it would explain the lack of houses.

Whatever the nature of the site before the castle was built, there can be no doubt that it was intended to be a highly impressive structure. Built out of Roman materials available nearby, it must have presented a bold aspect to the world with its layers of bright red tiles and

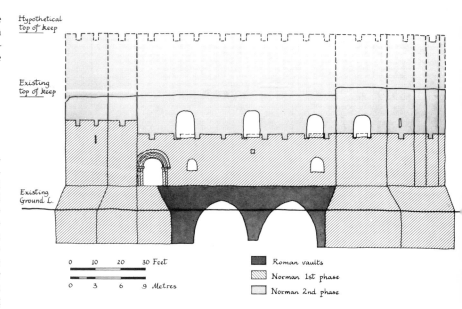

Sectional elevation of the keep from the south. The complicated history of the building beginning with the podium of the Roman temple at the base can be seen.

shallow buttresses as with the keep at Chepstow. Sadly, we need quite a lot of imagination to envisage the original majesty of the structure today; time and neglect have done their work all too well.

The keep was surrounded by a deep moat, the spoil from which was heaped against the bases of the walls. The surface of the underlying Roman masonry was revealed by the Normans, and the walls of the keep were bonded directly onto it. As first built, the keep was only one storey high, and the original crenellations can be seen embedded in the later walls. But this was probably a temporary setback since it seems more likely that the keep was intended to have three storeys from the first, of which only the lower two survive today. The fine doorway by which the keep is now entered is a later Norman alteration, the earlier doorway having been a rather simpler affair on the north side at first-floor level.

Also in Colchester is the ruin of the church of St Botolph's Priory. This was one of the

Map References: **St Botolph's Priory** TL 999249 (metric map 168. 1-inch map 162) **Castle** TL 999254
Locations: St Botolph's Priory is in guardianship and is open standard hours. It is on the south-east of the town centre and in the block between Church Street and Magdalen Street. The castle, now the museum, is situated in the centre of the town and the High Street.

earlier foundations after the Conquest, having been made in *c.* 1090, and was a house of Augustinian Canons. The existing nave with its handsome round pillars may well belong to the 11th century but the fine west end, unusually built in Colchester's 'vernacular' materials of flint with Roman brick dressings, is a fine composition of *c.* 1160. Here we see the lavish use of blank arcading which parallels the Cluniac work at Castle Acre.

43
Orford Castle and Church, Suffolk

There must have been a settlement at Orford before Henry II built his great castle here, for Orford was first granted a market in Stephen's reign. The site was attractive because it then had a good harbour by which the castle could be supplied and it was close enough to menace Hugh Bigod's principal East Anglian strongholds. It was the turbulent career of this Bigod, the Earl of East Anglia (see entry on Bungay), that prompted Henry II to establish a royal castle in Suffolk.

Orford Castle is interesting not least because it is the first castle for which detailed building accounts survive; we know that the castle was finished in 1173 at the substantial cost of £1,413 9s 2d. The housing of the gangs of workmen required for this huge project, the bringing of the stone by sea and the purchasing power of a royal castle and its garrison all conspired to make Orford a prominent place. We can only speculate on the townspeople's reactions when in 1173, the year the castle was finished, rebel barons including Bigod himself laid siege to it. Was the town destroyed at this time as well? Perhaps the local people came to rue the day that the king decided to make Orford his East Anglian seat!

Only the keep of Henry's castle remains, but this is of considerable merit by virtue of its innovative design. Whilst the 12th century was undoubtedly a time of experimentation in castle design, as the round tower at New Buck-

enham and the later work at Conisbrough and Pembroke demonstrate, the near-circular keep at Orford appears to have been the first royal departure from the traditional rectangular ground plan. That Henry was not in fact persuaded of the utility of the design is evident from his decision to return to a rectangular plan at Dover, built immediately afterwards. Although the keep is technically faceted, it is circular on the inside and effectively so on the exterior as well. It is provided with a wide battered base to deflect stones on to a besieger when dropped from above and it also has three large rectangular buttresses which, apart from affording extra accommodation, fulfilled the military purpose of enabling the defenders to bring some crossfire to bear on an attacker.

Access was provided via a stair contained within a forebuilding attached to one of the buttresses which opened at the top end into an entrance hall. There was also a lower hall and kitchen at this level, presumably for retainers.

The west front of St Botolph's Priory, Colchester; the blank arcading is ingeniously contrived of reused Roman bricks because of the shortage of local building stone.

Map Reference: TM 419499 (metric map 169. 1-inch map 150)
Nearest Town: Woodbridge
Location: Orford is on the River Alde on the Suffolk coast near Orford Ness. It is 12 miles (19.3 km) east of Woodbridge at the end of the B1084. The castle is in guardianship and is open standard hours and Sunday mornings from 9.30, April to September.

The first-floor entrance to Orford castle with its fine joggled lintel.

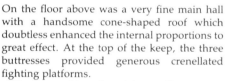

On the floor above was a very fine main hall with a handsome cone-shaped roof which doubtless enhanced the internal proportions to great effect. At the top of the keep, the three buttresses provided generous crenellated fighting platforms.

The keep, although architecturally impressive, seems to us to make more concessions to civilized living than to defence. The windows are relatively large but there are no proper arrow slits; the portcullis covering the gate was puny and the joggled entry arch is not strongly built. Additionally, a disproportionate amount of the structure is given over to the hall rather than to more serious occupancy. Nor were the surrounding defences particularly impressive. They have since disappeared, but a view dated *c.* 1600 shows a simple gateway through the outer curtain which is itself defended by square towers without arrow slits. All this suggests that, whilst a royal presence had to be maintained in East Anglia, it was as likely to be peaceful as purely military.

44
Framlingham Castle, Suffolk

Framlingham came into the possession of the Bigod family when it was granted to Roger Bigod by Henry I in about 1100. Roger's son Hugh was a turbulent baron, and in a long and tempestuous life played the part of traitor and rebel as occasion provided. He built a major castle at Bungay, in the entry for which his career is more fully described.

Little is known of the early history of the castle here at Framlingham although it is thought that there was a motte and bailey which was later remodelled to form a residence, perhaps in Hugh's time. Certainly in 1175 Henry II gave orders for Framlingham to be slighted, a job which was apparently efficiently accomplished by Alnodus the engineer in company with carpenters and masons. After Hugh's death in 1178, his son,

Orford keep now stands in splendid isolation having lost its encircling outer defences. The profligate use of imported ashlar for the wall facing marks this out as an expensive royal initiative.

Map Reference: TM 287637 (metric map 156. 1-inch map 137
Nearest Town: Saxmundham
Location: An attractive small town, Framlingham is 7 miles (11.2 km) west of Saxmundham on the B1119. The castle is in guardianship and is open standard hours and on Sunday mornings from 9.30 between April and September.

another Roger, rebuilt Framlingham on a substantial scale and it is to this rebuilding that most of the existing structure belongs.

It is probable that the area of the present inner bailey reflects the layout of Hugh Bigod's fortified residence. Fragments of two major buildings survive from that earlier period of the castle's history, which are generally interpreted as a hall and an adjoining chapel. The side wall of the hall, replete with two excellent round chimneys with smoke vents, can be seen built into the east curtain of the inner bailey. The chapel was to the south of it and its east wall is 'fossilized' in the later curtain. Nothing remains of the original fabric of the chapel, but the 'negative' imprint can be seen in the inner facing of the later curtain of three vertical pilasters. Both hall and chapel belong to the period 1150–60.

After Roger Bigod inherited the castle, he reconstructed it in a wholly new style – indeed, Framlingham is often described as one of the new generation of 'keep-less' castles. There is certainly no keep at Framlingham today, but it will be noted from the plan that the south-east angle of the otherwise ovoid inner bailey is noticeably angular; was this because there was a rectangular keep standing in this position at the time the curtain wall was built? Whether or not there was a keep, the technique of using many interval towers on the curtain does mark a move away from earlier defensive plans. Here the towers were an important element of the defence from the first and their sophistication shows that they were carefully designed for the defenders' advantage. In particular, the provision of arrow slits, lacking at the nearby royal castle at Orford, demonstrates the careful thought given to fields of fire at both ground and wall-walk levels. Additionally, the projecting towers themselves afforded flanking fire along the walls which would effectively hinder infantry assault. The use of removable wooden floors inside the towers meant that each section of the curtain could be isolated from the rest if it were overwhelmed by an attacker.

In these modifications, it has been suggested that the influence of foreign fortifications should be discerned. It is undoubtedly true that the Land Wall at Constantinople was considered a great marvel by Europeans and that the curtain wall at Framlingham does bear more than a passing resemblance to it. The dating of Framlingham to the 1190s fits exactly with men returning from the Third Crusade, having taken Acre and Jaffa in 1191.

45
Bungay Castle, Suffolk

The remains of Bungay Castle are rather neglected today, much overgrown and prone to frost damage, but their reduced state should not alter our appreciation that this was one of the major fortresses built and held by that same Earl Hugh Bigod who held the castles of Framlingham, Walton and Thetford. Bigod was one of the premier lords in the land and his life was marked by many schemes and ploys against various monarchs.

He had originally supported Stephen but rebelled against him in 1136; but before 1153 they were reconciled and he was made Earl of Norfolk and Suffolk (the East Angles). By 1154, Hugh was once more turning his coat, this time in favour of Stephen's successor Henry II. Henry became king in 1154, but already by 1157 Henry had to crush his untrustworthy subject by confiscating his castles. By payment of a huge fine in 1165, Bigod bought back Framlingham and Bungay but could not regain the others.

Also in 1165, doubtless anticipating further trouble in East Anglia, Henry began Orford Castle. In the event it was just completed in time, for rebellion broke out again in 1173. The revolt failed, and Hugh's castles were both demolished; he died a broken and disappointed man in 1176–7. For over 80 years Hugh Bigod had strutted across the political stage but in the end this great man gained little by his treachery.

It seems that Bigod began work on his great

The cylindrical chimneys of the now-vanished hall built in to the later curtain at Framlingham Castle.

Map Reference: TM 335898 (metric map 156. 1-inch map 137)
Location: Bungay is on the Suffolk/Norfolk border between Beccles and Harleston. The castle, in private ownership, is beside the market-place. The key is obtainable from the Cross Street Café on payment of a returnable £1 deposit.

keep at Bungay in 1165, the same year that Orford was started. The base of his keep can still be seen enclosed within the later 13th-century defences and consists of a 70-foot (21-metre) square of masonry with massive walls 18 feet (5.5 metres) thick. There was a forebuilding on the south side, presumably affording first-floor access, and the whole edifice would have rivalled the huge keep at Rochester. The scale of this building amply illustrates Bigod's overweening ambitions.

But after the collapse of the revolt in 1174, Henry determined that Bigod's power should be utterly broken and to that end he ordered the demolition of the castle here at Bungay in 1176. It seems that his orders were faithfully carried out and a tunnel was dug diagonally beneath one angle of the keep. This was done to undermine the foundations and usually such a tunnel would have been filled with brushwood, pig's fat and other combustibles and set on fire. The intense heat normally cracked the masonry above and so completed the work of destruction. For some reason the tunnel here was never fired and it remains today as a tribute to the ruthless efficiency of the siege warfare which became such a feature of military science during the Middle Ages.

46
Bury St Edmunds Abbey and House, Suffolk

Bury St Edmunds, the town where the bones of St Edmund are buried, features prominently in Domesday Book. This provides startling evidence of Norman initiative: 'now the town is contained in a greater circle, including land which then used to be ploughed and sown . . . Now altogether [there are] 342 houses in the land of St Edmund which was under plough in the time of King Edward [the Confessor]'. Domesday Book shows that Bury doubled in population and area between 1066 and 1086, and provides the further information that there were both French and English knights in the town. The total figure of households

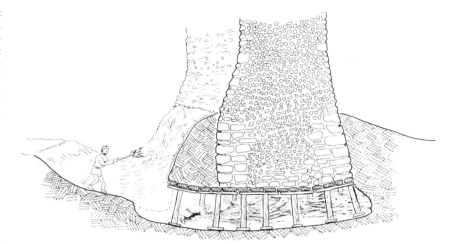

Artist's impression of a mining tunnel showing how the tunnel roof was supported by props until it had been packed with combustibles and fired.

Left: The Norman gateway at Bury St Edmunds into the monastic precinct; the wide arch and gablette at ground level may have been inserted into the tower c. 1170.

Map References: **Bury St Edmunds** TL 858642 (metric map 155. 1-inch map 136) **Little Saxham** TL 799638
Locations: The abbey lies at the centre of the town on Angel Hill. It is in guardianship and is open standard hours between October and March, and 9 a.m.–4 p.m., April to September. The Norman Gatehouse, called St James's Gate Tower, is next to St James's church. Moyses Hall, now a museum, is nearby in the marketplace and is reached by Abbeygate Street. From March to October its opening hours are 10–1 and 2–5, and from November to February 10–1 and 2–4.

Little Saxham is 4 miles (6.4 km) west of Bury. It can be reached from a turning south off the A45(T) to Newmarket.

would place Bury fifth in the national ranking of English towns. The great prosperity of the abbey of Bury was based upon its ownership of this burgeoning town.

Sadly, little remains above ground of the prodigious monastic church which took nearly a century to build and the nave of which had 12 bays. The great west doors, built in the time of Abbot Anselm (1121–48), were made by Master Hugh and it is said that 'as in his other works he surpassed everyone else so in the making of these gates he surpassed himself'. These wondrous gates were 'arte fusoria', made of bronze, and we must look to the beautiful doors on the churches of southern Italy to discover their parallels.

Bury St Edmunds consisted of more than the great church itself; the whole town reflected the power and prestige of the abbey. One of the most important survivals is the massive tower gate, which was to form the model for many later grand entrances. It is as large as many a keep elsewhere and its superbly designed decoration is a tribute both to the taste and wealth of its patrons. It has been claimed as the purest example of Norman architecture in England and, whilst this might be true, it ignores the fact that the gate is probably a composite work, the elaborate western arch and its gablette having been inserted into an earlier building.

The other Norman building of note in Bury is Moyse's Hall. This stands on the north side of the Beast Market which was the main market-place of the Norman town. The name 'Moyse's' – presumably because of its resemblance to 'Moses' – has encouraged the belief that it was built by a Jewish merchant, an idea familiar from Norwich and Lincoln. However, Moyse is still a Suffolk surname, and a man called Moyse may have owned the building during the 14th century. In fact it is more likely that the building was also a product of monastic enterprise since it occupies such a prominent position in the market-place. This was quite probably the toll house of the monastery where market dues were collected, a function also suggested for 'The Marlipins' at New Shoreham. The interior of the building, though rather altered, suggests that it was basically a first-floor hall, and one of the two ground-floor windows, which have been

replaced in modern times, may have acted as a 'business window' again by analogy with New Shoreham.

Before leaving the area, the visitor should see the excellent 12th-century round tower at Little Saxham near Bury St Edmunds. It has been suggested that the lower parts of the tower are late Saxon, but in view of the very regular construction throughout and the absence of any clear differentiation between the two stages, it seems most probable that all is Norman. Either way, the delicate blank arcading round the top of the tower is very fine and the quiet country churchyard in which it stands provides a pleasant contrast to the bustling town nearby.

47
Thetford Castle and Priory, Norfolk

At Thetford, which until the Conqueror removed the East Anglian see to Norwich in 1095 was a cathedral city, we find the remains of a large castle and an important Cluniac priory. The castle is a huge motte and bailey set within an earlier double-ditched enclosure, which has been proved by excavation to be an Iron Age hillfort. At the time of Domesday in 1086, Thetford was partly in the possession of the mighty Bigod family, but it seems unlikely that they founded the castle. Rather, it is probably a royal foundation made shortly after the Conquest and designed to control the important Saxon town of Thetford and its vast hinterland. There were no permanent buildings in the castle enclosure and even the motte was devoid of any large keep or similar structure. Thetford seems to have been established for purely military reasons, but with passage of time custody of the area fell upon the Bigods, thus rendering the castle unnecessary.

The second monument at Thetford is the Cluniac priory which has been efficiently robbed of its freestone dressings in this stone-less land. Roger Bigod, who fought with the Conqueror at Hastings, was beginning to fear his

Little Saxham tower outside Bury St Edmunds is well worth seeing: it dates to c. 1130.

Map References: **Priory** TL 865836 (metric map 144. 1-inch map 136)
Castle TL 875828
Locations: The castle is on the south side of the main A1066 road into Thetford from the east (Diss). It is in a park and is open at all times. The priory is on the A11 trunk road bypass on the north-west side of the town and is signposted. It is in guardianship and is open standard hours and Sunday mornings from 9.30, April–September.

reckoning with the Almighty. He took the standard protective measure of founding a priory in 1103–4 which was at first based on the old cathedral church in the town of Thetford itself. Later the monks decided to move out of the town and on 1 September 1107 old Bigod laid the foundation stone of the new church, only just in time since he died the following week! Even then, his last wish was not granted for instead of being buried here his corpse was whisked off to Norwich Cathedral.

Today there are extensive ruins of the monastery, though much of the surviving masonry postdates our period. During the 13th century in particular, a sequence of miracles involving the Virgin Mary resulted in a great upsurge of popularity for the priory and the original apsidal sanctuary was rebuilt. Parts of the chapter house, the south and west ranges and the base of the prior's lodging are 12th century, but most of the details have been robbed. We must turn to Castle Acre in order to see a Cluniac house in a condition which reflects its original splendour.

Despite its great size, it seems that Thetford motte supported only relatively small timber structures.

48
South Lopham Church, Norfolk

The huge tower of South Lopham church is quite out of scale with the modest nave and chancel. Why it should have been built on such a scale is a mystery; perhaps Lopham was intended for greater things after the church was given to Thetford Priory early in the 12th century. There had been a church here at Lopham in Anglo-Saxon times and parts of the north wall of the nave, including the small circular window at its west end, are of 11th century date.

Early in the 12th century the great axial tower was raised between the nave and chancel. This tower, with its bold horizontal divisions, small round-headed windows and blank arcades, bears more than a passing resemblance to some of the great Anglo-Saxon towers at sites like Great Tey (Essex), described in our

The style of the massive central tower at South Lopham seems closer to Anglo-Saxon than Norman styles of building.

Map Reference: TM 040818 (metric map 144. 1-inch map 136)
Nearest Town: Diss
Location: South Lopham is on the A1066 Diss to Thetford road, 5 miles (8 km) west of Diss. The village is at the junction of the A1066 with the B1113 and the church, easily spotted with its tall tower, stands beside the B road on the north-west side.

Guide to Anglo-Saxon Sites. Whilst the architectural details may be Norman, the architectural concept belongs to the Anglo-Saxon age.

49
New Buckenham Castle and Town, Norfolk

The approach to New Buckenham Castle is highly atmospheric: a set of creaking wrought-iron gates wreathed in barbed wire and a murky moat lend the place an air of forgotten mystery. This would doubtless have depressed the castle's founder, William de Albini II, who was, in the mid-12th century, bent on a policy of large-scale construction and aggrandizement. His castle at Castle Rising is now a ruin and here at Buckenham his castle and town are but earthworks in the first case and a mere village in the second; Buckenham is a grave of ambition.

New Buckenham supplanted nearby 'Old' Buckenham, which had been the original caput of the Albini family. In 1146 the castle at Old Buckenham was granted to the Augustinian order as the site of a priory on condition that the castle was demolished. This grant indicates that Old Buckenham had become obsolete and hence the new site was probably in use. This activity corresponds with the date of Castle Rising and the general similarities between Rising and Buckenham reinforce this conclusion.

As far as is known, New Buckenham was established on a 'green field' site. It consisted of a large circular ringwork castle with subsidiary baileys, in the manner of Rising, to the east and south-west. A small chapel, now a barn, was sited beside the outer gate into the baileys. East of the castle works a rectangular town enclosure, defended by a bank and ditch, was laid out with a grid of streets and a market-place. New Buckenham Castle probably also had a large park, traces of which can still be seen in the landscape around the site. This park, like the deer park at Kincardine, was

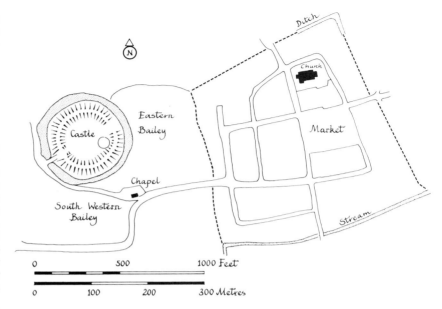

intended to be a game preserve as well as a source of wood and other supplies, a fact evidenced by the occurrence of a ditch inside the bank, as at Kincardine.

One of the most intriguing features of Buckenham Castle is the round keep. This structure, which survives as a circular foundation 70 feet (21 metres) in diameter with walls 12 feet (3.6 metres) thick, is a great puzzle. If, as has been claimed, it is part of William de Albini's original construction then it is the earliest English example of the sort of circular keep-tower or donjon later erected by William Marshall at Pembroke.

50
The Broadlands School of Sculpture, Norfolk

The little church at Hales is well known by virtue of its thatched roof; such roofs must have been a common enough sight during our

Plan of New Buckenham showing the relationship of the castle and the planned town.

Map Reference: TM 084904 (metric map 144. 1-inch map 136)
Nearest Town: Diss
Location: New Buckenham is about 7 miles (11.2 km) north of Diss on the B1077. The key to the castle enclosure is available from the Castle Hill Garage. The entrance to the castle is by a lane beside a farm building (in fact the old chapel) on the west side of the town.

period, but few churches possess them now. Here in the Broadlands of East Anglia, thatch is still used and hence we can imagine that Hales church must always have looked rather like this.

Apart from its thatched roof, Hales also has the distinction of being a largely intact mid-12th-century church, or at least the nave and chancel are of that date. When we come to the round western tower opinions vary and it is possible that it is about a century older than the rest. This is because it contains two double-splayed circular windows in its north and south sides which are of pre-Conquest character. These openings, familiar at Bibury (see our *Guide to Anglo-Saxon Sites*), have basketwork

placed round them in order to provide keying for wall plaster.

Apart from the tower, the nave of Hales church has two finely decorated doorways in the north and south walls. These provide the first evidence of the 'Broadlands School'. This group is represented by the doorways here as well as in two other churches in the area at Heckingham and Hellington. This alliterative group is distinguished by lavishly decorated doorways which make great play of disc and star patterns, double-cone motifs and other tricks of decoration. They are competently sculpted, if unusual, and it is possible that their richness owes something to the now-vanished Cluniac foundation at Thetford.

Map References: **Hales** TM 382973 (metric map 134. 1-inch map 137/126)
Heckingham TM 384988
Nearest Town: Beccles
Locations: Hales in on the east side of the A146 Beccles to Norwich road, about 6 miles (9.6 km) north-west of Beccles. The church is redundant but the key is available. Heckingham stands on its own by a farm surrounded by fields. It is about 1 mile (1.6 km) north of Hales.

Hellington TG 312030
Directions, 5 miles (8 km) SE of Norwich; take the A146 and turn north to Hellington on a minor road for about ½ mile (¾ km). The church stands on a slight hill.

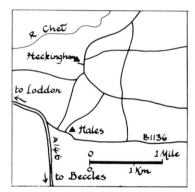

The southern doorway of Hales.

51

Norwich Cathedral, Castle and House, Norfolk

In view of the importance of Norwich, it is not surprising that the Conqueror took early steps to ensure its loyalty. A castle was built here soon after 1066 and we know that 98 houses were destroyed in the process. All that remains of William's castle are the earthworks of the baileys and, of course, the motte upon which the later keep stands. This keep was probably built during the latter part of the reign of Henry I, *c.* 1130. The keep looks rather 'new' today but the thoroughgoing restoration of 1834–9 seems to have followed the original design very closely. Since Norwich was retained as a royal castle, the elaborate surface decoration on the walls of the keep might have set the trend for decorated hall-keeps in East Anglia. Perhaps William de Albini did no more than follow royal precedent when he built Castle Rising.

Apart from the castle, Norwich also came to prominence during the Conqueror's reign by virtue of the new bishopric which was established here. It seems that William wanted to assure the loyalty and safe conduct of ecclesiastical as well as civil authority and to this end he relocated the old East Anglian bishopric here which had latterly been based at Thetford.

Bishop Herbert de Losinga laid the cathedral's foundation stone in 1096 and the presbytery came into use by 1101, a remarkably rapid piece of building. But after this promising beginning, the pace of work slowed and by the time of de Losinga's death in 1119 the church was built only as far west as the nave altar. It was left to his successor Eborard (1121–45) to finish the project. Norwich Cathedral is unusual because it was built on a new site and has not suffered substantial alteration since.

Finally, there is an interesting town house in Norwich which unlike so many 'Jews' houses' does have a direct link with a Jewish family. It is sad to recall that Jewish persecution has a long and dishonourable history in England and during the 12th century, when the power of the Church was strong, anti-Jewish feeling was institutionalized. We can find evidence for this in many ways, such as in the figure of 'Synagogue' on the font at Southrop, in the laws which forbade Jews to hold offices of state or authority and in the various recorded riots and expulsions. Whilst this may have been the 'official' position, we know that Jews were very important to the English economy since they, unlike Christians, were allowed to lend money. Great building projects often required short-term loans and we know that Jurnet Ha Nadib, who probably built the 'Music House' here in Norwich in the 1170s, lent money to King Henry II. Even more ironically, the family of the same name may have helped to finance the construction of the cathedral as well!

The Music House was a large L-shaped building with fine vaulted undercrofts and a first-floor hall, the lower parts probably given over to commercial affairs, as in the Southampton houses. The quality of the original masonry was very high and some of the details are paralleled in contemporary buildings at the cathedral, suggesting that the same masons may have been employed here. Although the house was remodelled and extended later, the undercroft of Jurnet's hall is well preserved and is now used as a rather cosy bar by the residential education centre which is based there.

52

Castle Acre Castle, Priory and Town, Norfolk

William de Warenne, Earl of Surrey and builder of the first castle at Conisbrough, was granted the site of Castle Acre by the Conqueror and evidently decided to make it the caput of his considerable East Anglian estates. Recent excavations of the castle at Castle Acre have revealed an unusual sequence of construction not paralleled elsewhere. The first phase, probably built during the 1080s, con-

Map Reference: TG 236089 (metric map 134. 1-inch map 126)
Locations: Norwich castle is on Castle Meadow and is now a museum, open weekdays 10–5, Sunday 2.30–5. The cathedral and close are open daily, 8–6.

'The Music House' is part of Wensum Lodge Residential Education Centre owned by Norfolk Education Committee and is situated on King Street which is on the south side of the city centre.

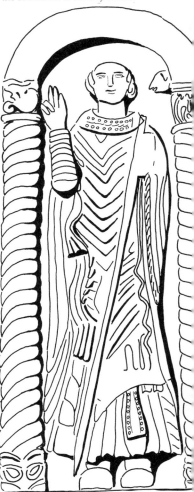

Above: The heavy 19th-century restoration gives Norwich Castle a very 'new' look, but the details seem to be accurate and hence it affords a rare opportunity for the visitor to see a Norman castle as it was intended to be seen: a shining symbol of the conquerors' power.

Left: This effigy was once thought to commemorate Herbert de Losinga, founder of Norwich cathedral, but its position in the exterior of the east end of the cathedral which was completed during his lifetime precluded this. Traces of blue and gold paint can still be seen on the surface of the carving.

sisted of a defended 'country house' which was two storeys high with an entrance at ground level. This extraordinary building stood inside a relatively slight bank on top of the motte; the general impression of domestic rather than military considerations being uppermost in the mind of the builder is reinforced by the discovery that the first-phase gatehouse was built of timber. Later, perhaps during the years of Stephen's reign, the bank was raised and crowned with a curtain wall and the walls of the house were widened internally, presumably to transform it into a 'keep'. Later in the 12th century work on the keep may have ceased, but the curtain wall was raised yet again and the defences were greatly strengthened. Had the 'keep' phase been completed, then a structure very like the one at Castle Rising would have resulted, but the sequence of construction here is unique.

Apart from the castle, the de Warennes also laid out a strongly defended town enclosure to the west. This had a bank and ditch round it, and it was evidently intended to contain a prosperous settlement. In both the scale of the castle defences (for there are two baileys in addition to the motte) and in the careful

Map References: **Priory** TF 814148 (metric map 132. 1-inch map 125)
Castle TF 817152
Nearest Town: Swaffham
Locations: Castle Acre lies on the north side of Swaffham some 3 miles (5 km) up the A1065 signposted off just to the north-east of the main road. It sits in the valley of the River Nar and is a defended town with a 13th-century gateway.

The priory stands on the west side of the village; it is in guardianship and is open standard hours and Sunday mornings from 9.30, April–September.

The castle, on the east side of the town, can be reached by a lane beside the Methodist Chapel. At the time of visiting, it was being consolidated prior to opening to the public as a guardianship monument.

Artist's impression of the 'country house' phase of the castle's development at Castle Acre.

arrangement of the town, we can see that the de Warennes intended Castle Acre to be a prominent place. The third element in this plan was, of course, the splendid Cluniac priory outside the town.

The de Warennes had cultivated a connection with the Cluniac order, and the first William founded the first Cluniac house in England at Lewes in 1077. This initiative was continued by the second earl, also called William, here at Castle Acre. He invited the Cluniac monks here in 1089, but the first site, which lay somewhat to the east of the present one and within the outer works of the castle, proved unsatisfactory. Within a year they moved to the existing site and began work on the church and the claustral ranges shortly thereafter.

Although the claustral ranges generally follow the plan and the extent of the Norman layout, they were remodelled extensively during the later medieval period. The principal Norman survival is therefore the church and in particular the spectacular west front. The decoration of the west front, with its lavish use of intersecting blank arcading and fine 'textured' work round the head of the door, marks the apogee of Norman surface ornament during the later 12th century; it is the external counterpart of the magnificent Cluniac interiors at Bristol and Much Wenlock.

53
Hindringham Coffer, Norfolk

Nothing of the structure of St Martin's church at Hindringham is of Norman date, but it contains a unique wooden chest which bears a scheme of Romanesque decoration. Whilst there is no direct dating evidence for the chest, or 'coffer' as it might be more accurately termed, the decoration strongly reminds us of the intersecting blank arcading which was so widely used in Norman sculpture. Also the occurrence of circular motifs on the legs or 'styles' of the coffer, which are painted rather

than carved, provides a further link with Norman decorative schemes.

The lock on the front could have been added later in view of the way it crudely effaces the decorative scheme, but it also serves to underline the antiquity of the piece. This is because the claimed examples of 13th-century coffers all have single locks whereas later examples generally have three or more, as required by later medieval ordinances passed to ensure the preservation of church valuables. Thus the single lock at Hindringham, even if not actually original, still supports a 13th-century date for the piece at latest. Other examples of 'early' chests are rather undramatic; at Bishop's Cleeve there is a coffer carved from a solid log with an early lockplate bearing simple punched motifs, whilst there is another early dug-out coffer at South Lopham.

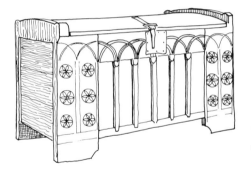

This wooden coffer at Hindringham is almost certainly of 12th-century date.

54
Burnham Deepdale: Seasonal Font, Norfolk

Apart from its fine Saxo-Norman circular western tower, Burnham Deepdale church contains the famous 'Seasonal Font'. This font, which stands at the west end of the nave, is decorated on three of its sides by carvings illustrating the 'Labours of the Months' as at Brookland. Here each month is depicted by a suitable activity and the Latin name of each is

Map Reference: TF 984364 (metric map 132. 1-inch map 125)
Nearest Town: Fakenham
Location: Take the A148 to Cromer from Fakenham for 5 miles (8 km) and then the minor road north to Hindringham which is a further 2 miles (3.2 km).

Map References: **Burnham** TF 804444 (metric map 132. 1-inch map 125)
Fincham TF 689065
Nearest Towns: Wells-next-the-Sea (Burnham), Downham Market (Fincham)
Locations: Burnham Deepdale is on the A149 Norfolk coast road between Wells-next-the-Sea and Hunstanton, 7 miles (11.2 km) west of Wells. Fincham is 5 miles (8 km) north-east of Downham Market on the A1122.

inscribed within an enclosing arcaded frame. Above the arcade are spirited carvings of lions and foliage. The whole is a pleasing rustic composition which belongs to the second half of the 12th century; another font of the same general character though with very different scenes can be seen at Fincham nearby and was probably made by the same man. Both fonts are carved from single blocks of Barnack stone.

The months are represented as follows:

JANUARIUS A seated figure 'keeping house' with his mead horn for comfort!

[F]EBRUARIUS A seated figure warming himself by the fire and wearing something that looks remarkably like a balaclava helmet

MARTIUS Digging the soil ready for planting

APRILIS Pruning trees

MAIUS A standing figure, possibly female, with a banner; probably representing the Rogationtide processions at that time of the year

JUNIUS Weeding with two hooked sticks

JULIUS Perhaps mowing grass with a scythe

AU[GUSTUS] Binding a sheaf of corn at harvest

SEPTEMBRIS Threshing corn with a flail

OCTOBRIS Grinding corn into flour with a quern

NOVEMBRIS Killing a pig before winter

DECEMBRIS A jolly scene of feasting at Christmastide; one diner has a straight-backed knife and there are loaves and perhaps fish on the festive board

These scenes occur on the north, east and south sides of the font, whilst on the west side the arcades are filled with foliage. The scenes give an interesting, if somewhat leisured, view of farming activities at different seasons of the year, and show some homely details such as the type of chair in use and a heart-shaped spade without a crosspiece at the top. Addi-

tionally, there is an indication of the elaborate ceremonial attendant upon Rogationtide which, with its preoccupation with prayers for the preservation and fertility of crops, must have been an important observance in such a rural community. But the specific meaning of each scene is less important than the overall message of the decoration, that God oversees all activities in all seasons and that whether at work or at home, He is ever-present.

Four of the 'Labours of the Months' on the 'Seasonal Font', Burnham Deepdale. From right to left they are: September – threshing, October – milling grain, November – killing a pig, and December – feasting.

55
The Norfolk Fonts

There are six fonts in this group, all situated in north-west Norfolk. The location of the school which produced them is not known, but the occurrence of one example at Castle Rising might suggest lay rather than ecclesiastical patronage. The fonts are distinguished by having round bowls set in square frames like the Tournai marble fonts and, also like the Tournai fonts, they are supported on four or five freestanding circular pillars.

Whilst these features suggest some links with foreign models, the decoration of the fonts is purely English. The wealth of abstract carving on their sides marks them out as masterpieces of their age and the Shernborne is the finest of all. Although they belong to a 'group' the details vary, with different com-

Map References: **Shernborne** TF 714325 (metric map 132. 1-inch map 124/125)
Toftrees TF 898276
Castle Rising TF 666249
Sculthorpe TF 899319
South Wootton TF 640228
Nearest Towns: King's Lynn, Fakenham
Locations: South Wootton is on the northeast outskirts of King's Lynn. Castle Rising is 4 miles (6.4 km) north-east of King's Lynn on the A149.

Shernborne is in Sandringham country, 2 miles (3.2 km) east of the A149.

Sculthorpe is on the north side of the A148, 1½ miles (2.4 km) east of Fakenham. The church is on the far north side of the village.

Toftrees itself is on the A1065 2 miles (3.2 km) south of Fakenham. The church is some way from the village up a lane signposted Shereford.

The amazing font at Shernborne has something of the air of a beast about to spring on its powerful short legs.

binations of cat heads, interlace and acanthus foliage being used on each. These motifs find parallels in Anglo-Saxon manuscript art and it does seem that a strain of local taste was maintained in Norfolk many years after the Conquest. At Toftrees, the pillars have fine floriate capitals and the interlace patterns are markedly angular, a feature of manuscript art. At Shernborne, the carving is deeper with the play of light caused by the overhanging rim being particularly effective; at Castle Rising, cat heads dominate the design. The fonts belong to the period 1160–80 and should be set beside the other groups in Buckinghamshire and Cornwall.

56
Castle Rising Castle and Church, Norfolk

Rather like the de Veres at Castle Hedingham, the de Albinis at Castle Rising came to sudden prominence during the Anarchy of Stephen's

reign. Whilst they were troubled times, men who sided with the right party were obviously set to profit from the conflict and William de Albini II also made a prudent marriage to Alice, widow of Henry I; the marriage was in 1138, and by 1141 he had been made Earl of Sussex. This was probably the time at which William de Albini II removed the castle of Buckenham to New Buckenham, founded a priory on the site of 'Old' Buckenham, and began the construction of the great hall-keep here at Castle Rising. It is perhaps unsurprising that a chronicler of Waltham Holy Cross records that he was 'intolerably puffed up'! The de Albini family had already left their mark on Norfolk since William II's father, another William, had founded a Benedictine priory at Wymondham, the great nave of which can still be seen. But at Buckenham and Castle Rising, William II was to overtop all previous achievement.

All three enclosures at Castle Rising were probably built at the same time; the largest oval one in the centre contained the keep and the lesser eastern and western baileys presumably held ancillary buildings. As first built, the keep would have dominated the town below the ramparts but later in the 12th century the bailey banks were raised, masking the view from below. A sidelight on de Albini's determination in building the castle is provided by the presence of a ruined early Norman church in the middle bailey. This had probably been the parish church, but de Albini demolished it and even used its north wall as a revetment for his bailey bank. He did, however, provide the inhabitants with the fine new church of St Lawrence which can still be seen.

The keep is unusual since it had only two storeys and hence looked more like a large version of a first-floor hall than a keep *per se*; also it has an uncommon amount of external decoration. The similarities between this structure and the postulated second phase at Castle Acre are striking, despite the fact that each had very different structural histories. The keep here at Castle Rising is basically thought to be of one build and to have been designed as a

Map References: **Castle** TF 666246 (metric map 132. 1-inch map 124)
Church TF 666249
Nearest Town: King's Lynn
Location: Castle Rising is 4 miles (6.4 km) north-east of King's Lynn on the A149. The castle is in guardianship and is open standard hours and Sunday mornings from 9.30, April–September.

Detail of the richly carved exterior of the hall-keep.

The impressive approach to the first-floor entrance of the hall-keep.

hall-keep from the first. It is likely that de Albini was following the trend set by Henry I at Norwich both in the design of the castle and in its external decoration.

The most famous view of Castle Rising is the one looking up the stairs contained within the forebuilding on the east side. This is appropriate since the approach was obviously designed to impress. The exterior of the forebuilding is enriched with blank arcading and the entrance vestibule at the top of the stair contains the superb doorway into the Great Hall which is decorated with nook shafts, roll mouldings and chevrons.

The principal accommodation was arranged on a *piano nobile* at first-floor level; apart from the Great Hall itself, a chamber, elaborate chapel, service rooms and a kitchen were also provided. One curious feature is the apparent absence of sleeping accommodation; presumably the lord slept in the first-floor chamber whilst other guests were lodged in buildings in the bailey. Later, some upper rooms were added, doubtless to compensate for this deficiency. The Great Hall has lost both floor and roof, which makes it difficult to appreciate its original quality, but the splendid details of the entrance lobby show the quality of de Albini's palatial keep.

57
Castor Church, Cambridgeshire

As the name suggests, Castor was an important Roman settlement and 'Castor ware' – a type of fine Romano-British pottery – is well known amongst students of Roman Britain. Later, during Anglo-Saxon times, a small nunnery was founded here by two saintly princesses, one of whom was Kyneburgha, to whom the church is dedicated. There are important fragments of 9th-century sculpture in the church, including a tympanum set into the later south porch. It was in the 12th century, however, that the church was rebuilt on a substantial scale and it is to this period that we

must now turn.

The most exciting evidence at Castor, now built into the south wall of the chancel, is an inscription which records that the church was dedicated in 1124. There was a church here before but we must imagine that the major rebuilding, the most splendid evidence of which is provided by the central tower, necessitated a re-dedication of the structure upon its completion. Indeed, the dedication slab itself appears to be a reused tympanum since the inscription is fitted rather awkwardly onto it.

The church of 1124 seems to have consisted of a nave, north and south transepts, a central tower and a chancel. Of this original layout, only fragments remain in the arms of the church, including a window in the west wall, a possibly repositioned south doorway and a fine pair of sedilia in the south wall of the chancel. The most important remnant is undoubtedly the superb central tower, which is not only richly decorated externally but also has a wealth of carving on the capitals of its supporting pillars. The capitals have a range of foliage, monsters and even fighting human figures. These figures remind us of the spirited knights on the chancel arch at Wakerley not far away, which were probably carved by the same sculptors. The undoubted quality of the work at Castor and its early date, evidenced by the lack of zigzag ornament, suggests that sculptors from here may have taken part in the somewhat later work at St Peter's Northampton.

Above right: The unique dedication stone which records that the church was dedicated on 17 April 1124. This unusually precise date is generally taken to include the splendid tower, thus providing a valuable fixed point in Norman architectural history.

Right: Central tower of Castor church showing the elegant belfry openings and elaborate surface decoration.

Map Reference: TL 125985 (metric map 142. 1-inch map 134)
Nearest Town: Peterborough
Location: Castor is 4 miles (6.4 km) west of Peterborough on the A47(T). Wakerley, which is mentioned in the text, is 13 miles west of Castor, in Leicestershire.

58
Ramsey, Thorney and Peterborough: The Fenland Abbeys, Cambridgeshire

The great abbeys of Peterborough and Thorney were, like Ely, founded during the 7th century and destroyed during the Danish holocaust of 870. They were similarly refounded during the later 10th century, at the time of the 'monastic revival', and it was as part of this same movement that Ramsey was founded in 969. Only Peterborough retains significant evidence of its Anglo-Saxon history (see entry in our *Guide to Anglo-Saxon Sites*) and all had total Norman rebuildings.

The earliest evidence is at Thorney where the nave, which is the only part remaining, was finished in 1108. The style is plain and majestic, a more civilized version of Blyth; decoration is limited to scalloped capitals. At Ramsey, little remains of the monastic buildings, but the parish church of St Thomas was actually the monastic hospital which, like the Hospital of St Thomas at Canterbury, was used for the accommodation of visitors. The plan of this building, like the ruined example at Ely, is effectively that of a church with a nave and aisles with a small attached chapel at the east end. Built in the last two decades of the 12th century, the hospital shows a fine progression from the Norman vaulted chancel at the east end to the Transitional nave arcade and the 'ultimate' Romanesque of the west front. Of the marvels of Peterborough, all we can say is that it has one of the most intact Norman interiors in the country and that the painted wooden ceiling of the nave, whilst much repainted, provides one of the most dramatic instances of late Norman decoration anywhere.

Why were these great monasteries located here in these fenny wastes? Originally it was doubtless the seclusion of the sites which attracted the religious. On these islands, for such they were, the monks could pursue their devotions removed from the trammels of earthly life. But later, despite being Benedic-

tine houses, a new emphasis on agriculture and above all on drainage and land reclamation was born. When we go to the sites of these Fenland abbeys, the landscapes in which they stand are as much a part of the record as the great churches themselves. Certainly some drainage had been done by the Romans before them, and more has been done since, but it was the monasteries that really blazed the trail into the Fens. They turned 'waste' into rich agricultural land and many of the embanked watercourses of the Fens can be traced back to the monks' initiative.

59
The Isle of Ely: Cathedral, Sculpture, Priory and Causeway, Cambridgeshire

Ely will be forever associated with the resistance of Hereward the Wake, 'Last of the Saxons', to the overlordship of the Conqueror, and there is no doubt that he and other Saxon leaders such as Edwin, Earl of Chester, and

Map References: **Ramsey** TL 291851 (metric map 142. 1-inch map 134/123)
Thorney TF 281043
Peterborough TL 193986
Locations: Ramsey, on the windswept fen, stands at the junction of the B1040 and the B1096. Thorney is on the A47(T) 6 miles (9.6 km) east of Peterborough.

Sombre simplicity of the nave at Thorney, c. 1105.

Prior's Door at Ely, c. 1140.

Morcar, Earl of Northumberland, sought refuge here in the midst of the swamps and marshes. Like Alfred at Athelney in Somerset they were safe from an enemy who did not know the ground and treachery alone was their peril; in the end, it seems that the monks of Ely, fearing the Conqueror's vengeance, may have betrayed the place. Whether or not this is true, the monastery was sacked by William's troops and a terrible price was exacted from the defenders of the island fastness. Ely fell in 1071, and the traditional story of its heroic defence, of William's use of the Black Arts to encompass its fall and of the final onslaught from Belsar's Hill along the still existing Aldreth Causeway is an exciting one. But Ely was already ancient before Hereward knew it.

It was to this place that St Etheldreda, daughter of Anna, King of East Anglia, came in 673. She too had been a refugee, from her husband Ecgfrith, King of Northumbria. The story of her flight is told in the entry on Stow in our *Guide to Anglo-Saxon Sites*, but it was here at Ely that she and her sisters founded a monastery. The little community flourished despite the death of its founder in 679 until the Danish raid of 870. Some communal life may have continued here afterwards, but it was not until 970 that King Edgar refounded the abbey.

All went well enough until the coming of the Normans and the siege of the Isle. Once the place was taken, William replaced the Saxon abbot Thurston with his kinsman Simeon; despite being 87 years old, this Simeon was evidently a vigorous man and he set about reorganizing the monastic estates and rebuilding the abbey on even more impressive lines. By the time of his death in 1093, he had laid the foundations of the present church and had probably completed the lower parts of the east end and transepts. By 1106 under his successor Richard, the translation of the bones of the Foundress could take place and in 1109 Ely became a bishopric. Setback was not long delayed, however, for under Abbot Nigel, Ely fared badly in the Anarchy of Stephen's reign. It was probably at this time that the motte was built at the south end of the cathedral close and in 1143 the notorious Geoffrey de Mandeville was invited to Ely to help defend the place against the king. Yet through all this muddle and mayhem, when 'men said openly that Christ slept, and his saints', the building of the cathedral continued. The incomparable Prior's Door, for example, dates to c. 1140. Finally, during the third quarter of the 12th century, the great cathedral was completed. It was altered later, of course, owing to the great popularity of St Etheldreda's shrine, but it retains much important Norman work including the exceptional western transept which was amongst the latest building in the 12th century.

Elsewhere in the Isle of Ely there are several interesting Norman sites. At Wentworth is the fine church dedicated to St Peter which, in the twisted columns of its south door, shows the influence of the monastic sculptors spreading out into the surrounding area. More important is the excellent sculpture of the patron saint St Peter which must, like the relief of St George at Fordington, have originally been more prominently displayed than its present position in the north wall of the chancel would suggest. The carving depicts St Peter standing beneath a portrait of the Holy City to which he holds the key; his name is cut into the arcade behind his head. This panel has twisted columns down the side which match those on the south door; plainly the church was built on a handsome scale during the mid-12th century.

At Isleham is well-preserved small priory church built during the later 11th century. It is entirely plain with herringbone work and provides an excellent foil to the decoration in the later abbey church at Ely itself. Finally, it is well worth visiting the Aldreth Causeway. The track runs out into the fen which is still quite swampy in one part just south of the village. When we walk this muddy track and speculate upon its place in the history of Ely, we can still get some feeling of the desolation of the place and of the difficulties encountered by the Conqueror when he decided to hunt down Hereward and his faithful fenmen.

Map References: **Ely** TL 540800 (metric map 143/154. 1-inch map 135)
Wentworth TL 480786
Isleham TL 642744
Aldreth TL 443732
Locations: Wentworth is 4 miles (6.4 km) west of Ely on the A142. Isleham is reached by taking the B1382 north-east out of Ely for 3 miles (5 km) and then turning south-east down the B1104 to Isleham which is a further 6 miles (9.6 km). Isleham is a guardianship site and the key has to be obtained in the village. Do not confuse with the grand parish church which has no Norman work.

Aldreth Causeway is reached from the larger village of Haddenham on the A1123. Aldreth is a tiny village 2 miles (3.2 km) south-west of Haddenham. Down the village street a T-junction is reached. Straight ahead is a green lane which in winter is very rutted and boggy. This green lane is the causeway which leads to the River Ouse and a bridge point.

Carved panel at Wentworth.

60
Burwell Castle, Cambridgeshire

Although over 30 miles (48 km) inland, Burwell enjoyed a vigorous waterborne trade in the past, in common with many fen-edge settlements. The name Burwell probably derives from the manor or 'burgh' spring, and this evidence of an Anglo-Saxon origin for a settlement founded on a spring site is emphasized by the name 'Spring Close' given to a field near the church. This field also contains the principal Norman evidence in Burwell which links the place with the notorious robber baron Geoffrey de Mandeville.

De Mandeville was an opportunist who effectively played both sides against each other during the Anarchy of Stephen's reign. By alternately supporting Stephen and Matilda, he built up a vast power base in the south-east of England. At one stage he was the sole representative of the Crown in Essex, Middlesex and Hertfordshire, as well as being custodian of the Tower of London; few brigands rose to the heights of Geoffrey de Mandeville. Eventually, after Stephen had stripped him of his offices in 1143, de Mandeville retreated to the swamps of East Anglia and led a ragged tail of desperadoes. They ravaged a wide area of countryside, sacked Cambridge and St Ives and used Ramsey as their base; the country for miles around was described as a 'desert' owing to their depredations.

At length, de Mandeville was hunted down by Stephen but, despite that monarch's best endeavours, he could not trap his quarry. Castles were built in the fenlands but, like Hereward the Wake before him, Geoffrey succeeded in eluding his pursuers – until, that is, he came to Burwell. In 1144, Stephen began a new castle here in order to contain his rebellious subject and de Mandeville, with characteristic audacity, determined to attack the place before it was completed. By one of those strange chances of Fate, Geoffrey was slain by an arrow which struck him as he was reconnoitring the position. Thus died one of the

greatest brigands of that unhappy time. But in the way of brigands, many felt some admiration for the man and after his death he was lamented as a good knight (by feudal standards) and one who had sadly died under pain of excommunication by the hand of a commoner.

The earthworks in Spring Close are therefore very closely dated, and they are unusual in being the remains of an unfinished castle. We know that this was not a 'green field' site before Stephen built his castle but that, like the monks of Byland, he had to clear his chosen location of villagers' houses. Foundations of two possible houses and the low banks of four or five closes round other houses can be seen on the site plan. The ditches and spoilheaps of the castle encroach upon these, proving that they existed before the earthworks were raised; the fishponds to the north-west of the site may be contemporary with the houses. We must trust that the villagers of Burwell were well compensated for the destruction of their homes in an enterprise which was never completed!

Map Reference: TL 585670 (metric map 154. 1-inch map 135)
Nearest Town: Newmarket
Location: The village is 4 miles (6.4 km) north-west of Newmarket on the B1103. A fine view of the castle can be gained from the church tower. The castle site is in green fields at the west end of the church beside a little road called Mandeville. Although large notices refer to private property, a public footpath goes past the site.

Plan of the earthworks at Burwell indicating the way in which King Stephen's castle was established over the site of earlier houses and gardens. The fishponds to the west are of uncertain date but they too could have existed at the time that the castle was built.

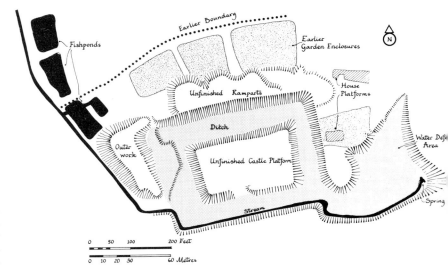

61

Cambridge: Round Church, House and Lepers' Chapel, Cambridgeshire

The Conqueror built a castle at Cambridge in 1068 as part of his policy of holding down his newly won territory. Earthworks are all that remain of his castle, but there are some interesting monuments from the later Norman history of Cambridge. The most famous of these is the 'Round Church' of the Holy Sepulchre which, like the examples at Northampton and Ludlow Castle, was inspired by the form of the Church of the Holy Sepulchre in Jerusalem. A charter of Ramsey Abbey records a grant in the time of Abbot Reinald (1114–30) to the 'Fraternity of the Holy Sepulchre' of the churchyard of St George and the neighbouring land for the construction of a church there 'in honour of God and the Holy Sepulchre'. The 'Fraternity' was probably the Order of the Knights Templar which was founded in 1118 (see entry on the Temple Church, London).

The Round Church, which is generally dated to around 1130, now appears uncompromisingly 'Norman' from the outside but this is largely due to a somewhat severe restoration carried out by the architect Anthony Salvin in 1841. Before his work, the building had been 'modernized' during the 15th century by the insertion of larger windows in the nave walls, the addition of a rather top-heavy lantern where the conical roof now stands and by the elaboration of the eastern parts of the church. Salvin altered much and restored more; the west door was apparently entirely rebuilt and the chancel was reconstructed. Despite all this, the interior of the round nave is substantially intact and the groined roof over the ambulatory around the central space is particularly fine. Enough remains for the quiet dignity of the original to be appreciated.

Elsewhere in the city there are various Norman fragments, but the most unusual are undoubtedly the 'School of Pythagoras' and St Mary's Chapel. The School of Pythagoras is actually a much-abused first-floor hall with a vaulted basement beneath. Two pairs of windows are the principal structural remains of what was presumably a private house. There are later additions comprising a 13th-century solar and a 16th-century west wing; the prominent buttresses are 14th-century additions.

Pride of place amongst the lesser Cambridge monuments must undoubtedly go to the Chapel of St Mary Magdalene which stands about a mile (1.6 km) from the city centre on the Newmarket road. The chapel served a large leper hospital, and this explains its location here outside the medieval city limits; fear of contagion was always very strong. Today the chapel is hemmed in by depressing railway relics, and it was actually restored in 1844 for use as a mission church to the men building the nearby Eastern Counties Railway. This was a late episode in a chequered history since it had earlier come to prominence as the centrepiece of the great Stourbridge Fair. The fair was held on the land around the chapel, and in 1783 we know that the chapel was sold for the purposes of drawing beer for the fairgoers and also of storing the stalls used there! The chancel was used as a 'flat' for the custodian of this booty and the place was evidently rather down at heel. Salvation came first with the 1844 restoration and later, when it was given to the University, it was fully restored by Sir Gilbert Scott in 1867. It can now be recommended as one of the finest small 12th-century chapels anywhere and its decoration may in part reflect its original function as a haven for the afflicted.

Grotesque leper's head from the Chapel.

Map References: **Holy Sepulchre** TL 449588 (metric map 154. 1-inch map 135) **Pythagoras Building** TL 445589 **St Mary's Chapel** TL 472595
Locations: Holy Sepulchre is on Bridge Street on the north side of the city. There is a multi-storey car-park in the block immediately behind.

Pythagoras Building is part of St John's College. Cross Magdalene Bridge up to the first set of traffic lights, turn left, then left again into a lane which leads into the College Backs. Pythagoras Building is in the courtyard on the right, surrounded by modern buildings. Access is through St John's walkways during working hours. Interior is modern.

St Mary Magdalene: take the Newmarket road 1 mile (1.6 km) from the city centre; immediately past the dual carriageway is a railway bridge; take a left lane turn to Barnwell Junction Station. The chapel is set well below road level. The key can be obtained from the old station house behind.

The Round Church; most of the external features date from the restoration of 1841, but the general appearance probably follows the original quite closely.

NORTHERN ENGLAND

85 ▲

• Buxton

84 ▲

83 ▲

Louth •

80

▲ Lincoln

86 ▲

DERBY-
SHIRE

NOTTING-
HAMSHIRE

82 ▲ 81 ▲

LINCOLNSHIRE

• Nottingham

Grantham •

78 ▲

79 ▲

STAFFORD-
SHIRE

• Derby •

88 ▲ 87 ▲

• Stafford

• Burton

LEICESTERSHIRE

77 ▲

76 ▲

Spalding •

• Leicester •

Oakham •

75 ▲

Birmingham

73 ▲ 74 ▲

EAST

WEST
MIDLANDS •

• Coventry

ANGLIA

72

NORTHAMPTON-
SHIRE

WALES

• Warwick

WARWICK-
SHIRE

71 ▲

Bedford •

AND

• Northampton •

THE MARCHES

Banbury •

BEDFORD-
SHIRE

70 ▲

BUCKING-
HAM-
SHIRE

67 ▲

HERTFORD-
SHIRE

OXFORD-
SHIRE

66 ▲

Oxford • 68 ▲

Aylesbury •

63 ▲

62 ▲

65 ▲

St Albans

69 ▲

64 ▲

0   10   20 Miles

0 10 20 30 Km

central
england

Central England

Introduction

It seems logical to begin at Berkhamsted since it was there that the Conqueror received the formal submission of the Anglo-Saxon leaders in 1066. We do not know what relationship the extant castle earthworks had to that great event, or whether they were even built then, but it does not seem too far-fetched to imagine that the relatively large bailey was designed to accommodate William's army. From Berkhamsted, William proceeded to London for his coronation on Christmas Day, 1066.

As far as we know, the Conqueror did not meet any significant resistance in the central region; no revolts are recorded and the relatively thin mantle of castles suggests that it was not thought necessary to hold the area in strength. One of the most important royal castles was at Lincoln, founded in 1068 and the scene of fighting during Stephen's reign. In Derbyshire, the small but well-sited castle at Peveril controlled the royal interests there. Elsewhere in the region, lords built castles to serve as caputs for their estates. At Oakham and Tutbury there were early motte and bailey castles whilst the motte and bailey at Hallaton may have been constructed during the troubled reign of Stephen (1135–54). At Newark, Alexander 'the Magnificent' built a fine castle beside the Trent, the gatehouse of which survives, and at Oakham, Wakelin de Ferrers built himself a superb aisled hall near the end of our period.

Lincolnshire can show rare evidence of domestic life in town and country during the 12th century. In Lincoln itself, there are the two splendid houses on the hill below the cathedral which are probably the best-preserved Norman town houses in England. Also in that city is St Mary's Guildhall, again a rare survival which reflects the prestige of one of the important guilds merchant of the early medieval city. These precious buildings, which are soundly constructed, comfortable and even quite richly decorated, are a clear indication of the heady days of Lincoln's early prosperity. Later, after the new bridge was built across the River Trent at Newark in 1179, Lincoln entered a long period of gradual decline. At Boothby Pagnell, also in Lincolnshire, we see the hall block of a country manor house which in the quality of its details and the soundness of its construction illustrates a more settled and prosperous version of rural life than the myriad cold castles elsewhere in the country.

The generally untroubled course of the Norman settlement in central England resulted in the early construction of important monastic churches and at St Albans and Blyth we have two fine 11th-century buildings. Blyth in particular is dark and holy with an almost barbaric quality about its severe interior. St Albans by contrast is lighter and more optimistic but it can boast no more elaboration than Blyth. From these austere beginnings, we see a rich flowering of major ecclesiastical architecture, including the near-perfect Norman interior at Southwell, the grandiose but overblown west front at Tutbury Priory and the unforgettable west front of Lincoln Cathedral. Impressive as this catalogue of major churches appears, it has at least two grievous gaps which can never be filled. One was the Cluniac monastery at Northampton which was one of the richest in the land, and the other is the abbey church at Sempringham. It is sad that nothing now remains above ground of that great medieval church which celebrated the only Englishman to found a monastic order, the Gilbertines. What we find at Sempringham instead is one of the most dramatic sites in this book, a forlorn part-Norman church standing in the midst of sweeping Lincolnshire cornfields.

In the same way that the 'ghost' of Gilbert's Sempringham can be seen in the fine work at the parish church on the site, the glories of the Cluniac house at Northampton can be glimpsed at second hand in St Peter's church there. The scintillating carving, owing more to the delicate flourishes of the metalworker than the ponderousness of stone, is a tribute to the Cluniac order's patronage of the arts in that city. A further advantage which Northampton possessed was shared by much of the region; this was the availability of good freestone for carving. Thus even at many relatively humble parish churches we find memorable sculpture; the bellringer at Stoke Dry, the mighty chancel arch at Tickencote, the tympana at Hallaton and Charney Bassett, the Aylesbury Group fonts and the more curious examples at Hook Norton and Youlgreave attest plenteous supplies of raw material. Similarly we see fine individual churches from the early simplicity of Tixover to the more developed styles of Melbourne, Stewkley and finally at Iffley, which is both a masterly essay in the Romanesque style and a precocious pointer towards the Gothic glories to come.

62
St Albans Cathedral, Hertfordshire

The abbey of St Albans may have been founded on the site of St Alban's grave outside the Roman town of Verulamium. Alban, the first English saint, was a soldier who died for the faith in Roman times, perhaps in the 3rd century. King Offa of Mercia founded the first monastery here in 793; it was refounded in 968 by King Edgar and retained its importance into the post-Conquest period. In 1077 Paul de Caen, who was rumoured to be the son of Archbishop Lanfranc of Canterbury, began building a major abbey church, parts of which remain.

St Albans is unusual since it was the only English medieval cathedral not to have been constructed of dressed stone. Instead, the principal building material was flint with Roman bricks reused from nearby Verulamium supplying the quoins and dressings. It was probably this shortage of freestone which precluded the use of any carved decoration in the Norman church; St Albans is notable for its lack of structural elaboration. Of de Caen's church, only the transepts, crossing and parts of the nave on the north side survive. These fragments, together with the fine crossing tower, provide a good impression of the grave majesty of the original structure. The interior would have been plastered as we see it now and traces of simple geometric painted decoration can be seen over the crossing arches. The carved shafts at triforium level in the transepts are probably reused Saxon work, again indicating the paucity of good stone near the site. Despite these disadvantages, the church was conceived and built on a noble scale, a fitting tribute to England's protomartyr.

63
Berkhamsted Castle, Hertfordshire

After the Conqueror's victory at Senlac Field near Hastings on 14 October 1066, the Anglo-Saxons had to make up their minds which way to jump. Were they to embrace William as their new ruler and thereby attempt to gain the best terms possible, or should they continue to resist? Many made up their minds quickly and

Map Reference: TL 145070 (metric map 166. 1-inch map 160)
Location: The cathedral is on the south-west side of the modern city near the city centre.

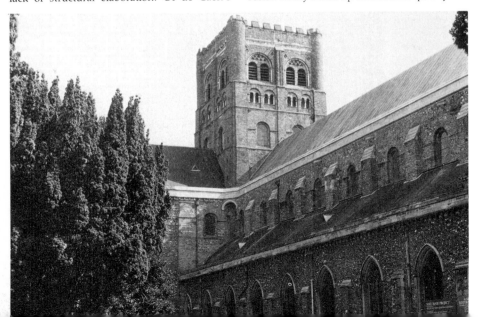

The central tower of St Albans; almost all the details are executed in reused Roman tiles owing to the shortage of local freestone.

decided on the former course; in the words of the Norman chronicler Guy de Amiens, 'citizens flocked to William's camp like flies to a running sore'. Winchester, ancient capital of Wessex, recognized the Conqueror as did many others, but London remained suspiciously quiet. This was not necessarily because the citizens were bent on resistance but rather because they suffered from divided counsels. In the end they half-heartedly elected 'boy Edgar', as the Anglo-Saxon Chronicle calls him, to be Harold's heir, but when William began his march inland early in November and began to devastate the country, they found themselves in danger of being blockaded in London.

Accordingly, the leaders made a virtue of necessity and went to meet William with an embassy of peace. The Anglo-Saxon Chronicle records that when William came to Berkhamsted he was met by all the men of mark who remained in London and 'they gave him hostages and swore oaths of fealty, and he promised to be a gracious lord to them, though at the same time his men plundered all they could'. The Chronicle laments the fact that peace had not been made sooner in view of the depredations which William's army had already made on their march inland, and we can imagine that this evil beginning did not make men more optimistic about life under their new Norman lords.

Berkhamsted then was the scene of one of the major events of early Norman history in England and it must have stood as a symbol of loss to the Anglo-Saxons. Robert de Mortain, who subsequently held the place for the king, dug in behind a fairly powerful set of earthworks and it is to this later period of Norman history that the existing remains may belong. The castle as it stands today is a large motte and bailey with a wet moat around it. Later, probably in the period 1155–80, the motte was crowned by a sub-circular stone ringwork and the bailey was defended by a stone wall. Here are the remains of an archetypal Norman castle on what must have been for the Anglo-Saxons at least a place of evil reputation.

Map Reference: SP 996083 (metric map 165. 1-inch map 159)
Location: The castle is signposted from the town centre. It is on the north-east side of the town, past the public school and beyond the main railway line. It is a guardianship site open standard hours.

Plan of the castle; the curious 'lumps' on the outermost bank are thought by some to be a legacy of the siege of the castle which took place in 1216.

View of the bailey from the top of the motte. Note the wide wet moat on the left-hand side and the later stone curtain wall on top of the bailey bank on the right.

64

Fingest Tower, Buckinghamshire

The massive flint tower of Fingest church is a puzzling structure since it appears to be unique in Norman England. The closest parallels are perhaps the 10th-century tower naves of Anglo-Saxon churches, of which the most celebrated example is Earls Barton. The date of the tower is difficult to determine because although the paired belfry lights in the top stage are of early 12th-century character, there is a change in build between this work and that below which might suggest that the lower part is earlier. The Norman chancel, which was narrower than the tower, has now become the nave and a full ritual chancel was added during the 13th century.

Whether these 'tower naves' had some defensive role, as has been claimed for the Anglo-Saxon examples, is difficult to determine. What we can say about Fingest is that it appears to carry on a pre-Conquest structural tradition, and that this sense of continuity appears to have also been strong elsewhere in Buckinghamshire, as the carvings at Dinton and Stone indicate. Fingest also reminds us of that other enigmatic Norman tower at West Malling in Kent, which was reputedly built by Gundulf in *c.* 1090; if that was indeed the tower of St Leonard's church there, then it might have influenced this tower as well.

65

The Aylesbury Fonts, Buckinghamshire

There are eight fonts in this group, of which the example at Aylesbury itself is the finest. The fonts are of the 'chalice' type – they look like large versions of metal cups rendered in stone. Certainly the symmetry and rounded fluted shapes of the fonts strongly remind us of metal prototypes, and there is something of the Grecian about their form. The font at Bledlow seen in the half light looks more

Map Reference: SU 777911 (metric map 175. 1-inch map 159)
Nearest Town: High Wycombe
Location: Fingest can be approached by a minor single-track road off the B482 Stokenchurch to Marlow road, or from Watlington by minor roads leading through Christmas Common and Turville for some 5 miles (8 km) to Fingest. The shortest road from the B482 is not marked; it is first left after Stokenchurch and is just before Cadmore End. Fingest is 1½ miles (2.4 km) down this road. The church is in the centre of the village.

The 'tower nave' of Fingest church harks back to Anglo-Saxon church planning.

The font at Aylesbury possesses the characteristic fluted 'chalice' shaped bowl which was the hallmark of the Aylesbury Group fonts.

Map References: **Aylesbury** SP 818139 (metric map 165. 1-inch map 159)
Great Kimble SP 825060
Bledlow SP 778022
Little Missenden SU 921990
Great Missenden SP 900010
Buckland SP 888125
Houghton Regis TL 018240
Weston Turville SP 859103
Nearest Town: Aylesbury
Locations: These sites represent the best examples of the group and are to be found in an area to the south and east of Aylesbury.

18th-century than Norman! It is possible that the source of these designs was the great abbey at St Albans, for the delicate filigree work round the rim of the font at Aylesbury would have been entirely appropriate to a gold reliquary or shrine. It is possible that the Bledlow font is the earliest of the group since it is much the least accomplished.

66
Dinton and Stone Carvings, Buckinghamshire

The two churches at Dinton and Stone stand quite close together in the Buckinghamshire countryside. Both contain highly unusual carvings of the 1130s which were probably made by the same man. They are particularly interesting because there are various details of the iconography which hark back to the pagan period. An earlier version of the same vigorous style of carving can be seen on the tympanum at Leckhampstead (Buckinghamshire) which forms a further link in this chain of bizarre beasties.

The font at Stone consist of a cylindrical tub which is decorated round the top with a rather languid two-strand interlace band which links it directly with the outer zone of the tympanum at Dinton. Beneath are strange interlacing circles and knots of billeted ribbons which owe much to manuscript illustrations. Between these strands is a rich variety of human heads and figures, beasts with knotted tails, snakes and perhaps fishes.

At Dinton, the tympanum over the south door contains an unusual scene of two lions or dragons eating fruit from a Tree of Life. This strange design is interpreted by an inscription beneath the panel: PRAEMIA PRO MERITIS SI SUIS DESPERET HABENDA AUDIAT HIC PRAECEPTA SIBI QUAE SINT RETINENDA – 'If any should despair of obtaining reward for his deserts let him attend to the doctrines here preached and keep them in mind.' This articulates with the two creatures since it underlines the sustaining nature

of the church which is illustrated literally above. On the lintel beneath the tympanum is a further curiosity. A great curling-tailed dragon with gaping toothed jaws menaces a diminutive angel who fends off the outsize beast with a cross. Here again we see a literal interpretation of Christianity – the symbol of the cross holds back the Evil One. Such carvings as these are revealing; few could have understood the Latin inscription, but all could 'read' the pictures.

Map References: **Dinton** SP 767110 (metric map 165. 1-inch map 146)
Stone SP 784123
Nearest Town: Aylesbury
Locations: Dinton is on the A418 4 miles (6.4 km) south-west of Aylesbury. The church stands by a fine manor house. Stone is also on the A418 3 miles (5 km) south-west of Aylesbury. Leckhampstead (Bucks), which is also mentioned in the text, is 20 miles north of Dinton and Stone, 3 miles north-east of Buckingham.

Were it not for the fact that the Dinton tympanum has an inscription which 'interprets' its imagery, it would be as much of a mystery as the font at Stone.

The extraordinary font at Stone with its riotous and incomprehensible decoration.

67
Stewkley Church, Buckinghamshire

The mid-12th-century church of St Michael at Stewkley is an excellent example of a small Norman three-cell parish church. Although restored during the last century, the work was generally well done and there is no excessive neatness about the building. Stewkley is a smaller version of the axial tower plan at Iffley and it is interesting that the advowsons of both churches were given to Kenilworth Priory before the end of the 12th century. As with many Norman towers, the one here at Stewkley impresses by its bulk; it is a powerful piece of masonry and the rather desultory intersecting arcading round its top does nothing to diminish its force. The openings in the tower are small, just enough to provide light to a stair and to emit the notes of the bells. The other openings in the church have chevron decoration and their neat ashlar dressings must have complemented the plastered exterior as at Iffley.

Internally, all is holy darkness with robust figure carving, further chevrons round the windows and a fine string course which is a more elaborate version of the external one. The chancel arch is particularly splendid with beak heads, further chevron moulding and a zigzag-decorated hood mould. Beyond, the chancel has a ribbed vault and here, rather than simple square or rolled ribs, we find lozenges. A ghost of colour is provided by some later painted foliate decoration on the vault and this serves to remind us of how dramatic such an interior would have been. Here in the chancel there are angle shafts bearing the vaulting ribs, a handsome east window and an elaborate string course. If we close one eye we can still see the colour and the flickering candlelight; what marvellous shrines these little Norman churches must have been!

Map Reference: SP 852261 (metric map 165. 1-inch map 146)
Nearest Town: Leighton Buzzard
Location: Stewkley is on the B4032 between Linslade and Winslow, about 5 miles (8 km) from Linslade. The church is in the centre of the village.

The chancel and central tower of Stewkley church with their restrained mid-12th-century decoration.

68
Iffley Church, Oxfordshire

The celebrated church at Iffley is the best example of late Norman decorative exuberance in England. Built by the St Remy family who granted land and paid for a priest here, the church was constructed substantially as we see it today between 1175 and 1182. The Norman plan consisted of a nave and chancel with an axial tower between; there may originally have been a further eastern compartment beyond the chancel. The features of particular importance are the west front and the chancel arch. Recent restoration has improved the appearance of the west front very considerably and we now see the stone dressings as they were intended to be seen – against a crisp background of wall plaster.

The great west door is sandwiched between two niches; there is a circular window above, restored in 1858, and three further windows above a string course echo the rhythm of the lower three openings. The doorway itself has continuous chevrons and beak heads – there are no capitals or columns. The flowing lines of the door complement those of the circular window above and the similar openings in the

Map Reference: SP 527035 (metric map 164. 1-inch map 158)
Nearest Town: Oxford
Location: Iffley is in the southern suburbs of Oxford although it was originally a separate settlement. From the centre of Oxford, where Norman remains can also be seen at the castle and the cathedral, take the Iffley Road from Magdalen Bridge. Iffley church is a turning to the west off this road about 2 miles (3.2 km) from the city centre.

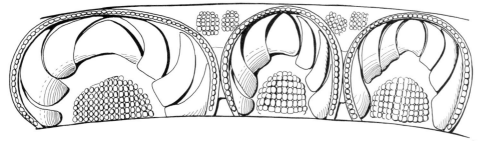

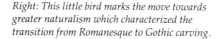

upper storey; likewise the chevron motif occurs on the inner angles of the pilasters down each side. There is a feeling of Gothic line about the west front, and Iffley looks forward to the Gothic style in other ways as well. But it is a Transitional building, looking backwards as well as forwards; the north and south doorways into the nave still have regular nook shafts and elaborate freestyle capitals.

Inside, the chancel arch dominates the scene. This is a massive construction with, round the head, a unique scheme of 'sunflowers' carved on it. An important feature of this arch is that the faceted nook shafts on its western face are made of polished black stone, probably Tournai marble; a similar material was used for the fine square font. These shafts are the earliest-known use of black marble in an English architectural composition and provide another example of Iffley's advanced style. In the hollows separating the paired columns supporting the chancel arch is a delicate carving of a bird standing on a nest; this hint of naturalism again prefigures Gothic models. Iffley is often claimed as one of the last fully Romanesque buildings in England. Whilst this may be true, we can detect many harbingers of the new Gothic style.

Above: The unique 'sunflower' motifs on the chancel arch.

Right: This little bird marks the move towards greater naturalism which characterized the transition from Romanesque to Gothic carving.

The richly decorated west front, recently restored to something more nearly approaching its original condition by the addition of render which covers the rubble walling.

Alexander the Great prepared to mount heavenwards, borne up by hungry griffins.

69
Charney Bassett Tympanum, Oxfordshire

St Peter's Church at Charney Bassett was apparently rebuilt during the early 12th century and the tympanum which is now built into the north wall of the chancel is of the greatest interest. The early-12th-century tympanum is very well carved in quite high relief and with controlled assurance. It consists of an outer beaded border with a projecting head in the centre at the top. In the outer zone is a tight stylized leaf border. On the main panel is a scene of a crowned king shown between two griffins; he clutches their manes and he is shown sitting in a chair.

This scene probably illustrates the legend of the Flight of Alexander the Great. In this story, Alexander was borne up to heaven by hungry griffins who were themselves lured upwards by meat impaled on spears just beyond their reach. Rather like the tales in the Bestiary, this tale was used to demonstrate a Christian idea, in this case Man's hunger for the beauty of heaven. But by some the meaning was reversed and it was regarded as an instance of vaunting pride.

Various dissenting voices have been raised against the idea that it depicts Alexander but no other has been plausibly suggested. There are other bits of evidence which tend to support the idea, however. In the first place, the church was given by Ralph Bassett to the priory at Abingdon in the 1120s, and this gives some context for such an elaborate meaning. Similarly, the style of the carving shows influence from nearby Reading Abbey, again suggesting some monastic patronage. Finally, we know that the image was popular during the 12th century since Henry de Blois, Bishop of Winchester, owned a piece of metalwork depicting the legend. Charney Bassett is another example of the filtering downwards of complicated iconography during the great period of interest in Classical ideas.

Map Reference: SP 381945 (metric map 164. 1-inch map 158)
Nearest Town: Abingdon
Location: Charney Bassett is reached directly from the A420 Oxford to Swindon road. 10 miles (16 km) from the ring road in a south-westerly direction, after Kingston Bagpuize, take the turning south to Charney Bassett. The church is at the end of the village beside the ancient Charney Hall, now owned by the Society of Friends.

Right: Aquarius the water carrier is menaced by Sagittarius on the font at Hook Norton.

70
Hook Norton Font, Oxfordshire

Parts of the church of St Peter at Hook Norton are certainly Norman and traces of early wall-paintings have recently been found on the chancel walls. It is the font which claims our attention, however, for it is a rustic version of more splendid schemes elsewhere. The 12th-century carver of the font was evidently aware of the significance of the iconography in use at such sites as Malmesbury and he might have seen lead fonts such as the one at Brookland, but unfortunately his skill was limited. Here we see a local attempt to convey vigorous meanings but the effect is one of caricature.

The designs on the side of the cylindrical font include a figure of a centaur labelled SAGITTARIUS aiming his arrow at a figure carrying water skins representing Aquarius. In this use of the Signs of the Zodiac we see the implicit statement that God oversees all seasons and that they exist as part of His plan. Apart from the Zodiacal signs, there is a Tree of Life and a rather jolly representation of Adam and Eve, presumably a reference to the power of baptism to release men from the taint of Original Sin. Above the figures is a band of foliate decoration reminiscent of the lead fonts, whilst below is a zone of roundels.

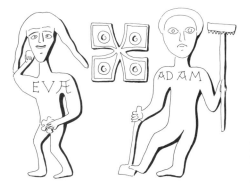

71
Northampton Churches, Northamptonshire

Northampton was an important borough in the pre-Conquest period, and it was here that the famous Council was held in 1164 after which Thomas à Becket had to flee from Henry II's wrath. Northampton had a royal castle, its huge market-place grew up in Norman times and it had one of the most important Cluniac monasteries in the land. Sadly, the castle and St Andrew's Priory have gone but Northampton retains two important Norman churches. The first of these is St Peter's, which stands close to the site of the castle; it was reputedly founded on the site of a Saxon minster by an Earl of Northampton, one of the de Senlis family, and may also have benefited from the Cluniac decorative tradition in the town.

From the outside, St Peter's looks interesting but unimpressive; this is because the fine western tower was rebuilt in rather a muddled fashion early in the 17th century and there was also a later restoration in 1851. Internally, however, all is light; St Peter's is one of the finest decorative compositions to have survived from the mid-12th century. Notice first the use of alternating nave piers, a technique normally reserved for major churches such as Durham. Here, round and quatrefoil shafts

Map Reference: SP 355331 (metric map 151. 1-inch map 145)
Nearest Town: Chipping Norton
Location: From Chipping Norton, take the A361 Banbury road for 3 miles (5 km) in a north-easterly direction, then follow the signs northwards up a minor road to Hook Norton.

Adam and Eve – presumably their presence on the font at Hook Norton recalls the power of baptism to cleanse the taint of sin.

Map References: **St Peter's Church** SP 750603 (metric map 152. 1-inch map 133) **St Sepulchre's Church** SP 756613
Locations: Both churches are in the city centre, St Peter's on the Marefair and St Sepulchre's on Sheep Street.

alternate, the round shafts having decorative collars half-way up, a technique noticed at Tyninghame. The nave arcade is decorated with markedly angular chevron ornament executed in contrasting voussoirs of white limestone and brown ironstone. One half-bay of the original six double nave bays disappeared during the 17th-century rebuilding of the tower, as indicated by the awkwardly placed windows at the west ends of the clerestories. The capitals of the nave pillars are decorated with foliage and animals in a rather formal style reminiscent of metalworking. The tower arch, which must have been reset, has lost nothing of its grandeur; the shafts have lattice, chevron and twisted decoration and the three orders of the arch have deep chevron moulding.

A further important survival is a richly decorated slab in the south aisle. This is covered with complicated decoration including a human mask from which foliate tendrils curve round to form panels inhabited by backward-biting beasts, a knotwork roundel and further animals. This extraordinary slab seems too elaborate to have been a simple grave-marker and it is possible that it covered the relics of the mysterious soldier–saint Ragener who was venerated in St Peter's church in pre-Conquest times. Two fonts outside Northampton may also have been made by masons of the St Peter's school; it seems that the nave capitals, slab and fonts together comprise the products of a major school of carvers who looked to Reading and oriental textiles for their designs and may have earlier worked at Castor in the same county.

Also in Northampton is St Sepulchre's church which, as the name suggests, was based on the circular plan of the Holy Sepulchre in Jerusalem. This church was built at about the same time as the circular chapel at Ludlow Castle, although on a somewhat larger scale. The Ludlow chapel has no internal colonnade but here the nave was provided with a concentric vaulted aisle like the Round Church at Cambridge. Unfortunately the vault seems to have proved too heavy for the outer wall for

it was replaced by pointed arches during the 13th century. The sturdy round pillars survive and Norman windows together with sections of corbel table can be seen in the side walls of the chancel. The church was apparently founded by Simon de Senlis, Earl of Northampton, who had taken part in the First Crusade in 1095, and it was doubtless his intention to build this church as a monument to that high endeavour.

One of the delicately carved capitals of the nave arcade; the lightness of the style suggests that it might owe something to filigree decoration of metalwork.

72
Berkswell Crypt, West Midlands

The chancel of Berkswell church is of considerable interest since it was built on rather a lavish scale during the 1180s, and features such unusual details as the use of half-round pilasters and simply decorated though generous windows with nook shafts. The whole is built in good ashlar and was obviously intended as a showpiece. This impression is heightened when it is realized that underneath the chancel is an intriguing crypt.

This superb slab may have covered the grave of the mysterious soldier–saint Ragener whose cult was important at Northampton in pre-Conquest times.

Map Reference: SP 244791 (metric map 139. 1-inch map 131)
Nearest Town: Coventry
Location: Berkswell is west of Coventry, 5 miles (8 km) from the city centre. It can be reached directly from the A452(T) Birmingham to Kenilworth road or by the A4023 from Coventry. The church is in a pleasant setting beside the hall in the centre of the village.

The presence of this crypt, which appears to be of two phases, raises the obvious question of why it was built. The western octagonal part is the earlier and must surely be a reliquary crypt, but whose relics did it contain? The easterly extension takes the form of a small vaulted chapel and appears to be an after-thought, added when the octagon was refurbished. Perhaps the name Berkswell holds the key to the problem. It means 'Bercul's Well', and the settlement may thus be the site of an early conversion centre dating back to Anglo-Saxon times. Perhaps this Bercul was an Anglo-Saxon missionary who baptized dwellers in the remote Forest of Arden, in which the settlement lay. There is a restored stone tank in the churchyard which is reputed to be 'Bercul's Well'; were his relics displayed in the crypt beneath the later church? We will almost certainly never know.

View looking eastwards from the octagonal crypt into the chapel beyond; was this the burial place of Bercul whose name is commemorated in the placename?

A corbel head from the chancel.

73

Hallaton Castle and Tympanum, Leicestershire

Hallaton Castle is an almost perfect little motte and bailey tucked away down a quiet valley. As far as we know, the defences were never rebuilt in stone and it was probably not occupied for very long. There appears to have been no settlement immediately around the site and its position here is something of a puzzle. The site was dug into during the last century and quantities of iron slag were found in the make-up of the defences; this has led to the suggestion that the castle was sited so as to guard nearby ironworkings. Whilst such an explanation is possible, it might be more believable if gold rather than iron were being mined. The winning of iron was a long and complicated process (see entry on Bentley Grange) and hence a would-be attacker would have better tried to intercept the movement of the finished product rather than to attack the workings themselves.

It probably makes more sense to see the Hallaton site as one of the many castles raised during the Anarchy of Stephen's reign in 1135–54. For the year 1137, the Anglo-Saxon Chronicle records that 'every powerful man made his castles and then held them against [the king] and filled the land full of castles. They oppressed the wretched men of the land hard with work on the castles, and when the castles were made they filled them with devils and evil men.'

The Peterborough Chronicle records for the same year: 'and men said openly that Christ and His saints were asleep'.

After the period of the Anarchy, the chronicler Robert de Torigni records that 1,115 castles were destroyed after the peace which brought Henry II to the throne. Doubts have been expressed about this figure, but there can be no doubt that large numbers of relatively short-lived castles were built during those troubled times. Such castles are often called 'adulterine', which means they were built ille-gally, i.e. without royal permission. Control of castle-building was a prudent precaution since it effectively restrained all save the most 'trusted' lords from defending themselves. However, during the Anarchy the system broke down and all sorts and conditions of men built themselves castles.

Apart from the castle, the church at Hallaton is of interest since it contains what is perhaps the finest Norman carving in the county. Little of the existing fabric is Norman, with the exception of elements of the late-12th-century north nave arcade, but in the north porch is a tympanum with a spirited rendering of St Michael and the Dragon. St Michael is shown with his archangelic wings and a fine circular fluted shield, plunging his spear into the dragon's mouth. Notice that in the folds of his cloak he holds the souls of the faithful and that they lurk in safety behind his shield, but above the dragon and to the right are other souls who must be evildoers. Here is a symbolical representation of the saving power of the Church and its saints which parallels the image at Dinton. This carving was probably executed whilst Hallaton Castle was occupied; what other interpretations might have been placed on this symbolism whilst 'Christ and His saints were asleep'?

Map Reference: SP 786966 (metric map 141. 1-inch map 133)
Nearest Town: Uppingham
Location: Famous for its Easter Bottle Kicking event, Hallaton is reached by minor roads south from East Norton which is 5 miles (8 km) west of Uppingham on the A47(T). To find the castle, go past the church on the left to a dead end beside the house. At the end of the road is a footpath sign with a left fork to Cranoe and right to Goadby. The right fork affords a good view across the river to the earthworks. The left fork crosses the river but there is no actual right of way to the castle site.

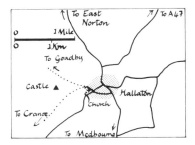

St Michael defeats the Dragon and guards the diminutive souls of the Faithful behind his fluted shield.

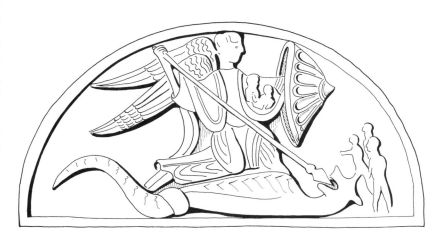

Above: Hallaton castle motte viewed from across the little valley in which it stands. Thawing snow shows up traces of ridge and furrow cultivation which could be contemporary with the castle.

Right: The ill-favoured bellringer amidst a mass of foliage, grotesques and animals which came straight out of the dreams (or nightmares?) of the 12th-century carvers at Stoke Dry.

74

Stoke Dry Carvings, Leicestershire

The church of St Andrew at Stoke Dry was in a sad state of dissolution and decay until a few years ago when a gallant restoration project was undertaken by the inhabitants of this tiny village. We know of no more satisfactory church interior than this one; we can only thank its saviours.

Upon entering the church, all the proportions are Gothic and it is at first difficult to see anything Norman at all. The principal Norman evidence is detailed rather than large-scale and consists of a few pieces of decorated string course in the chancel and the responds of the chancel arch. This may sound little enough but the shafts of the arch are covered with extraordinary freestyle carving.

There are several rather grand pieces of

Norman sculpture in Rutland churches – we think of the small figures at Uppingham, the work of Essendine and, of course, Tixover and Tickencote. It is evident from the period range of these pieces that Rutland was able to patronize good sculptors throughout our period. But of all these we feel that the laurel must go to the pillars at Stoke Dry. The more you look at them, the more you see. Apart from the famous bellringer and the devil near him, there is a strange human head which emerges from foliage and which finds its closest parallel on a Roman capital at Cirencester. This early picture of 'Jack in the Green' and the other creatures on the columns seem to us to come out of the great imaginative reservoir of the 12th-century carvers. They are of a piece with the Alkborough Maze and the other half-pagan observations which were held in rural areas. The roots of the foliage on the Stoke Dry pillars reach into the remotest past.

Map Reference: SP 855968 (metric map 141. 1-inch map 133)
Nearest Town: Uppingham
Location: A charming little village close by the Eyebrook Reservoir, Stoke Dry is 2 miles (3.2 km) south of Uppingham, just to the west of the A6003 to Corby.

Map Reference: SP 971998 (metric map 141. 1-inch map 123)
Nearest Town: Uppingham
Location: Tixover is 8 miles (12.8 km) east of Uppingham on the A47(T). It lies just to the south of the main road and is a lovely peaceful place. The church is about a half-mile (0.8-km) walk from the village in a south-westerly direction along a field track. A large notice outside one of the houses on the main street indicates the location of the key and it is wise to pick it up before starting off!

Now deserted, the little church of St Mary formerly stood within a small village.

75

Tixover Church, Leicestershire

St Mary's church stands in tranquil isolation to the south-west of the little village of Tixover. The church was not always so isolated – in the fields around it there are scatters of medieval pottery, and a Roman villa site to the north hints of a long span of occupation in this favourable location. It is likely that a change in the road alignment during the later medieval period resulted in a shift away from the original village site to its present more easterly position. Recent road works resulted in the discovery of medieval occupation near the later road line, which appears to fit this general theory.

Whatever the reasons, the result is the survival of a splendid early-12th-century church in an idyllic setting. The tower in particular with its tall and well-proportioned belfry lights is reminiscent of the more elaborate though less satisfactory tower at South Lopham. Inside, the tower arch is a robustly decorated piece, having five shafts with crudely carved capitals and no fewer than seven roll mouldings round the head. The south door by which the church is entered is perhaps an alteration of a late-12th-century opening with good waterleaf capitals. The whole is a delightful survival, marred only by the rather unfeeling stove pipe which rises up the east side of the tower.

76

Oakham Castle, Leicestershire

The hall was built for Wakelin de Ferrers, lord of the manor of Oakham Lordshold in the years after 1180. The hall would have been only one element of Wakelin's quarters, however; this was a public space for feasting, dispensing justice and for other matters of general concern. By this time the lord would have slept in a separate block of buildings which probably resembled the existing camera block at Boothby Pagnell. Even the hall is not complete. There are blocked doorways on both the ground and first-floor levels at the 'low' end of the hall which presumably led to a kitchen, buttery and pantry on the ground floor and a suite of private rooms above.

Map Reference: SK 882089 (metric map 141. 1-inch map 122)
Location: The Castle Hall is in the centre of the town behind the Butter Cross Market-Place. The castle grounds are well preserved and the fine hall is open daily, free of charge.

Unlike the first-floor halls at Christchurch and Boothby Pagnell, Oakham hall is built on the ground and it has an aisled plan. This emphasizes its public rather than private function and the original position of the doorway in the south-east angle of the building would have assured the visitor of an impressively long vista up to the dais end of the hall. In this connection it is fitting that the use of the hall as a courtroom should have continued; something of the majesty of the original has been retained.

The basic plan of the hall consists of four bays divided by six cylindrical pillars surmounted by foliate capitals. Above each capital, facing in towards the hall, is a figure of a musician, four human and two animal. The occurrence of the animal musicians here echoes the work of the Kentish School of sculptors and this parallel is strikingly reinforced by the marked similarities between the capitals and corbels at Oakham and those in the choir of Canterbury Cathedral. This is an exciting observation, and the suggestion that some of the sculptors employed on William of Sens' choir at Canterbury also worked at

Oakham would account for the high quality of the work here.

After the Conquest, the manor of Oakham was retained by the Crown until the early 12th century. We know there had been a hall here at the time of Domesday Book in 1086. The hall referred to was probably made of wood and may have stood in a motte and bailey castle. The banked enclosure in which the present hall stands is probably the bailey of an early castle and slight traces of a motte with a ditch can be detected in the south-east corner. There is a further, outer, bailey to the north of the main one called 'Cutts Close' and between the two are some medieval fishponds. As far as we can tell, the defences were not reconstructed during our period, but in the 13th century a stone curtain was added to the inner bailey and it was strengthened by two round towers, the bases of which can still be seen on the west side near the church. At the time the hall was built, Oakham Castle was perhaps equivalent to the first 'country house' phase at Castle Acre; it was a pleasant and civilized place in which courtly life could better be pursued than in a constraining keep.

Above: Corbel from the hall.

Below: Sculpture of a musician which surmounts one of the capitals of the hall arcade.

Interior of the famous castle hall; the horseshoes on the wall were donated by any peer of the realm who entered the county of Rutland. On the left is the seating for the court which continues a tradition of the administration of justice in this building which is 700 years old.

77

Tickencote Church, Leicestershire

Tickencote is celebrated for its extraordinary chancel arch. This gargantuan construction is totally out of scale with the small two-cell church in which it stands, but further reflection reminds us that this is merely a prodigious example of a wider phenomenon. Many small Norman churches and chapels, such as Kilpeck, Barfreston and Kempley, are richly decorated either with sculpture or painting in great profusion. Perhaps the builders economized on the scale of the churches in order to lavish more attention upon the finishes.

The chancel arch consists of six deeply cut orders decorated with beak heads, castellations, grotesque heads, enriched chevrons and a sort of stepped abstract motif; the hood mould is also decorated with double billeting. Despite the fact that the arch is out of scale and badly erected, as the misshapen appearance indicates, the carving is finely executed and several of the heads in particular are very lively. On the north side are a king and queen, a 'Green Man' with a sprig of foliage issuing from his mouth, a muzzled bear and what could be a foreshortened elephant.

Less well known are the other features at Tickencote. The chancel is unique in Norman England since it has a sexpartite vault with a charming vaulting boss at the centre which bears animal heads in a similar style to the work at Kilpeck. Also, although imaginatively restored during the 18th century by S.P. Cockerell, some elements of the exterior, including the half-round shafts in the manner of Berkswell, appear to be original. From around 1200 comes the small square font with its delicate blank arcading and stubby engaged legs; but the rest of the work at Tickencote has proved

The gargantuan chancel arch at Tickencote Church with its serried rows of beak heads, chevrons and castellations.

more difficult to date. The full-blown beak heads and other ornament point to a date in the 1160s, but the chancel vault was unknown even in English cathedrals before William of Sens used it at Canterbury in 1175; Tickencote is indeed a puzzling place!

78

Boothby Pagnell Manor House, Lincolnshire

The important remains of the manor house at Boothby Pagnell supply some of the elements missing from Oakham Castle. At Oakham we have the main hall though without any domestic accommodation whilst here at Boothby Pagnell we have the domestic block without the hall. The hall at Boothby would not, of course, have been on the scale of that at Oakham, and it was probably built in timber. Before considering the evidence here in more detail, we must dispose of the myth that Boothby was an 'unfortified' site. The shallow course of a substantial ditch can be seen to the south and west. Such a ditch would have had a bank beside it, and the two elements would have

Map Reference (Tickencote): SK 900095 (metric map 141. 1-inch map 123)
Nearest Town: Stamford
Location: The pretty little village of Tickencote lies perilously close to the busy A1, 2½ miles (4 km) north-west of Stamford. Watch out for the Tickencote signs carefully as from most directions it is necessary to approach via Great Casterton. Many is the time that we have whizzed past Tickencote on the A1, unable to reach it directly!

Above right: This superb 12th-century fireplace at Boothby Pagnell has a joggled lintel and a lightly 'keeled' roll moulding across its front. To the left can be seen a blocked Norman window, and on the extreme left is a timber studded screen which probably dates to the 15th century.

provided an effective defence. We cannot be certain just how large the enclosure was but it possibly included the area now occupied by the later manor house to the east. The enclosure would have contained, apart from the existing camera block, a hall, kitchen, servants' lodgings, a brewhouse, stables, storeplaces and all the other structures consonant with the kind of high quality lifestyle which the existing building attests.

The camera block has been extended later on its west side, but apart from this it is singularly intact. It consisted of two basements at ground-floor level which were entered by two doors in the east front; the central door survives intact, but the more northerly, which gave access to the smaller chamber beneath the solar, has been altered to form a window. On the first floor, which was reached by a stair case in the same position as the existing one, were a hall and solar divided by a stone wall. The small domestic hall has a magnificent fireplace with a joggled lintel supporting a smoke hood. The timber-framed partition across the south end of the hall probably reflects the original arrangement; the smaller chamber might have been used as a wardrobe for clothes. The solar would have been used by the lord and his lady for sleeping in, and the hall would have been a cosy retiring place for the lord and his family.

Externally the two-light windows are particularly fine. Note that each has small circular holes drilled through it at sill level to drain water which had condensed on the window glass. On the west side the round chimney is

very well preserved and the whole hearth and chimney arrangement must be the best Norman example in the country. One further point concerns the roof; this was much steeper than at present, probably to facilitate drainage from a thatched roof covering. An earlier, steeper, roof angle can be seen 'fossilized' by a chase in the south side of the Norman chimney. This fact makes it likely that the hall originally rose into the roof space without a ceiling above it.

Nothing is known of the owners of the manor house at Boothby Pagnell. The estate was owned at the time of Domesday Book in 1086 by Gilbert de Gand, who was the man who provided Gilbert of Sempringham with funds for his abbey. By the time the hall was built in around 1200, the place probably belonged to the de Boothby family, who probably took their name from the village, but the Pagnell element did not exist before the 14th century when the place passed by marriage to the Pagnells. Whoever did build Boothby Pagnell manor house was probably also responsible for some of the work in the parish church of a similar date; church and manor house together give a picture of quiet plenty in the late 12th century.

Map Reference: SK 970307 (metric map 130. 1-inch map 123)
Nearest Town: Grantham
Location: From Grantham take the A52 out of town to the first major roundabout, then go straight on to the B1176 to Bourne. Boothby Pagnell is the second village along this road – some 3 miles (5 km). The manor house is in the grounds of the early 19th-century hall opposite the church; the site is in private ownership and it is necessary to write in advance for permission to visit.

Imaginative reconstruction of the original appearance of the manor house surrounded by a moat with ancillary buildings.

79

Sempringham and St Gilbert, Lincolnshire

Sempringham today consists of a small and much-restored Norman church standing in the midst of large arable fields. The village of that name has long since vanished and the place would qualify as yet another deserted village site like Tixover, were it not for the remarkable story of St Gilbert of Sempringham.

St Gilbert was born here at Sempringham in 1083 or thereabouts. He was the crippled son of the lord of the manor and was devout from an early age. He went to study in Paris and on his return he founded a school in which he taught boys and girls from his native village and lived in poverty. Later he was ordained priest and entered the household of the Bishop of Lincoln; at one time his patron was Bishop Alexander 'the Magnificent' who was responsible for the elaborate west front of Lincoln Cathedral. Later he returned to Sempringham, despite having been offered an archdeaconry, and seven village women whom he had earlier taught made known their desire to live secluded lives in the service of God. Gilbert, who was by this time lord of the manor, caused small cells to be built for them to the north of the parish church. Other women joined the first seven and lay sisters were recruited to minister to their needs. In 1147 Gilbert went to Cîteaux, the home of the Cistercian order, to ask them to take over the rapidly expanding group of religious. The Cistercians declined his offer, but Pope Eugenius III made him the head of a new (Gilbertine) order.

The new order proved popular in eastern England and canons and lay brothers also joined; the canons were necessary because the nuns could not celebrate Mass for themselves. In 1164, Gilbertine monks helped Thomas à Becket to escape the wrath of Henry II after the Council of Northampton, but Gilbert was forgiven when he said that his first loyalty was to God and the Church rather than to the Crown. The Gilbertine monasteries were unusual since they were 'double houses' for both sexes. This requirement was reflected in the unique plan of the Gilbertine churches which were divided down the centre by a high wall with canons on

Map Reference: TF 105325 (metric map 130. 1-inch map 123)
Nearest Town: Billingborough
Location: The church of Sempringham is 1 mile (1.6 km) south of Billingborough, on the west side of the B1177 Bourne road; it stands out on its own amongst the fields about 1 mile (1.6 km) off the road up a trackway. Cars can be taken up the track and there is a small car-park near the church. Before going up the track, collect the key from the house opposite the end of the track. While visiting the church also look at the holy well in the south-east corner of the churchyard, date unknown. The site of the abbey shows as a mound in the fields to the south-west of the church.

The church at Sempringham appears as a ship in a sea of golden barley; 'bright robes of gold the fields adorn, the hills with joy are ringing, the valleys stand so thick with corn that even they are singing'.

one side and nuns on the other. Gilbert continued his devout ways until his death in 1189, by which time 13 monasteries had been founded, although none now survives above ground. Gilbert was canonized in 1202 by popular request and his relics were venerated in the abbey church here at Sempringham which he had built.

So Sempringham is one of the most unusual sites in this book; it was the birthplace of the only Englishman to found a monastic order and the site of a great abbey church; but all that remains is the lonely parish church, parts of which were built during Gilbert's lifetime. The village which stood around it has disappeared apart from a few bumps in the field to the north-west of the church, whilst the site of the abbey church, which was as long as Sherborne after it was rebuilt during the 14th century, is marked by a mound in the fields. But in the fine stonework of the church we get some slight impression of the splendid works which stood here, and as we pass through the firwood door, which still retains fine Norman ironwork, we can remember Gilbert of Sempringham and be thankful.

80
Lincoln Castle, Cathedral and Houses, Lincolnshire

Some of the Anglo-Saxon history of Lincoln is outlined in our *Guide to Anglo-Saxon Sites*, and that story is compelling enough. Norman Lincoln has left us with a rich and remarkable legacy of monuments, however, attesting its substantial economic prosperity during our period. Today, the city is dominated by the magnificent cathedral, and this seems a good place to begin. At a council held at Windsor in 1072, it was decreed that episcopal sees should be moved to larger towns, as with the move of the East Anglian see from Thetford to Norwich, and in the case of the vast diocese of Dorchester on Thames the bishopseat was moved to Lincoln. Construction of the new

cathedral began on the site of St Mary's minster almost immediately, and the new church was consecrated in 1092. A fire in 1141 resulted in extensive damage and it was Bishop Alexander, builder of Newark Castle and called 'The Magnificent', who refurbished the structure.

Only the west front remains as witness to the Norman splendours of the cathedral, but it tells an interesting story. It is basically a work of the first Norman church built by Bishop Remigius, and was originally very severe. After the fire, Alexander elaborated the front by inserting ornate doorways into the existing recesses, raising the central recess and adding the carved frieze. He also replaced the timber nave roof with a high stone vault. The frieze in particular repays careful examination; it depicts Noah and the Ark, his family and animals as well as Daniel in the Lions' Den and the Harrowing of Hell. Judging by this spectacular west front, the rest of the cathedral must have been as magnificent as Alexander's sobriquet suggests, but it was severely damaged by an earthquake in 1185 and most of the rest of the church was rebuilt.

Panel showing the Ark, Noah and his family leaving the Ark, and God's covenant with Noah. Both these carvings come from Bishop Alexander's magnificent embellishment of the west front of the Cathedral.

Map Reference: SK 977719 (metric map 121. 1-inch map 113)
Locations: The Norman Guildhall is on the south side of the city on the High Street. The two Jews' Houses are both on Steep Hill below the cathedral. One is an arts centre, the other an antique shop.

Daniel in the Lions' Den; the lions look remarkably cheerful, or perhaps they are meant to be growling at the serene Daniel in their midst.

Inside the church are two interesting objects, however, both of which are made of Tournai marble. The first is the font which belongs with the 'Hampshire Fonts', being an import of mid-12th-century date. The second is a tombstone that bears a fine carving of a Tree of Jesse on the front. Since a small fragment of a similar design appears on the west front, and because the stone is evidently of the highest quality, the art historian Dr Zarnecki has suggested that this could be the tombstone of Bishop Alexander himself.

Near the cathedral in the upper city is Lincoln Castle. This was founded in 1068 by the Conqueror, and 166 houses were destroyed during its construction. Lincoln is unusual in having two mottes within its large bailey, one surmounted by a shell keep and the other by a rectangular tower. Whether the first castle was built of stone is difficult to say, but by 1115 it was certainly stone built, and much of the curtain wall survives from that period, as do the east and west gates. The presence of two mottes is curious but it has been suggested that the Lucy Tower, which is the shell keep, replaced the earlier tower which was possibly damaged in the siege of Lincoln Castle in 1140 during the Anarchy of Stephen's reign.

Apart from the cathedral and the castle, which represented Church and State in the early medieval city, Lincoln was also a flourishing mercantile centre. At the time of the Conquest, the population of the city was probably around 6,500, which put Lincoln in the first rank of late Saxon towns. After the foundation of the castle, the town suffered a setback and its population seems to have declined sharply to around 4,500, but by the mid-12th century as many as 7,000 people probably lived in the city. All went well, trade prospered with Lincoln's fairs being major events, and Lincoln scarlet and green cloth was famous throughout Europe. Suburbs grew up beyond the Roman walls at Newport in the north, Wigford in the south, Newland in the west and Thorngate in the south-east. It was in Thorngate that many foreign merchants lived. In Wigford was St Mary's Guildhall, and on the 'Steep' below the cathedral a large Jewish ghetto came into being.

This activity has left important evidence for us to see. St Mary's Guildhall is a unique 12th-century building, L-shaped in plan, of which the main western range survives. The existing work is of the highest quality with excellent decoration and details in keeping with its function as the headquarters of one of the city's most powerful institutions. Two of the houses inhabited by the merchants who belonged to this or similar guilds can be seen in the upper city. These are the Jew's House and Aaron the Jew's House, both on the steep hill up to the cathedral. There are strong traditions of Jewish ownership of these houses, but unlike the Music House at Norwich there is no direct evidence here beyond the names. What is clear is that Lincoln was a major market centre during our period, as the high standard of these houses attests.

A reconstruction of the altered two-light first floor window of the Jew's House.

The late 12th-century Jew's House on the steep hill below the cathedral. The vertical projection above the door was a chimney and the round-headed windows of the first-floor hall can be seen on either side.

81

Newark Castle and Town, Nottinghamshire

The principal Norman survival at Newark is the castle gatehouse, which was probably built by Bishop Alexander 'the Magnificent' who was also responsible for the west front of Lincoln Cathedral. In about 1133, Alexander received a licence from Henry I to turn his fishponds into a moat and to build a rampart. By 1138 the place could be described as 'a magnificent castle of very ornate construction'. It is virtually certain that this fulsome description included the fine stone gatehouse. Apart from the gatehouse, little is known of the internal arrangements of the early castle although some moulded voussoirs preserved there are thought to have come from a free-standing chapel. The quality of the gate and the size of the enclosure compare with the work of Roger, Bishop of Salisbury, at Sherborne and this might give some idea of the original appearance of Newark. This splendid castle caught the attention of King Stephen in 1139, and he is reputed to have imprisoned Alexander without food until he relinquished the castle to him. It was probably not until after Alexander's death in 1148 that the castle was finally restored to the see of Lincoln.

The gatehouse incorporated a keep above in the manner of Richmond (North Yorkshire), which contained a chapel and what might have been a smaller room for a chaplain. The first floor was lit by relatively large decorated round-headed windows which were remodelled in the 16th century. These windows, together with the decorated string course at sill level, show the quality of Alexander's work. The whole is fronted in fine jointed ashlar, though the back is made of rubble with ashlar dressings; when first built, this handsome portal would have looked just as fine as the work at Sherborne.

The town of Newark probably owes its shape to this same Bishop Alexander; we know that he reorganized the town of Sleaford in Lincolnshire and the majestic market squares located west of the parish churches in both towns form a link between them. That Newark church was rebuilt on a substantial scale at this time is evidenced by the great crossing piers which still stand. A further feature which suggests a major Norman church is the presence of a small Romanesque crypt under the chancel which apart from being a mark of quality in its own right also suggests that the Norman chancel reached as far east as the present one. All these signs indicate that Newark, situated as it was on a bridgepoint of the Trent on a main north–south route, was a flourishing place during the 12th century.

Map Reference: SK 796540 (metric map 120. 1-inch map 112)
Location: The castle is on the north-west side of the town, standing beside the River Trent in a municipal park.

Artist's reconstruction of the probable original appearance of the castle gatehouse before it was altered during the 16th century.

82
Southwell Minster, Nottinghamshire

Southwell Minster was founded during the 10th century though almost all the Saxon building has disappeared (see our *Guide to Anglo-Saxon Sites*). By 1108–14, Southwell had become the mother church of Nottinghamshire and actually owned about half the county. It seems likely that a major programme of rebuilding was initiated under Archbishop Thomas of York in 1108, for at that time Southwell, though influential in its own right, was still part of the diocese of York. Building seems to have gone on with few interruptions until 1145–50 and virtually the whole of the existing nave, transepts, crossing tower and western towers belong to that period. One curiosity about the plan of Southwell is that excavations have revealed a square-ended chancel whilst the transeptal chapels were apsidal; it would have been more normal for all the terminations to have been apsidal at such a date.

Assuming that work started on the chancel, which has since been replaced, the earliest part of the Norman building is the crossing which dates to 1120. This is a remarkable structure and its scale dwarfs that of the nave, with its gigantic arches rising through to the clerestory level. The east and west arches have composite piers and on the capitals of the eastern piers are important 'historiated' scenes which are amongst the earliest in England. The term 'historiated' means that the capitals are decorated with scenes which tell a story. In this case the scenes are: The Last Supper, an Annunciation scene, The Entry into Jerusalem, the Agnus Dei and The Washing of the Feet. These carvings are important because they mark the break between the 11th-century geometrical or foliate motifs and 12th-century attempts to give sculpture a narrative and didactic character.

Apart from this detailed treatment, the nave and crossing at Southwell are all about architectural mass and space. The nave arcade is relatively thick and low but does not have any sense of ponderousness. In the few years since Blyth was built, English architecture had changed profoundly; from the craggy grimness at Blyth we enter a new period of lightness and movement at Southwell.

Blank arcading in the north porch.

The serenity of Southwell with its near-perfect Norman proportions.

Map Reference: SK 702538 (metric map 120, 1-inch map 112)
Location: The minster is at the centre of the town.

83
Worksop Priory, Nottinghamshire

The three Nottinghamshire churches of Blyth, Southwell and Worksop together illustrate the principal phases of Norman ecclesiastical architecture. From the starkness of Blyth we proceed to the graceful rhythms of Southwell with its careful decoration, and from Southwell we come here to the nave of Worksop Priory which was built in the years 1170–80. Worksop is a rather mannered composition which, although well executed, has little life about it. An attempt was made to enliven it, however, as indicated by the use of alternating octagonal and round pillars and the eccentric placing of the clerestory lights above the nave pillars. But these details cannot compensate for the dull uniformity of the nailhead decoration or the stylized 'fragments' of foliate decoration which adhere to the capitals of the nave arcade. If this seems unkind, it is only because we sense a style which has gone beyond its peak; this is the last gasp of the Romanesque here in the East Midlands before the fresh air of Gothic blew through the land.

Twin 12th-century towers at the west end of the nave, Worksop Priory.

Map Reference: SK 500789 (metric map 120. 1-inch map 103)
Location: The priory is on the south side of the town on the A620, set behind a gate-house in a large churchyard.

The dull perfection of 'ultimate Romanesque' at Worksop.

84
Blyth Priory, Nottinghamshire

Blyth Priory was founded in 1088 by Roger de Busli, Lord of Tickhill. Tickhill was a compact lordship which controlled the roads south from York; the remains of the castle there can still be seen at the centre of the village, which lies just over the Yorkshire border to the north of Blyth. Blyth lay on a major north–south route and we know that the priory had the right to levy tolls from travellers on all food-stuffs, livestock, wool and timber which passed through the town. De Busli gave the site at Blyth to the Benedictine Abbey of the Holy Trinity at Caen. Little time was lost in the construction of the priory church, for the style of the nave, which is the only part to survive, belongs to the years around 1090. The nave is in a grim Norman style which finds its closest parallels in France; thus it belongs to the period before the Anglo-Norman style began.

What remains of the priory church are six of the seven bays of the nave, and fragments have been found which show that the church had a distinctive plan of an apsidal presbytery flanked by square-ended chancel chapels with further aspsidal chapels beyond. This arrangement indicates the French influence on the building since the most similar plans are at Caen itself and at Bernay in Normandy. Similarly the severe and forceful style of the existing nave and north aisle are French-inspired, as are the use of half-shafts on the inner faces of the piers and the plain open arches in the triforium gallery. Decoration is

Map Reference: SK 624873 (metric map 120. 1-inch map 103)
Nearest Town: Worksop
Location: Blyth is just off the A1 to the west. The church is on the north side of the town. While visiting Blyth, notice also the small stone house, claimed as the Norman Hospital of St John, which incorporates 12th-century masonry in its fabric. The single-storey building is on the green, facing south, beside the main road.

restricted to small highly stylized faces on the simple voluted capitals and, at the bases of the shafts, hollow mouldings with two rolls beneath. Blyth Priory is a fascinating place to visit since it conveys the atmosphere of 'dark holiness' of early Norman interiors more faithfully than anywhere else.

Above: One of the rudimentary capitals in the nave with mask-like face and simple volutes at the angles.

Left: The austere 11th-century nave arcade at Blyth Priory.

Above: This small building on the village green at Blyth is reputed to be a 12th-century hospital; certainly the doorway could be a reset Norman archway.

85
Peveril Castle, Derbyshire

Peveril Castle is small but strongly sited and it was the most important castle in Derbyshire. Soon after the Conquest, William Peverel was made bailiff of the royal manors in north-west Derbyshire and this was his caput. It appears that the first castle was built of stone, perhaps unsurprisingly in view of the surroundings; herringbone masonry can still be seen in the curtain wall which was presumably his work. Also 11th-century are the foundations of two small buildings in the south-east angle of the bailey. The east–west structure was perhaps a chapel whilst the other may have been part of a hall-block. Early in the 12th century the west curtain was added to the earlier northern defence.

In 1155 William the Younger, who inherited his father's offices, fell spectacularly from grace on account of his poisoning Ranulf, Earl of Chester; this bizarre crime resulted in the forfeiture of his estates to the Crown. So it was that Henry II erected one of his characteristic keeps here at Peveril in around 1176. This act must have been partly dictated by the recent rising in which Henry Ferrers of Tutbury had been involved.

The keep stands across the curtain wall on the highest point of the site and commands extensive views of the valley below. It is a small building of three floors with customary access at the first floor; constructed of good ashlar, it has the characteristic angle and middle buttresses of the period. This keep would have been small by the standards of the time and we must imagine that the earlier hall-block would have remained in use. Later, during the 13th century, more lavish accommodation was built in the north-west angle of the bailey. The place seems to have continued in use until the 15th century but it was probably more used as

Map Reference: SK 150827 (metric map 110. 1-inch map 111)
Nearest Town: Castleton
Location: Up in the Peak District, Castleton is on the A625 between Sheffield and Chapel-en-le-Frith, 7 miles (11.2 km) east of Chapel-en-le-Frith. The castle is up a steep hill on the south side of the town and is in guardianship. It is open standard hours and Sunday mornings from 9.30, April to September. There are wonderful views from the castle, which is just as well in view of the climb up there!

a hunting lodge than as a military base.

The town of Castleton below the castle plainly takes its name from the site and was probably founded during the 12th century. Castleton was perhaps a planned town since the elements of a minor grid system can be detected in its streets and part of a town ditch survives on the west side.

86
Youlgreave Font, Derbyshire

The famous font at Youlgreave actually came from its daughter-church at Elton from which it was summarily ejected during an early-19th-century restoration. It was brought to Youlgreave by the then vicar who put it in his garden. Later the importance of the piece was recognized and the fickle inhabitants of Elton demanded its return, but a substitute was made for them and Youlgreave retained its prize!

The font is a circular tub with a small, subsidiary bowl, the whole set upon round detached shafts; it is generally dated to around 1200. The particular interest attaches to the presence of the smaller bowl and to the iconography of the decoration. The smaller bowl, which has no drain, was either for holding the oil of the chrism with which the catechumen was anointed before baptism or else it was designed to catch the drips of water from the baby's head afterwards. Either explanation seems possible and both have medieval authority.

To turn to the iconography, apart from sprigs of foliage which might represent a Tree of Life, the main interest attaches to a carved salamander which appears upside-down under the smaller bowl. Salamanders were credited with the power to pass unscathed through fire and this property meant that they were used as an allegory for the virtuous man. The prophet Isaiah said of the just man, 'When thou walkest through fire, thou shalt not be burned'.

Henry II's keep on the highest point of the site of Peveril Castle. Most of the facing stones have been robbed, exposing the rubble core.

The use of the salamander might also allude to the cleansing power of the Holy Spirit which descended as fire. The salamander is shown in the usual manner, inspired by the Bestiary, with a knot in its tail and the legs set well forward. This is another example of the use of imagery by the 12th-century Church.

Map Reference: SK 201643 (metric map 119. 1-inch map 111)
Nearest Town: Bakewell
Location: Take the A6 Matlock road from Bakewell for 2 miles (3.2 km). Turn south on the B5056 and after 1 mile (1.6 km) take the minor road west to Youlgreave which is a further mile. The church is at the centre of the village.

Design from the font which looks rather 'Art Deco'.

The font at Youlgreave with the curious projecting subsidiary basin on the left-hand side.

87

Melbourne Church, Derbyshire

Map Reference: SK 389250 (metric map 128. 1-inch map 120)
Location: Melbourne is 7 miles (11.2 km) south of Derby just off the A514. The church is on the south side of the town beside the hall.

When the see of Carlisle was founded by Henry I in 1133, the living of Melbourne church formed part of the original grant. As is discussed in the entry on Carlisle, the foundation of the see was part of Henry's attempt to stabilize relations on the western end of the Border, but he must have known that Scottish pressure would be maintained on Carlisle itself. In 1136, the Scots retook Carlisle for a time and the first bishop, Adelulf, had to flee southwards. This event seems a likely scenario for the construction of Melbourne church on the scale that we now see. If it was indeed built for a dispossessed bishop, then its noble proportions would have been entirely appropriate.

The church is remarkable not only for the scale and complexity of its plan but also for its completeness. Apart from the fact that the west end was probably not finished, perhaps owing to the death of Adelulf in 1156, the structure is, inside at least, substantially as it was built. The plan consisted of a relatively broad nave entered through a western narthex with north and south aisles terminating in apsidal chapels and with an apsidal chancel. Unusually, there are two western towers, as at Southwell, in addition to the more normal crossing tower. The nave is lined by closely set round piers with a clerestory gallery above; this feature, like the narthex, attests the high quality of the structure. There is a good deal of heavy zigzag on the nave arcades, but the overall effect is one of unadorned mass. The crossing arches mostly have simple cushion capitals but those in the east have freestyle foliate scrolls with grotesque masks, cats and human figures – all very barbarous.

Respond of the chancel arch with lively beasts.

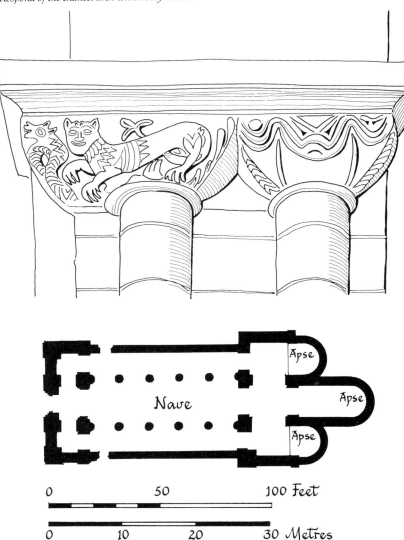

Plan of the church as originally built with three apses at the east end.

88

Tutbury Castle, Priory and Town, Staffordshire

Tutbury was granted to Henry, Earl Ferrers, in 1071 by the Conqueror and he apparently made it his caput. Before Norman times Tutbury had been a Saxon burgh and was an important bridgepoint across the River Dove. A motte and bailey castle was established here during the 11th century and it was probably rebuilt later in the 12th. The foundations of a small two-cell chapel can be seen in the bailey. After the 3rd Earl Ferrers was involved in a rising against Henry II in 1174 the castle was besieged, and destroyed in 1175–6. Later it was rebuilt and remained in desultory use until it was restored as a folly during the 18th century.

Below the castle lies the town of Tutbury; at the time of Domesday Book in 1086, we learn that there were 42 men who devoted themselves entirely to trade. This is a large total and compares favourably with substantial towns elsewhere; it seems that Tutbury's trade was well stimulated by the Conquest. An interesting feature of the town is that its plan, like Pleshey's, seems to follow the line of the castle defences since it has a semicircular shape. Part of the early bank and ditch called the 'Park Pale' can be seen to the south of the castle and this might help to explain the town's shape. But whether this was actually a huge outer bailey rather than a castle park of the sort which existed at New Buckenham is difficult to say.

Some time between 1080 and 1085, the 1st Lord Ferrers founded a small Benedictine priory below the castle which was a dependency of St Pierre sur Dives in Normandy. Part of the nave dating to c. 1130 survives with fine quatrefoil pillars; all traces of the claustral buildings on the north side have disappeared.

The particular interest of Tutbury church is the west front which has a richly decorated doorway of five orders dated to around 1160. Whilst the work is of an impressive scale, the details are rather poor; emaciated beak heads on the second order are a sad echo of the beginnings of the style even though they are executed in alabaster here. This is the earliest structural use of alabaster and it foreshadows the great medieval industry based at Nottingham. Inside, the church is bright and strangely majestic. The eastern apse was rebuilt by G. E. Street in 1867 but it probably marks the site of the 11th-century termination, for the later church was certainly longer.

Map Reference: SK 211291 (metric map 128. 1-inch map 120)
Nearest Town: Burton upon Trent
Location: Tutbury is on the border between Staffordshire and Derbyshire on the south side of the River Dove. It is 3 miles (5 km) north-west of Burton upon Trent on the A50. The Park Pale is in open space on the south side of the town surrounded by a modern housing estate.

West front of the priory church below the castle.

NORTHERN ENGLAND

Anglesey 112▲

Denbigh
Chester
CLWYD
GWYNEDD
▲113
Wrexham
CENTRAL ENGLAND

Dolgellau
SHROPSHIRE
111▲
Welshpool
Shrewsbury
Newtown
90▲
89▲
▲91
▲92
▲93
Kidderminster
POWYS
110▲
HEREFORD & WORCESTER
▲94
•Worcester
95
Cardigan
Hereford
DYFED
▲96
Brecon
▲97 ▲98
▲99
▲100
Carmarthen
GLOUCESTERSHIRE
▲109
Monmouth
Gloucester•
▲101
Pembroke
GWENT
▲103
102▲
108▲ ▲107
WEST GLAMORGAN
Swansea
MID GLAMORGAN
Newport
104
106 105
SOUTH GLAMORGAN
Cardiff
SOUTHERN ENGLAND

0   10   20 Miles
0 10 20 30 Km

wales and the marches

Wales and the Marches

Introduction

Whereas the Norman Conquest of England was accomplished after one epic battle, give or take the odd rebellion such as that led in the Marches by Edric the Wild, the doughty Welsh held out for over 200 years! It was not until the fall of Llywelyn ap Gruffydd (the Last) and the Statute of Rhuddlan in 1284 that the subjection of Wales was accomplished. This was a remarkable outcome, for at first it appeared that Wales would fall quite quickly. Recovery was swift, however, and by the opening of the reign of Henry I in 1100 a form of stalemate had developed in which the upland kingdoms of Gwynedd and Powys held the Normans at bay. The Normans overran the low-lying lands of the south and transformed ecclesiastical and secular authority there, but in the north traditional Welsh culture held sway.

The Conqueror obviously anticipated trouble from the Welsh after his victory at Hastings since he created three large earldoms at Chester, Shrewsbury and Hereford through which the military situation was stabilized. These three bases, together with the great port of Bristol, acted as the 'jumping off' points for the invasion of Wales. Assaults were launched along the north and south coast plains as well as in the middle March in the area around Montgomery. But it must have been realized at an early stage that the process was going to be protracted, and as a result we see in the Marches the densest collection of motte and bailey castles in Norman Britain.

The Marches presented the Norman kings with a problem. Since Wales was a dangerous neighbour, the Marcher province was critical to the defence of the realm. In order to defend it, strong lords were needed with adequate forces. But those same lords, who came to be known as the king's 'overmighty subjects', could become so powerful as to threaten the king himself. Hence royal policy was always geared to achieving a balance between the needs of defence and control. This resulted in an unusual amount of personal power being vested in the Marcher lords whereby they controlled their subjects as petty kings. This strange and perilous society has left an interesting legacy of monuments which, apart from the ubiquitous castles, includes fortified towns and villages as well.

But whilst this situation of siege and uncertainty applied to the early Norman period, by the mid-12th century the Marches appeared more secure. Early patronage of the Church is evident at the monastic centres of Worcester, Tewkesbury and Much Wenlock, and even at Chepstow Fitz Osbern founded a priory. It was during the early 12th century that the pace of monastic foundation began to quicken and at Leominster, Haughmond and Buildwas we see new foundations established in the countryside. These large-scale ecclesiastical ventures may have encouraged other Marcher lords to look to their spiritual welfare, for it is a remarkable fact that these wild border lands can show a rich legacy of smaller churches, many of which contain major artistic works.

The early stages of restrained ecclesiastical architecture are represented by Peterchurch and Moccas, simple in detail yet impressive in plan. From these austere beginnings there was a dramatic explosion of artistic endeavour in the Marches. It was almost as if the Marcher lords attempted to compensate for their barren and circumscribed lives by vying with each other to commission beautiful buildings. Chief amongst this movement was the Herefordshire School of sculptors who, even during the dark days of Stephen's reign, produced some of the most spirited and satisfying carvings to survive from Norman Britain. It is a constant source of wonder when we visit these often small and remote churches in the middle March that we should find works of art bursting with energy and inspired by exemplars as far removed as France and Spain. But if sculpture holds the laurel, the paintings at Kempley and Claverley show us a further manifestation of this artistic endeavour. Whilst they cannot compare with the refined metropolitan styles of Canterbury or Sussex, they are nevertheless a welcome indication that not all life in the Marches was dedicated to death and destruction.

When we look across the border into Wales, we see a range of secular and religious sites broadly similar to those in the Marches. Chepstow is now in Wales, of course, and it formed the base for the westward advance. Further west, we see the three lordships of Ogmore, Coity and Bridgend in which the liegemen of the Fitz Hamons, Lords of Glamorgan, 'dug in' on their new estates with castles and set up the machinery of manor and borough. The manors ensured that the land was efficiently farmed and the boroughs enabled the lords to control the trade in their lordships. Manorbier and Pembroke further west still were larger feudal centres, with Pembroke in particular acting as a strong fastness to guarantee the security of the westernmost Norman settlements, and ultimately as a base for the invasion of Ireland.

Behind the military conquest and the civil settlement came

various religious orders. At Chepstow and Ewenny the Benedictines established priories, but further west the Cistercians were more important. The relationship between the Cistercians and the Norman settlement was curiously ambivalent. Whilst they were undoubtedly a 'foreign' and even a French order, their emphasis on labour and simplicity of lifestyle commended itself to the Welsh. So it was that Strata Florida became more of a Welsh cultural centre than a Norman one; in this the Cistercians followed the pattern of other orders in southern Scotland. Cistercian monasticism did not recognize simple political divisions; it was a European movement.

Further north in Wales, we enter the historic kingdom of Gwynedd, stronghold of the Welsh princes and beyond the strict ambit of the Norman settlement. But if there was no formal Norman presence in Gwynedd, Romanesque artistic influence is clearly detectable. At Penmon Priory on Anglesey we see a superb example of Romanesque architecture in the transepts and interesting details like the dragon tympanum. Penmon is thus a rare survival of the architecture of the independent Welsh nation during our period. Even more remarkable, not least for its setting, is the splendid shrine of St Melangell, a monument unique in Britain and as delicate a piece of work as will be seen anywhere. Perhaps that Romanesque shrine deep in its secret Welsh valley illustrates more graphically than anything else the fine balance which Gwynedd maintained between independence and cultural enrichment.

89
Claverley Wallpaintings, Shropshire

The wallpaintings at Claverley have been the source of some debate since there are at least two theories as to their meaning. One fact which is clear is that they date to around 1200 and they are some of the liveliest and most secular Romanesque paintings to have survived. It is fortunate that when they were discovered in 1902 they were so well treated; many another cycle of paintings has not fared as well either before or since. The paintings occur above the north nave arcade and a severe crick of the neck is apt to develop after a close inspection.

When the paintings were found, their resemblance to the Bayeux Tapestry encouraged the belief that they too depicted the Battle of Hastings. This conjecture was strengthened by a reference in the 12th-century 'Roman de Rou' to an exploit by Roger de Montgomery, who later owned Claverley, which turned the tide of battle at a critical moment. That Roger or rather one of his descendants should wish to record this feat of arms seems reasonable enough, so the paintings were seen as a kind of thank-offering.

Later, however, it was suggested that they represented the symbolic conflict between the Virtues and Vices which was contained in the poem 'Psychomachia' and which is illustrated elsewhere in this book under the entry for the Virtues and Vices fonts. In this case the celestial conflict was rendered as a fight between mortal knights, a vehicle of communication which would have been familiar to the congregation.

Whilst it is impossible to be sure which of these theories is true, the balance of the evidence probably favours the earlier one. This is because on the Southrop font and elsewhere there is a clear physical distinction between the

Left: Detail of one of the combat scenes in the panels; it is uncertain whether they represent real or mythological conflicts.

Virtues and the Vices. There, for example, each Virtue and Vice is clearly labelled and, as if to underline the distinction, the vanquished Vices are shown as cowering figures with distorted features. At Claverley, however, we could not distinguish between the two. Accordingly, it is perhaps improbable that it portrays a divine conflict, but merely an earthly one.

Map Reference: SO 792934 (metric map 138. 1-inch map 130)
Nearest Town: Bridgnorth
Location: From Bridgnorth travel east on the A454 for 3 miles (5 km) and then turn south-east on a minor road to Claverley, a further 2 miles (3.2 km). The church is in the middle of this very attractive village.

The ghostly procession of knights above the north nave arcade – their position high up off the floor doubtless helped them to survive.

90
Three Shropshire Monasteries

The three sites of Buildwas, Haughmond and Much Wenlock are close together in space and time but they illustrate very different principles of monasticism in their architecture. Buildwas was, like Byland, a daughter house of the great abbey of Furness in Cumbria. It was founded in 1135 as a Savignac house, the robust principles of that order being given architectural expression in the robust simplicity of the nave pillars, the restrained scalloped capitals and the square-ended presbytery and transeptal chapels. The whole aspect of the site

12th-century seal of Buildwas Abbey.

is one of simple severity, a place offering few distractions from the contemplation of God.

At Haughmond, also founded in 1135 which marked the beginning of the Anarchy of Stephen's reign, we find a more 'middle of the road' establishment. This made concessions to taste and decoration since the doorways into the chapter house and the cloister have deeply recessed orders of moulding and nook-shafts, but the quality of the detailing is little better than might be expected in a good quality parish church.

It is with Much Wenlock that we enter a different world. Founded in 1070 by Roger de Montgomery, Earl of Shrewsbury, we can see in the scintillating interlaced decoration of the chapter house and in the figured panels of the lavatorium a completely different approach to monasticism. Wenlock was a Cluniac house and so belonged to an order which rejoiced in the elaboration of its liturgy and buildings. The abbey of Cluny itself, which was in Burgundy, has been described as 'a world in itself, given wholly to the worship of God in a setting of incomparable splendour'. There could be no greater contrast than between the austerity of Buildwas and the celebration of Wenlock.

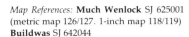

Map References: **Much Wenlock** SJ 625001 (metric map 126/127. 1-inch map 118/119) **Buildwas** SJ 642044 **Haughmond** SJ 542152
Nearest Town: Shrewsbury
Locations: All three sites are ancient monuments and are open standard hours. Much Wenlock is 12 miles (19.3 km) south-east of Shrewsbury on the A 458. The priory is on the north-east side of the town (beware of the one-way system). Buildwas is 3 miles (5 km) north-east of Much Wenlock. It lies on the B4378 close by its junction with the B4380 Ironbridge to Shrewsbury road beside the River Severn. It is well signposted. Haughmond is 3 miles (5 km) north-east of Shrewsbury on the B5062. It sits on a slope overlooking the town of Shrewsbury and is also well signposted.

The stark majesty of Buildwas, a remarkably perfect survival of a simple Savignac house; this monastic order later merged with the Cistercians, and shared the same abhorrence of architectural ostentation.

Haughmond chapter house entrance. The standing figures between the columns were added during the 14th century.

A carved panel from the cloister lavatory at Much Wenlock. It dates to c. 1190 and depicts two prophets standing under arcades.

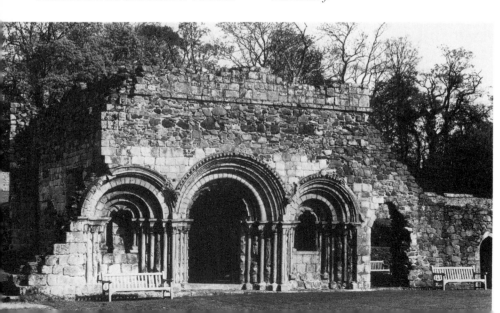

The ringwork at one end of More village is marked by low earthworks. Both castle and village defences made extensive use of water, and it seems likely that this boggy low-lying site was chosen for that reason.

91

More Castle and Village, Shropshire

The site of More is interesting since, like Kilpeck, it shows us a small defended settlement dependent upon a castle. In the Marches, it was as important for a lord to defend his retainers as himself, for without them he could not have worked his estates and hence he would have had no revenue. The village at More was probably founded soon after the Conquest and its axial plan with a ringwork castle at one end and a church at the other suggests a planned layout. The site is quite low-lying and can still be boggy in wet weather – a fact reflected by the placename which means 'moor' or marsh.

As you walk over the site you will see low mounds and ditches on either side of the approach road which mark the sites of the houses within the ditched enclosure. At the far side the mound of the ringwork can be clearly seen with a bailey in front; the mound has a deeper ditch round it which still contains water. There is a stony bank round the edge of the mound which indicates the former presence of stone walls. Later, when times were more peaceful, the villagers moved out of

these damp and unpleasant conditions to the higher ground around the church which was doubtless more comfortable.

An unusual piece of historical evidence enshrines the creation of the lordship of More in the reign of Henry I, of which More itself was presumably the caput. The Lord of More was a Constable of the royal army and was charged with the command of 200 foot soldiers whenever the king crossed the Welsh border in hostile array. Furthermore he was to march in the vanguard of the host and with his own hands to carry the king's standard.

92

Heath Deserted Village, Shropshire

Heath Chapel is well known as an atmospheric Norman site, situated as it is in a remote location high on the Clee Hills of Shropshire. Less well known is the existence of a deserted medieval village around the chapel, the subtle earthworks of which can be particularly well seen to the north of the chapel. Heath village was founded during the 12th century at a time when marginal land – the name means exactly what it says – was being pressed into cultivation.

The chapel was built, probably around 1150, to serve the new community and it remained a chapelry of the mother church of Stoke St

Map Reference: SO 340915 (metric map 137. 1-inch map 129)
Nearest Town: Bishop's Castle
Location: More is 2½ miles (4 km) north of Bishop's Castle just off the A489 road from Newtown to Ludlow. The castle site lies in a field to the south-west of the village and can be reached by a footpath from the minor road which runs north-west out of the village. The footpath is found by a narrow stile on the left-hand side of the lane. In the field you can see the remains of an early road which leads straight on to the site.

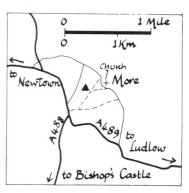

Map Reference: SO 557856 (metric map 137. 1-inch map 129)
Nearest Town: Craven Arms
Location: From Craven Arms, take the B4368 to Diddlebury then turn east into Diddlebury (which has an interesting Saxon church) and along minor roads. After 2 miles (3.2 km), take the south turn to Peaton and then east turn to Bouldon. Heath Chapel stands in a field on the north side of the road about 1 mile (1.6 km) from Bouldon.

The famous chapel of Heath, built in the mid-12th-century but standing in splendid isolation since the surrounding village was deserted during the 14th century.

Milborough. That the settlement never prospered is evident from the facts that the chapel was never extended later and that already by 1327 there were only seven families living here. Heath Chapel with its simple almost homely details and plain interior is a small monument to the heady days of 12th-century prosperity and population growth before the setbacks of the 14th century; climatic deterioration and soil exhaustion doubtless hastened the end of the village which it served.

93

Ludlow Castle and Town, Shropshire

After the Conquest, Ludlow was granted to the de Lacy family, and an earth and timber castle was probably constructed here soon afterwards. No pre-Norman settlement is known at Ludlow, and it seems that the town was established during the 11th century. Certainly the plan of the town is composed of regular elements, and when the outer bailey of the castle was enlarged to its present extent in 1180 or thereabouts, part of the grid pattern of streets to the south was obliterated. Nothing is left of the earliest castle, but in 1120 a great entrance-keep, similar to that at Richmond (North Yorkshire), was built by Hugh Lacy. This keep can still be seen, although the proportions of the lofty first-floor hall have been destroyed by later alterations, and the original gate passage was blocked later in the 12th century.

One of the most important surviving features at Ludlow is the famous circular chapel in the inner bailey. The form of this structure has inevitably invited parallels with Templar churches such as the 'Round Church' at Cambridge. On the basis of its architectural details,

Ludlow town plan. The castle fits neatly into the top left-hand corner of the town plan, but it appears that not all the town was laid out in Norman times. The original axis is marked by the wide market-place linking church and castle, with the southern extension towards the river being a later medieval expansion.

Map Reference: SO 508745 (metric map 137. 1-inch map 129)
Location: Close by the border between Shropshire and Herefordshire, the fine Marcher town of Ludlow has an imposing site beside the River Teme on the A49 between Hereford and Shrewsbury.

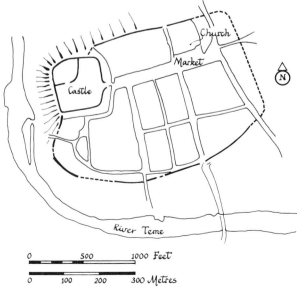

this chapel was probably built in the 1120s, which might seem a little early for such contacts when we remember that the Templars were founded only in 1118. Perhaps round churches had been in vogue amongst the knightly class ever since the First Crusade of 20 years earlier.

Only the nave of the chapel still stands, looking like a small circular keep except that it has a fine west doorway with three orders of chevron moulding about its head, and a billet-moulded string course whizzes round at what would ordinarily be first-floor level. In fact the church was open to the roof and the windows high up in the walls would have allowed shafts of light to fall into the space below. The inner face of the wall has fine blank arcading and seats around it and the chancel arch is enriched with three orders of moulding and nook-shafts. There are traces of plaster inside and out and we can be assured that the chapel would have looked very neat and trim when it was in use. The foundations of the chancel are marked out in the grass on the east side, and it appears that an apsidal sanctuary was replaced by a square one here as elsewhere. The first-floor windows had glazing bars, probably for

Circular chapel at Ludlow Castle. The arch on the right led into the now-vanished chancel, the angled roof scar of which can be seen above the doorway.

stained glass, and the whole impression is one of a lordly building.

94
The Herefordshire School of Sculpture, Hereford and Worcester

It is difficult to understand why a sculptural school of the competence and originality of that based in Herefordshire during the mid-12th century should have begun at all. It is doubly difficult when we realize that this occurred during the Anarchy of Stephen's reign, and that this remote part of western England was by no means isolated from its effects. Indeed the castle near Castle Frome church, where one of the finest pieces of carving is located, was actually destroyed at this time. A further remarkable aspect is that so many of the products of the school survive; they can be seen in over a dozen different locations and include virtually complete schemes of structural decoration at Kilpeck

Shobdon arches, re-erected as a folly after the church built by Oliver de Merlimond was replaced during the 18th century. Although much weathered, the outlines of many of the spectacular carvings can still be discerned.

Map References (metric/1-inch map numbers follow each entry in parentheses):
Rowlestone SO 374270 (161/142)
Castle Frome SO 665459 (148/142)
Leominster SO 498593 (148/129)
Stretton Sugwas SO 460420 (148/142)
Fownhope SO 581343 (148/142)
Brinsop SO 442448 (148/142)
Eardisley SO 312491 (148/142)
Chaddesley Corbett SO 891736 (139/130)
Shobdon SO 401629 (148/129)
Aston Eyre SO 655940 (138/130)
Kilpeck SO 446305 (148/142)
Stottesdon SO 672829 (138/130)
Rock SO 731711 (138/130)
Locations: The churches are easy to find, in their respective villages, with the following exceptions.

Shobdon ruined church is in the grounds of Shobdon Court on the north side of the village. The ruins are set at the top of a long ride. Leominster Priory is on the north-east edge of the town. Brinsop church is signed to the right off the road leading to the village. It is a private gated road but you can go through here to get to the church which is set in a delightful apple orchard. Stretton Sugwas church is signed off the main A438 road.

The Eardisley font is remarkable for the vivacity of its figures, both these fighting warriors and the Harrowing of Hell scene.

Castle Frome, font depicting the Baptism of Christ and the Symbols of the Evangelists. The heads of the figures supporting the font are similar to the corbel heads at Kilpeck.

and Rowlestone, details at Stretton Sugwas and Shobdon and incomparable fonts at Castle Frome, Chaddesley Corbett and Stottesdon. In all these ways the school is unusual, but beyond this its products are also dignified by a sparkling originality and diversity which command both admiration and respect.

Some of the influences acting on the school are clear enough. There is documentary evidence that Shobdon church was commissioned by Oliver de Merlimond, chief steward to Hugh de Mortimer, Lord of Wigmore. This patron also decided to take the pilgrimage road to Santiago de Compostella in Spain and it is

suggested that en route he or his followers took close account of the buildings they saw. De Merlimond's church at Shobdon, sadly demolished during the 18th century, was obviously a showpiece. The surviving fragments, re-erected to form a 'viewstopper' in the later park there, show such a profusion of decoration as to exceed all normal bounds of taste. Plainly de Merlimond was intent on constructing a major monument, an idea that accords well with the suggestion that his trip to Compostella influenced the school. An echo of the Spanish style is seen in the highly stylized figures placed unusually on the shafts

Tympanum at Rowlestone showing Christ in Majesty in a mandorla supported by four angels.

of the chancel arch at Kilpeck, a technique first used at Compostella itself. We know that on his return from Spain de Merlimond passed through south-west France, and at Brinsop and Stretton Sugwas we see images used on tympana which are paralleled in a single structure at Parthenay le Vieux near Poitiers.

Thus some foreign influence on the school is certain, but this does not account for the existence of a group of sculptors who could take up and adapt these new styles. In view of the proliferation of the works of the school, a major patron seems likely. The most probable milieu is a monastic one, since monasteries were great consumers of the applied arts. The closest parallels in a monastic context occur on the west front of Leominster Priory. There are problems with this attribution, since the dedication date of Leominster is 1131, which is a little too early, but as the evidence occurs on the west door it might be that it was not completed until some time after the main body of the church, as at Selby. Leominster is a strong contender for two other reasons: it was a daughter house of the great Cluniac abbey at Reading, and so belonged to an order celebrated for its patronage of the arts; and secondly, certain details of the sculpture such as the use of hatching were brought to Leominster from Reading, and later occur in the work at Shobdon.

There are further elements in the Herefordshire work. The first of these are hangovers from the earlier Anglo-Norman styles, the 'bed rock' of the sculptors' experience. These account for the corbels and jutting heads at Kilpeck and on the base of the font at Castle Frome. Similarly we must not ignore the effects of the mythological and allegorical sources such as the Bestiary and the Zodiac which played such an important part in east Yorkshire 20 years later. These can be seen in the medallions round the head of the south

The font at Chaddesley Corbett, superbly proportioned with fine relief carving.

The Stretton Sugwas tympanum; this design, like that at nearby Brinsop, is derived from western French originals.

Capital from Leominster Priory; notice how the treatment of the hair 'beehive' style is copied on the tympanum at Rowlestone.

These birds from Rowlestone have a rather contemporary feel about them, reminiscent of the design of postage stamps, perhaps.

door at Kilpeck, for example, where a mermaid jostles the sign of Pisces and on the tympanum is a Tree of Life.

But the undoubted 'uniqueness' of the school derives from the occurrence of Celtic images in the repertoire. The absence of straight lines, the excess of decoration on some of the fonts and the sinuous tendrils and tails have their origins not in Europe and the relics of Classicism but in the old gospel books of Ireland and in the rich metalwork of the Celtic regions. This surely is why the Herefordshire School has fascinated so many scholars; it had a direct link backwards into a past which seems remote to us now but which was doubtless very real to the dwellers in these western lands.

It could only have happened here in Herefordshire where all the necessary elements met together. The purchasing power of the monasteries and lay patrons, the rich imagery they brought with them, the presence of capable sculptors and the easily worked yet durable sandstone which they used and, finally, the imaginative traditions of the Marches which those same sculptors were heir to – all these factors conspired to make the school possible. But as with the 'Golden Age' of Northumbria, the whole was infinitely greater than the sum of its parts.

95
Worcester Cathedral, Hereford and Worcester

Wulfstan, Bishop of Worcester, was a remarkable man not least because he was a Saxon bishop who retained his position after the Conquest until his death in 1095. He became prior of the small Benedictine priory here in 1062, and was both prior and bishop at the time of the Conquest. He was amongst the first of the Anglo-Saxon bishops to submit to the Conqueror, and was held in such esteem that he both continued his offices and had popular support. Wulfstan was no lickspittle – he was a forceful man who, amongst other achieve-

Map Reference: SO 850545 (metric map 150. 1-inch map 130/143)
Location: The cathedral is at the centre of the city on the south side.

The Baptism of Christ at Castle Frome. Note the Hand of God above Christ's head and the 'mound water which was required by 12th-century seemliness to hide His nakedness.*

Interior of the chapter house at Worcester Cathedral; the banded stone work of the walls and the pattern of the blank arcading anticipate the later glories of Much Wenlock and Bristol.

ments, preached so strenuously against the slave trade from Bristol to Ireland that it was abolished. Another sidelight on this interesting man is that he apparently enjoyed a truly Anglo-Saxon love of hospitality. William of Malmesbury relates that, 'though temperate in his own habits, he prolonged his entertainments from high noon to sunset'.

Wulfstan's greatest memorial is the superb crypt at Worcester. This was begun in 1084, and was designed as an impressive setting for the display of the relics of his predecessor St Oswald. This structure, which must rank as one of the most atmospheric Norman spaces in England, consists of four open aisles of seven bays, each of which culminated in an apse at the east end. The aisle columns are austere with plain cushion capitals, but the shadows cast by the groined vaults make interesting patterns, and we can well imagine the wonder which the place would have induced in the minds of pilgrims visiting St Oswald's shrine.

The second major building at Worcester is the chapter house. This belongs to the early 12th century and was the first to have a single freestanding column at the centre supporting a radiating vault. There is delicate blank arcading round the walls which is neatly emphasized by the use of contrasting bands of greenish and white stone in the panels of the arcades. There is a feeling of movement in the wall arcades and, whilst not as rich, they prefigure the later work in the chapter houses at Bristol and Much Wenlock.

96
Peterchurch and Moccas Churches, Hereford and Worcester

Star motif from Peterchurch which is common to both sites.

These two churches provide an impression of the state of Norman architecture in the central Marches about 20 years before the luxuriant Herefordshire School began in the 1140s. Peterchurch in particular is a large and elaborate structure; it is the only Norman parish church in England to have four compartments, yet it is of an unremitting plainness. The original windows are small and simple and the internal arches where they survive have only a minimum of ornament on them. The overall impression is of starkness, almost of bleakness, but also of great size and majesty with arches diminishing towards an apsidal sanctuary, the floor level rising and everything oriented on a great line eastwards. It is effective and architecturally refined but uncompromisingly plain. Externally decoration is confined to a string course round the apse with cable moulding on its underside and, over the south door, a much weathered tympanum.

At Moccas (the name means 'swine moor' in Welsh), the church is considerably smaller but otherwise very much the same. Unusually it is built of tufa, a light and porous limestone-based material which is very easily carved. Yet despite this quality, there is a paucity of decoration. There is a string course round the apse and there are weathered tympana over the north and south doors upon which weathered figures and animals can be vaguely discerned. The two internal arches have simple chevron decoration and on the capitals of the chancel arch is a simple star motif which matches that at Peterchurch.

Map References: **Peterchurch** SO 345385 (metric map 161. 1-inch map 142) **Moccas** SO 355426
Locations: Peterchurch is on the B4348 up the Golden Valley. It is most easily reached from the A465 Hereford to Abergavenny road at Pontrilas. There take the B4347 north-west up the Golden Valley and Peterchurch is reached in 9 miles (14.5 km). Moccas is in the adjacent valley. From Peterchurch take the minor road east to Tyberton and the B4352 north-west to Moccas which is a further 3 miles (5 km). The church stands in the grounds of the hall.

Ground plan of Peterchurch.

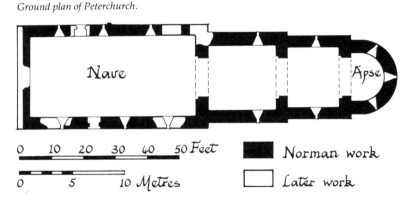

97
Longtown Castle and Town, Hereford and Worcester

Longtown was one of the many castle boroughs founded by the Normans in the Marches which represented the aspirations of the Marcher lords to introduce a market economy into their newly won lands. Some of these boroughs thrived but Longtown, which was founded later than most on a bleak ridgetop site on the fringe of the Black Mountains, never prospered. Today the site is merely a village, a physical sign of failure just as the town of Ludlow symbolizes success.

A castle was under construction at Longtown between 1185 and 1195 and the existing

Map Reference: SO 321201 (metric map 161. 1-inch map 142)
Nearest Town: Abergavenny
Location: From Abergavenny take the A465 to Hereford. After 6 miles (9.6 km), at Pandy take the minor road north to Longtown. The castle is on the west side of the road half-way up the long steep village street.

motte is probably of that date. The fine cylindrical keep on top of the motte has been the source of some debate; some claim it as part of the recorded building campaign, and there are Romanesque openings in it. Others see the keep as a later structure altogether with the possibility that the earlier details were reused. Certainly the rounded plan and buttresses might be more at home rather later. Before the keep is a stone wall dividing it from the bailey; there is a gateway with two solid rounded towers reminiscent of the late 12th century entrance at Conisbrough. A puzzling feature is the presence of an enclosure three acres (1.2 ha) in area which straddles the road beside the castle. The enclosure is rectangular in plan and was for long thought to have been part of a Roman fort. It is now accepted as an extension of the castle defences, probably designed to control traffic along the road.

View of the circular keep at Longtown Castle across the outer bailey; the gate, defended by two towers, is visible at the extreme right.

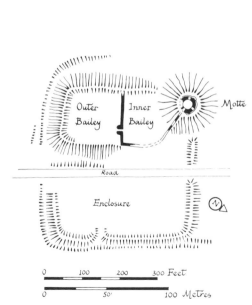

Plan of Longtown castle showing the large enclosure which straddles the road.

98
Kilpeck Church and Town, Hereford and Worcester

Even before Norman times there had been a religious settlement of some sort at Kilpeck as the name, which probably means 'the cell of St Pedic', indicates. Indeed, part of the celebrated church (see entry on Herefordshire School) is of pre-Norman date, since there is a megalithic quoin at the north-east corner of the nave as well as about four feet (1.2 metres) of the rough rubble wall of an earlier church. Apart from this, there is little other evidence of the nature of the early settlement.

After the Conquest, Kilpeck was granted to William Fitz Norman and it was probably he who was responsible for the main secular works there. These consist of a motte and bailey castle to the west of the church and a large rectangular 'village' enclosure to the north-east of it. The motte and bailey, which has only scanty traces of its stone walls

Map Reference: SO 446305 (metric map 148. 1-inch map 142)
Nearest Town: Hereford
Location: From Hereford take the A465 towards Abergavenny. Kilpeck is signposted off this road about 7 miles (11.2 km) along. It is about 1 mile (1.6 km) south-east off the main road.

remaining, consists of a mound with a small shell keep on top with a kidney-shaped inner bailey to the east and a sub-rectangular outer bailey to the south.

The enclosure to the north-east of the church is substantial in scale and was almost certainly intended to contain a small town rather than a village. Traces of the defences can be seen on three sides, and at the north-west and south-east angles in particular the bank and ditch can be clearly seen on the ground. Inside the enclosure, slight remains of rectangular house platforms and roads can be seen to the north-west of the road leading to the church. Later still, during the 12th century when Hugh de Kilpeck built his splendid church, a small cell of Benedictines was founded here as a dependency of Gloucester Abbey. Traces of the priory building can be seen to the south of the church near the house which is still called 'The Priory'.

All this information helps to put the church at Kilpeck in its context. It is very easy to go to this small hamlet today and wonder why such a marvellous church was built in such an

Kilpeck's south door surmounted by a tympanum containing a Tree of Life and flanked by superb intertwining scrolls and snakes.

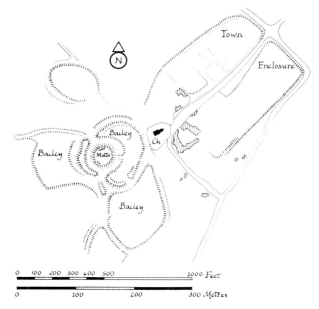

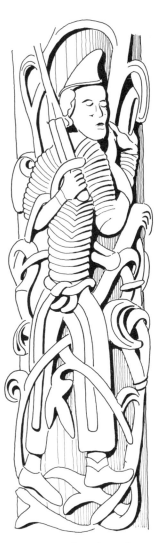

Detail of a warrior from the south doorway of Kilpeck church.

Plan of the Kilpeck earthworks showing how the famous church is just one element of a complex Norman settlement. The church stands between the castle and the town.

One of the many figure corbels on the exterior of Kilpeck church; they are exceptionally varied and depict a wide range of creatures, real and imaginary.

Three of the Apostles from the side walls of the chancel at Kempley; they look upwards towards the vision of Christ painted on the ceiling.

isolated spot. Yet if we look at the evidence 'on the ground' we can see that Kilpeck was much more important in Norman times than it is today, and in the castle next to the church we have the residence of a patron who could afford to build such an ambitious structure. Hugh de Kilpeck was a kinsman of Earl Mortimer to whom Oliver de Merlimond, first lay patron of the 'Herefordshire School', was steward. By these links, we can begin to reconstruct the process by which the products of the Herefordshire School were commissioned.

99
Kempley Wallpaintings, Gloucestershire

The church of St Mary at Kempley has, like others in this book, been deserted by its village. The original structure of two cells probably dates to the 11th century and it is to that period that the excellent south doorway with its Tree of Life tympanum belongs. This carving, together with the decoration on the chancel arch, stems from a local school of sculptors who worked in the Marches before the later Herefordshire School came into existence. Unusually this early church has retained its original wooden door and iron fittings as well as the early nave roof. Later in the 12th century the church was somewhat altered and the interior was sumptuously decorated.

Kempley church is justly celebrated for its splendid wallpaintings. In the barrel-vaulted chancel in particular an almost complete cycle survives and traces of contemporary work can still be seen in the nave. The paintings, which used earth colours including yellow, red and grey with black and white for details, were executed in fresco. The best way to see the Kempley paintings is as they were originally intended to be seen – by candlelight. Once the eyes have adjusted from the bright outdoors to the gloom within, the warm radiance of the colours gradually floods back. We sat entranced in the chancel as minute by minute the details gradually emerged; thanks to the care

Map Reference: SO 670312 (metric map 149. 1-inch map 143)
Nearest Town: Ross on Wye
Location: From Ross, take the A449 for 5 miles (8 km) in the Ledbury direction. Kempley is signed off the road and is a further 2 miles (3.2 km) in a south-easterly direction. Kempley church is an Art Deco–William Morris revival structure – the ancient church is about a mile (1.6 km) north of the village on a minor road, and is signposted in the village.

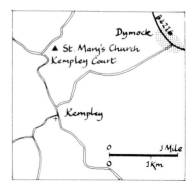

of modern restorers there is no harsh retouching here, just the mellow tones of the Norman composition.

At the summit of the vault is Christ in Majesty, His feet resting on a rainbow and His hand raised in blessing. Surrounding Him are the Symbols of the Evangelists, the eagle and angel to right and left above with the lion and ox below; the ox is particularly well figured. The Sun and Moon, twelve gold candlesticks, two cherubim and two seraphim as well as the Virgin and St Peter, fill the rest of the vault. The whole is a dramatic rendering of the Revelation of St John the Divine; what more suitable subject could there be for this 'heavenly vault'?

On the side walls of the chancel are pictures of the Twelve Apostles seated under an architectural arcade, six on either side. St Peter is shown holding his keys next to what is perhaps a representation of the Heavenly City of Jerusalem over the north window; opposite is a picture of Bethlehem over the south window. The window splays themselves contain effective chequer designs whose perspective emphasizes the depth of the openings. To the east of the windows are further standing secular figures, one with a pilgrim's staff and hat, perhaps representing the commissioner of the paintings. On the east wall there are three roundels above the small central window which contain angels holding scrolls. To the south of the window is a picture of a bishop with crozier and mitre; the northern figure was unfortunately lost when a memorial tablet was fixed to the wall.

100

Tewkesbury Abbey, Gloucestershire

Tewkesbury, with Gloucester, shows us how magnificent the early south-western Benedictine abbey churches could be. Only the nave remains to indicate the quality of the original work, but it has tall drum piers which soar upwards towards Hugh Despenser's splendid

14th-century roof. The abbey was founded in 1087 by Robert Hamon and by 1102 building was sufficiently advanced for a community to move here. The eight bays of the nave, which are practically unornamented, date to this period.

Externally, the tower and the great west front were amongst the latest parts of the church to be completed, and their quality owes something to the marriage of Fitz Hamon's heiress Mabel to Robert of Gloucester who was a wealthy patron of churches. The tower is the largest and one of the finest of the 12th-century towers with generous belfry openings and much blank arcading. It is with the huge six-ordered arch of the west front that we see the scale of the 'giant orders' at Tewkesbury. Unhappily, the window which it contained blew down in 1661, but the scale of the opening is still arresting. It has been suggested that the west end was designed for towers rather than the present small turrets, but the vertical proportions are still highly impressive. At Tewkesbury, we see early Norman architecture at its most grave and superhuman; it is a superb setting for worship with the insignificance of man being contrasted with the splendours of God's house.

The majestic central tower of Tewkesbury Abbey with its rich arcaded decoration.

Map Reference: SO 890324 (metric map 150. 1-inch map 143)
Location: The abbey is in a prominent position on the south side of the town.

101

Elkstone Church, Gloucestershire

St John's church is delightfully set in rolling Gloucestershire countryside and the high quality of its carving makes it a rewarding place to visit. The Norman church consisted of a nave and chancel with an axial tower. The tower was taken down during the 13th century and there are some later additions such as the west tower and the south porch, but much of the Norman work survives. There is a fine and well-preserved corbel table on the side walls of the nave with a collection of birds, beasts, grotesques and Zodiacal signs. The south porch contains a superb mid-12th-century tympanum which bears a very delicate carving of Christ in Majesty. The signs of the Four Evangelists are shown to each side of the Christ figure and the Agnus Dei hovers at His right hand. He is shown with a nimbed halo above which the Hand of God descends. There are roundly carved beak heads around the top of the tympanum and the work has a lightness of touch more reminiscent of chased metalwork than stone carving.

Nor does the church disappoint inside. The chancel arch is restrained but grand; notice the label-stops in the form of wolf heads which continue an Anglo-Saxon tradition. The vaulted tower space acts as an antechamber to the sanctuary which was evidently square-ended from the first. In the east wall is a single round-headed window with deeply cut chevron and palmette decoration and a fine foliated drip mould above. The sanctuary vaults spring from brackets bearing the Signs of the Evangelists of which only the Lion of St Mark has escaped the attentions of the Iconoclasts. Looking up at the sanctuary vault, we see one of the finest Romanesque vaulting bosses in England. It dates to about 1180 and consists of a head with four mouths from which the ribs of the vault emerge. A belt at the centre of the

Eastward view into the sanctuary.

design was probably intended to convey a sense of security not only by 'tying in' the roof but also by ensuring that the beast did not escape!

Vaulting boss in the sanctuary; the belt at the centre of the design seems to keep the beasts in check!

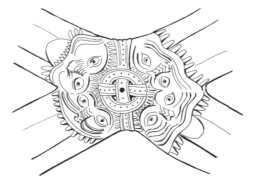

Right: Wolf head label stop on the arch into the tower space; this motif continues local Anglo-Saxon traditions.

Map Reference: SO 967123 (metric map 163. 1-inch map 144)
Nearest Town: Cheltenham
Location: Elkstone is 6 miles (9.6 km) south of Cheltenham. It can be reached from the A436 to Cirencester, along a minor road south signposted to the village. The church stands on its own in a beautiful churchyard on the south side of the village.

102
'The Virtues and the Vices' Fonts, Gloucestershire

At Southrop and Stanton Fitzwarren are two fonts, probably carved by the same man, which illustrate the conflict of the Virtues and the Vices. The fonts date to the latter part of the 12th century and take their imagery from a poem called the 'Psychomachia' written during the 4th century by Prudentius. It told how the Virtues, symbolized by armed virgins, vanquished the appropriate Vices in single combat. After the victories, the Virtues then went on to build the Heavenly City, the new Jerusalem, the buildings of which are probably depicted on the Southrop font. There is evidence from many 12th-century sites of the influence of earlier Classical ideas on the Church but nowhere is it more apparent than on these fonts; they are the physical product of the '12th-Century Renaissance'.

At Stanton Fitzwarren ten trefoiled arches hold images of eight Virtues trampling their Vices underfoot as well as Ecclesia and a figure of a six-winged Seraph with a drawn sword, symbolizing the Fall of Man. On the Southrop font there are only five Virtues and Vices with the additional subjects of Moses, Ecclesia and Synagogue. The last pair are symbolized as type and antitype, for whereas Ecclesia, representing the clear vision of Holy Church, gazes serenely out before her, Synagogue is literally 'benighted' by ignorance since the pennon of her broken lance covers her eyes and the crown falls from her head.

The Virtues and Vices are similarly opposed both visually and morally. At Stanton Fitzwarren the names of the Virtues are carved neatly above the relevant arcade whereas the Vices' names are relegated to the fields of the panels. At Southrop this is taken a stage further since the names of the Vices are carved backwards, as if to make mock of their pretensions. On both fonts the Virtues are depicted standing erect above their foes who are shown as crumpled defeated creatures with grotesque faces.

Both fonts are so charged with iconographical meaning that it comes as something of a surprise to discover a 'slip' at Southrop: Paciencia (Patience) is shown flogging Ira (Anger) in a most unsuitable manner!

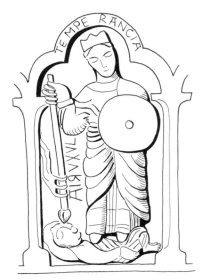

Map References: **Southrop** SP 202034 (metric map 163. 1-inch map 157)
Stanton Fitzwarren SU 179901
Nearest Town: Cirencester
Locations: From Cirencester take the A417 east for 8 miles (12.8 km) to Fairford. At the far end of Fairford take the north-east turning to Southrop which is a further 2½ miles (4 km). Stanton Fitzwarren is just north of Swindon (about 3 miles (5 km)). Take the A361 in the direction of Burford and then the minor road to the north-west signposted to Stanton Fitzwarren.

Left: Figure of a cherubim at Stanton Fitzwarren.

Below left: Temperance overcomes Excess at Southrop.

Below: The splendid font at Southrop; note how 'Patience' flogs 'Anger' on the right in a most unsuitable manner!

103

The Severn Valley Fonts, Gloucestershire

Lead fonts were perhaps originally inspired by Continental prototypes in either lead or bronze. At least one lead font, at Brookland, was probably imported from France during the 12th century and bronze fonts were being made in what is now Belgium. Bronze was an expensive material, and hence the more easily worked lead was perhaps an acceptable substitute. Here in Gloucestershire there is a remarkable group of six lead fonts which were all apparently made in the same mould.

That lead fonts should occur in Gloucestershire is not surprising in view of the presence of the Mendip lead mines which had been worked at least since Roman times. The riverine distribution of the group suggests that these heavy yet fragile objects were transported via the River Severn and that these villages availed themselves of these local products. The fonts were probably cast on a sand bed into which stones bearing the decoration carved in reverse had first been pressed. After casting, the long strip of lead was made into a circle and a round base plate was soldered on.

The group belongs to the mid-12th century and details of the decoration can be paralleled in various English manuscripts. The design consists of a band of palmette decoration round the top which is similar to that on the stone font at Southrop. Below is an arcade containing alternating seated figures and spiral scrolls; the figures may be prophets since they are shown alternately with open and bound books. The pillars and arches of the arcades are ornamented with pellets, chevrons and scallops and the bases have small interlace designs on them. The fat spiral scrolls have richly foliated terminals and the whole effect is one of stylishness and vigour. The slightly tapering sides of the fonts ensure that they catch the light and they are undoubtedly very satisfying objects.

Map References (metric/1-inch map numbers follow each entry in parentheses):
Frampton on Severn SO 744069 (162/156)
Sandhurst SO 828234 (162/156)
Siston ST 689752 (172/156)
Tidenham ST 556958 (162/155)
Oxenhall SO 711267 (162/155)
Gloucester Cathedral ST 831188 (162/143)
Locations: A good example of the group in an attractive setting can be found at Frampton on Severn, a place which was an important port during the Middle Ages. From the A38 Gloucester to Bristol road take the B4071 north-west to Frampton. Turn south into the village along the magnificent open green to the church which is at the far southern end of the village.

Detail of the font at Frampton-on-Severn showing a figure of a prophet seated under the architectural arcade.

104

Chepstow Castle and Priory, Gwent

William Fitz Osbern was one of the Conqueror's most trusted lieutenants, and he was made Earl Palatine of Hereford within a few months of the Battle of Hastings. Domesday Book records that 'Earl William built the castle of Estrighoiel' (Chepstow), and since he died fighting in Flanders in 1071 we know that Chepstow is the earliest stone castle in Britain. Apart from the magnificent castle, Fitz Osbern also founded a priory at Chepstow, parts of which remain. Here we see the classical combination of interests on the part of a Norman lord: the castle built for his protection, the priory for his soul, and the town for his insurance.

Chepstow was carefully sited for more than commercial considerations, however; it was in what must have been the front line of Fitz Osbern's conquests. He had conquered the Welsh parts of Herefordshire a few years before and now looked towards the rich coast

Map References: **Castle** ST 533941 (metric map 162. 1-inch map 155)
Priory ST 536940
Location: Chepstow Castle is a guardianship site and is open standard hours and Sunday mornings from 9.30, April–September. The Priory, now the Parish Church of St Mary, is on the east side of the old town, on Church Street next to a large car park.

plain of Wales. His new castle was on the Welsh side of the Wye at a point where the main road into Wales crossed the river and to which supply boats could come at all times of the year from Bristol. Chepstow was conceived as the springboard for further westward expansion and even by the time of his death in 1071 William had probably conquered the whole of the modern county of Gwent both 'beneath the wood and above it'.

What then remains from William's time at Chepstow? The first and most dramatic monument is the castle. This was exceptional in two ways: first, because it was built in stone from the beginning, and secondly, because its kernel was a hall-keep rather than a motte or a ringwork. The keep is a most distinguished building which can even boast some decoration at a time when most castles were strictly functional. Although heightened later, the keep as first built had only two storeys, with the lower being used as a store and the upper as a large hall. It was entered at first-floor level up a flight of steps from the middle bailey via a door with a decorated tympanum. The hall floor has since disappeared but at the far end, where the dais would have been, there are four arched openings with two circular lights above. The openings still bear traces of what might be their original painted plaster since the white diaper decoration on it is the 'negative' of the design on the tympanum. There is a fragment of cable moulding on the capital between the left-hand pair of arches and here and there you can see blocked Norman arches. A further feature of the keep is the use of bright red tile bonding courses at intervals through the structure. These tiles, presumably Roman material robbed from a site nearby, lend the yellowish walls some additional colour and the whole makes a very effective architectural composition when viewed from across the river. Apart from the keep, there would have been other buildings in the two baileys to each side. These would have included a kitchen and a camera, since no trace of either exists in the hall-keep itself.

Later the castle passed by marriage to Wil-

liam the Marshal, builder of the Great Keep at Pembroke Castle. At about the same time as he was building Pembroke in 1190, William undertook work at Chepstow too. The east wall dividing the lower and middle baileys is his work, and in it we can detect the same individuality as at Pembroke. The wall is the first recorded use of fully rounded mural towers and of purpose-designed shooting slits.

The other Chepstow monument is the priory church of St Mary. This is by no means as impressive as the castle, but it provides another sidelight on the process of Normanization. As at Ewenny, the priory at Chepstow was a Benedictine house but in this case the mother house was not English but at Cormeilles in Normandy. In 1060, Fitz Osbern had founded a rich monastery at Cormeilles and nothing could be more logical than to grant the monks a further site here at Chepstow.

It appears that the priory may never have been finished, or at least not on the scale that was intended, for soon after the foundation Roger, William's son, was deprived of his earldom for his part in an unsuccessful rising against the king. The nave survives, a substantial structure of six bays which, remarkably, was designed to be vaulted in stone from the first. The vault has collapsed long since, but enough remains on the side walls to trace the line of the cross-arches and groined vaults between them. The massive lower parts of the composite piers of the crossing can still be seen inside the church. The crossing tower fell in 1700 and it probably demolished most of the presbytery – certainly nothing east of the crossing is original. The nave probably dates to the 1120s and the decorated west front is slightly later. Although this work is impressive, excavations on the car-park south of the church in the 1970s revealed a fairly shabby collection of claustral buildings and it does therefore appear that the place never really prospered after the fall of the Fitz Osberns.

The priory church from the south-west; the western tower is post-medieval, but the fine western doorway and the large arches which formerly opened into the south aisle are all Norman.

The keep from the middle bailey; the topmost storey is a later medieval addition.

105

Ewenny Priory, Mid Glamorgan

The church at Ewenny was rebuilt by William de Londres, Lord of Ogmore, early in the 12th century and was granted by him to Gloucester Abbey. In 1141, his son Maurice confirmed the grant and also founded a small priory attached to the church. Parts of both men's work are visible in the existing building; the simple and austere nave belongs to William's original church whilst the transepts and unusual vaulted presbytery mark the larger scale of the monastic church. Gloucester was a Benedictine abbey of 'Black Monks' and they were the obvious choice for Maurice. The Benedictines benefited from the incursions into Wales and they were as alien to the Welsh church as was the bishopric of St Davids. The introduction of such an influence into their territories helped the Norman lords to 'civilize' their new subjects.

Ewenny is often cited as an example of a fortified monastery, because there are castellated walls and a gatehouse on the main north front. This notion was strengthened by the knowledge that the Benedictines were unpopular amongst the Welsh and hence might be more prone to attack. The main eastern 'defended' enclosure dates from the later 12th century, as do the cores of the north and south gates, but the 'fortification' of the site was either decorative or else it was never finished. For all its impressive crenellations at the front, the 'back' of the defences on the east side is composed of nothing more substantial than a precinct wall with neither towers nor crenellations. It is difficult to account for this show of military might – perhaps the prior of Ewenny was another of those mighty churchmen intent upon keeping up appearances!

The priory church from the north; note the roof scar of the now-vanished north transept and the wide arch which opened into it.

Map Reference: SS 912778 (metric map 170. 1-inch map 154)
Nearest Town: Bridgend
Location: Ewenny lies 1 mile (1.6 km) south of Bridgend on the B4524. The priory, which is on the north side of the village, is down a narrow lane and is well signposted. It is in guardianship and also the nave is used as the parish church. It is open Monday to Friday, 8–4.30.

This handsome slab commemorates the priory's founder; although he died in the mid-12th-century, the form of words used and the style of the decoration show that it was carved c. 1200. It reads: 'Here lies Maurice de Londres, the Founder, God reward him for his work. Amen'.

106

Ogmore, Coity and Bridgend Castles, Mid Glamorgan

The three castles of Ogmore, Coity and Bridgend together comprise a strategic unit within the great lordship of Glamorgan. Their position fossilizes one stage in the process of the subjugation of the south coast plain, probably the time after which Robert Fitz Hamon, who became Earl of Gloucester following the fall of the Fitz Osberns of Chepstow, had overrun the whole Welsh territory of Morgannwg. Fitz Hamon built his castle at Cardiff, where it can still be seen inside the walls of the Roman fort. In order to control his new territory, he established his more trusted followers in smaller lordships, each of which had its own castle as its caput. In this way, each man had a vested interest in defending his own land, and hence his loyalty was secure.

But at the western end of the territory there had to be a stronger arrangement capable of withstanding external pressure. This need was met by the establishment of three castles in close proximity. The first was probably Coity, since it controlled strategic routes from the unconquered western lands. Later the new castle at what was to become Bridgend was added to it and by 1116 William de Londres was established at Ogmore. The 'front line' did not last long, however, for by 1130 Richard de Granville built a castle further west at Neath and later still Swansea was fortified. The old front line became an in-depth defence, useful to check large-scale risings and also to control east–west traffic.

But whilst the south coast plain was Normanized to form an 'Englishry', the uplands in the northern part of the lordship were not brought fully under Norman control. These areas remained as 'Welshries' in which life carried on very much as it had before the Conquest, with the difference that they now paid tribute to Norman rulers rather than the native Welsh leaders.

In the Englishry, knights and freemen held their lands directly from Fitz Hamon. The land would be granted to the knights on condition that they would either render military service, normally for 40 days, or else they would go on guard duty in the lordship or in the castle itself. In this way the lord was assured of a military force for the defence of his lordship. Further down the feudal hierarchy those same knights had castles and manors of their own and received dues from their own tenants. A further mechanism for revenue raising was, of course, the borough. Trade was channelled through the boroughs and the burgesses who enjoyed the monopoly of trade had to pay for the privilege. Thus the feudal pyramid was assembled, with each element owing duties of loyalty and service to the stratum above; Fitz Hamon, of course, owed his to the king who was next only to God.

107

Manorbier Castle, Dyfed

Manorbier is famous as the birthplace of Gerald de Barri, better known as Giraldus Cambrensis,

Map References: **Ogmore** SS 882769 (metric map 170. 1-inch map 154)
Newcastle (Bridgend) SS 902801
Coity SS 923816
Nearest Town: Bridgend
Locations: Ogmore is south-west of Bridgend, standing beside a ford on the Ewenny river. It is reached by the B4524. Newcastle is situated next to the church on a hill above the town. From the town centre, take the Port Talbot road, turn right up St Leonard's Road, up the hill, right into West Road as far as the square where the castle is situated. The key is available from a house nearby at the following times:
Apr–Sept Weekdays 10–7 Sun 2–7
Oct–Mar Weekdays 10–Dusk Sun 2–Dusk
Coity is 1½ miles (2.4 km) north of Bridgend in the direction of the M4, Junction 36. The castle is open standard hours.

Ogmore Castle with the stepping stones marking the strategic ford which the castle guarded on the left-hand side.

monk and chronicler of 12th-century Wales and England. Giraldus's 'Itinerary Through Wales' provides a unique account of Welsh life and society during the 12th century. The book is a record of Giraldus's tour through Wales with Archbishop Baldwin when he preached the Third Crusade in 1188. Otherwise, Giraldus was a turbulent man and his vigorous fight for the independence of the see of St Davids from the primacy of Canterbury set him against both ecclesiastical and lay authority.

That Giraldus loved Manorbier is evident from his 'Itinerary'. In it he claims Manorbier as 'the pleasantest spot in Wales', praising its 'excellent' defences and providing homely details of an orchard, a fine fishpond, a vineyard and a wood with hazel trees of remarkable height.

Manorbier Castle, where Giraldus was born in 1146, is interesting because rather like Richmond (North Yorkshire) it has a decidedly domestic air about it. Although it had formidable defences, the kernel of the place was not a grim keep but a small and civilized house. This had a hall with a fine fireplace with a chapel and solar en suite; it must have been a pleasant spot, reflecting Manorbier's position tucked away on the south coast. The castle was never attacked by the Welsh after it was built, and it must have provided a comfortable and secure environment for its most famous son who was in any case of Welsh descent on his mother's side. Rather like St Gilbert of Sempringham whose parentage also crossed the cultural divide, Giraldus was popular with the native people. He records that even after the Chapter at St Davids Cathedral had basely deserted him, 'the laity of Wales stood by me'.

108
Pembroke Castle, Dyfed

The great citadel of Pen-fro, which means 'land's end' in Welsh, was established by Roger de Montgomery after the death of Rhys ap Tewdwr, King of Deheubarth, in 1093.

Map Reference: SS 046976 (metric map 158. 1-inch map 151)
Nearest Town: Tenby
Location: Manorbier has a delightful coastal setting just to the south of the A4139 some 5 miles (8 km) west of Tenby. The castle is open to the public daily between 11 and 6 from 19 May to 30 September.

Manorbier castle seen from the church across the valley; the residential accommodation can be seen on the left-hand side.

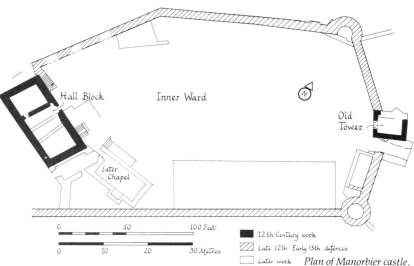

Hall Block   Inner Ward   Old Tower

Later Chapel

0 · 50 · 100 Feet
0 · 10 · 20 · 30 Metres

■ 12th Century work
▨ Late 12th-Early 13th defences
☐ Later work   *Plan of Manorbier castle.*

Rhys's death fighting near Brecon meant that south-west Wales lay open to the Norman onslaught and this base beside the navigable Milford Haven was crucial to Norman control. Pen-fro was not the westernmost point of Wales but it was the best port in the area; this was the key not only to Pembroke's vital significance in the history of Norman Wales but also to the conquest of Ireland.

The first castle which Roger built had earth and timber defences and may have reused the site of an earlier Welsh stronghold. This slight-sounding castle must have been quite strong however since it held out during the great revolt of 1094 during which many Norman gains were recovered by the Welsh. Later, in 1105, Giraldus Cambrensis's grandfather became castellan of Pembroke for the Crown. This was because Arnulf, Lord of Pembroke, had taken part in a revolt against the new king Henry I, and his lands were forfeit thereafter. The defences were put in hand, probably being rebuilt in stone, and the new town was also defended. We know the town was in existence by then and various English and Welsh sources mention the Flemings of Pembroke, so this place was also colonized by Frenchmen as Carlisle had been before under William Rufus. It seems that the Flemings were particularly introduced to control and organize the important wool industry.

The next great threshold in the Norman history of Pembroke, and the one which has left most for us to see, was the glittering reign of William the Marshal, a man who rose from humble origins to become the greatest English knight of his age. William first attracted royal attention by unhorsing Richard Lionheart during a skirmish. His dizzy rise to fame is underpinned by his marriage to Isabel de Clare, daughter of Richard 'Strongbow', Earl of Pembroke and Scourge of Ireland. William the Marshal set about building a castle at

Pembroke fit for his ambitions. In the closing years of our period he began work on the inner bailey and it was not until around 1250, after his death, that the great project was finished.

The most impressive survival of William's castle is the Round Keep. It is a prodigious thing, abnormal in its size, its place and in its design. When we compare Pembroke keep with the royal initiatives at Orford and Conisbrough, we realize something of the power of William the Marshal. He was potentially a great traitor, foremost amongst the king's 'over-mighty subjects', but he was evidently a loyal man and it is this quality as well as his undoubted prowess at arms and his chivalry which have assured his celebrity both in his own lifetime and ever since.

Left: this great natural cavern called 'The Wogan' beneath the castle acted as a store room or boat house.

Map Reference: SM 981016 (metric map 158. 1-inch map 151)
Location: Pembroke Castle is in the town centre at the west end of the main street and is open to visitors at the following times:
Winter Mon–Sat 10–4
Summer (Easter–Sept) Sun–Sat 10–6
The castle is closed on Christmas Day, Boxing Day and New Year's Day.

The great domed keep – a prodigy of military architecture built by a peerless knight.

109
St Davids Cathedral, Dyfed

One of the major effects of the Norman incursion into Wales was the reorganization of the Church. The Church became, whether intentionally or not, an instrument of influence and control in both England and Wales. Churchmen were often great magnates in their own right and, with a few notable exceptions, normally sided with the Crown. The Welsh Church before the Normans had consisted of a loosely knit structure of *clas* or 'mother churches' with some parish churches. There was no rigid territorial basis to these divisions, however, and no larger provinces analogous to the bishopric existed. Religious practices varied from place to place and, although the Welsh Church did acknowledge the supremacy of Rome a few years before the arrival of the Normans, the whole structure would have been entirely alien to the Norman clerics.

Early in the 12th century bishoprics were established based on St Davids, Llandaff, Bangor and, in 1143, St Asaph as well. After the appointment of Norman bishops to St Davids in 1115 and Llandaff in 1116, the sees recognized the primacy of the Archbishop of Canterbury and a formal parochial structure was introduced in the conquered parts of Wales. Here at St Davids, then, we have an alien presence in a conquered land. The Norman cathedral was a symbol of this great restructuring of the native Church.

Work started on the Norman cathedral in 1176 under the direction of Peter de Leia, a bishop appointed to the see by Henry II. The circumstances of his appointment were unfortunate since four nominees of the canons of the Cathedral, including Giraldus Cambrensis, had been curtly refused by Henry; it is perhaps unsurprising that de Leia was unpopular in his new bishopric! Nothing daunted, he set about

Map Reference: SM 751255 (metric map 157/138. 1-inch map 151)
Location: Right on the western-most promontory of Wales, St Davids Cathedral is beautifully set.

Storm clouds gather over the cathedral which was itself accorded a stormy reception when it was founded by the Norman conquerors.

building a church suited to its cathedral status, and although the chancel and crossing were later destroyed by the collapse of the central tower, the nave of his church has survived. This is a massive six-bay structure with arches that are rather too low for their width. There is much decoration, as we might expect of a man who had been prior of Cluniac Much Wenlock, but it is in a style which was already archaic in England – although it was not built until 1190–1200, it still uses zigzag ornament, albeit in a rather developed manner. An undercroft of the 12th-century bishop's palace survives under the later palace to the west of the cathedral.

110
Strata Florida Abbey, Dyfed

The name is a Latin rendition of the Welsh *strat fflur*, which means the 'flowery valley'. This is an idyllic name for an idyllic place; few Cistercian houses can be more delightfully situated than Strata Florida.

The abbey was founded in 1164 by a Norman, Robert Fitz Stephen, but in that same year the Welsh under Lord Rhys ap Gruffydd began the reconquest of Dyfed and later, in 1184, it was the Lord Rhys rather than the Norman Robert who endowed the new foundation. This conflict of lay interests points up the ambivalent position of the Cistercians in Wales. Whilst undoubtedly a 'foreign' order, being based at Cîteaux in Burgundy, they were nonetheless distinguished in the minds of the Welsh from their Anglo-Norman enemies. Strata Florida, remote from the influence of the English houses, went on to become a vital centre of Welsh nationalism and culture.

The ruins of the Romanesque abbey church built under the patronage of the Lord Rhys in the years after 1184 are for the most part unimpressive. The church was cruciform in plan with three square-ended chapels in each transept; they now have fine late medieval floor tiles in them. At the west end, however, the handsome west door survives, bearing a highly original scheme of decoration.

A further aspect of the site is the presence of a number of medieval gravestones in the angle of the south transept and the presbytery. Two of the stones have interlace ornament of pre-Norman character (though presumably of the 12th century), but the majority are undecorated. These are probably the burial places of some of the Welsh leaders who are known to have favoured Strata Florida, and they provide a unique glimpse of the appearance of an early medieval cemetery.

Map Reference: SN 746657 (metric map 135. 1-inch map 127)
Nearest Town: Aberystwyth
Location: From Aberystwyth, take the A4120 to Devil's Bridge then turn south down the B4343 for about 9 miles (14.5 km) to Pontrhydfendigaid. From here Strata Florida is signposted; it is a further mile (1.6 km) east up a minor road.

This unique doorway into the west end of the abbey church resembles the doors at Iffley and Malmesbury in its absence of capitals and continuous orders, but its details resembling ammonites are unparalleled.

Reconstruction of St Melangell's shrine, a rare example of such an object.

local lord sought to shoot a hare whilst out hunting. He was so surprised by her interruption of his sport that he gave her land here to form a small community and St Melangell 'of the Hares' lived her life here, dedicated to the quiet contemplation of God.

Nothing remains of her original church or other buildings, but in a small chamber called Cell y Bedd, the 'room of the grave', at the east end of the church stand the remains of a shrine erected to her memory in 1160–70. This object, which is a unique survival of a type of Romanesque shrine well known from documentary sources, is a fine piece of work. It was carefully reconstructed in 1958 to the great credit of the local authority which undertook the work.

The shrine stands on a base with a roll moulding round the upper edge; the main body of the structure rests on six paired columns with fine acanthus capitals. The upper part, where the original stone survives, is decorated with shallow foliate motifs. The ridge-shaped finial bears similar decoration as well as crockets with tight sprigs on them. The whole is a delicate piece of work and its quality bespeaks the great reverence in which the saint was held.

Map Reference: SJ 024265 (metric map 125. 1-inch map 117)
Nearest Town: Bala
Location: Llangynog is on the B4391, 12 miles (19.3 km) south-east of Bala. At Llangynog collect the key (next to the post office) and take the delightful minor road up the valley. The church is at the end of the valley road (2 miles/3.2 km).

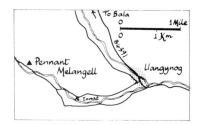

111
Pennant Melangell, Powys

The site of St Melangell's shrine is one of those very special places which leave a mark on the mind long after you have visited them. Situated in a deep valley with towering craggy rocks above, the place has a feeling of immense age and mystery. St Melangell came here from Ireland, perhaps during the 8th century, and is said to have intervened when a

112
Penmon Priory, Gwynedd

St Seiriol's church, pleasantly situated beside the Menai Straits, exemplifies the remote and dramatic sites beloved of the early Celtic monasteries. Although the early history of Penmon Priory is obscure, it must presumably have been the site of an early Welsh monastic community of the Celtic type in which stone or wooden cells clustered about a church within a

Map Reference: SH 630807 (metric map 114. 1-inch map 107)
Nearest Town: Bangor
Location: Penmon is on the coast of Anglesey at the east end of the Menai Straits. It has dramatic views across the water of Conwy Bay. From the Menai Bridge, take the A545 to Beaumaris. Carry on along the coast on the B5109 and then take the minor roads signposted to Penmon.

The site of the priory from the west with the waters of the Menai Straits in the background.

llan or enclosure. By the mid-12th century the nave of the monastic church had been built and later, probably around 1170, the church was extended to form a cruciform structure, parts of which still survive. In 1237 an Augustinian cell was founded and the modest claustral range dates from that period.

The nave retains its original single-splay windows and the south doorway is a notable composition with nook-shafts and a tympanum with, appropriately, a fierce dragon upon it. The crossing is fine though on a small scale; the northern transept was rebuilt as a vestry in 1855, but the southern one is fortunately preserved. This has excellent blank arcading on two sides, the pillars of which are enriched with faceting, chevron moulding and, in one case, candy twist; the heads are decorated with very light and effective chevron moulding. The capitals on the nave arch into the crossing are very curious; the stylized grotesque on the north side and the small carving of a man on the south are both highly stylized and probably reflect Celtic influence.

St Seiriol's church is a tribute to the power and prestige of the kingdom of Gwynedd under the able leadership of her king, Owain Gwynedd. The quality of the later work at Penmon is very fine and shows how the native rulers of Wales, as in Scotland, took up the fashions of their Norman neighbours. But even as Penmon was being built, the order achieved by Owain Gwynedd was threatened; he died in 1170, and the kingdom was again torn by strife between his sons.

Tympanum with weathered dragon and interlace decoration.

113

Tomen-y-Rhodwydd Motte and Bailey, Clwyd

The castle at Tomen-y-Rhodwydd must serve to illustrate the vast number of motte and bailey castles in the Marches. A distribution map shows that they were astonishingly numerous and some at least, such as this one, were probably built by the Welsh themselves. Many motte and bailey castles were established in the early years of the Conquest and may have been abandoned fairly soon thereafter. Others, like Hen Domen near Montgomery, stayed in use for a hundred years and more. In certain areas, such as eastwards of Montgomery and along the line of what is now the A5 road between Llangollen and Betwys-y-Coed, we can see defensive systems of mottes sited so as to control a particular area prone to attack. The motte and bailey could be built speedily out of simple materials and, once built, it could be held by a handful of men against all save the most determined attacker.

Here at Tomen-y-Rhodwydd we can see the typical plan of a 'pudding basin' motte which would have had a timber tower on top with an embanked bailey yard below and a deep ditch enclosing the two elements. Here the original structure was probably of wood, but later stone walls were built as is indicated by stones sticking out of some of the banks. The site was strong and easily held, close enough to the road to monitor its traffic and capable of controlling a considerable area of territory. The motte and bailey is deservedly the hallmark of the Normans; it enabled them to hold down large areas of land with relatively few men.

Map Reference: SD 177516 (metric map 116. 1-inch map 108)
Nearest Town: Ruthin
Location: From Ruthin take the A525 south, towards Wrexham. The castle is beside the A525 on the north side, just south-west of the junction with the B5431, 7 miles (11.2 km) from Ruthin and about 1 mile (1.6 km) west of Llandegla. Watch out for the earthworks which can be seen from the road. There are lay-bys either side of the road, so parking is no problem.

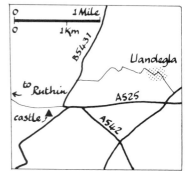

The hump of the motte on the left flanked by its deep surrounding ditch on the right.

northern england

SCOTLAND AND THE BORDERS

CLEVELAND

▲124

• Northallerton

▲122

119 ▲ • Scarborough

▲125

▲123

121 ▲

NORTH YORKSHIRE

▲120

Harrogate

York •

118 ▲

HUMBERSIDE

• Lancaster

▲132

▲131

117 ▲

130 ▲ 128 127

WEST ▲ • Leeds ▲ ▲

• Hull

Preston •

YORKSHIRE 126

LANCASHIRE

116 ▲ • Scunthorpe

GREATER
MANCHESTER

▲129

SOUTH
YORKSHIRE

MERSEYSIDE

▲115

Sheffield

▲

CHESHIRE 114

WALES

• Chester

AND

CENTRAL ENGLAND

THE MARCHES

0   10   20 Miles

0   10   20   30 Km

Northern England

Introduction

The Norman history of the north had an inauspicious beginning. After 1066, the area was still unsubdued and in 1069 a general rising was led by Edgar 'the Aetheling', scion of the ancient line of Kings of Wessex. The English rebels were joined by Danish forces led by King Swein's two sons, and this mixed host set about the newly built castle at York. Having reduced and plundered York, they moved southwards into Lincolnshire, but they got no further since William marched rapidly northwards, forcing the Danes to take to their ships in the Humber.

This threatening situation provoked a characteristically resolute response from the Conqueror. His line of march was marked by hellish scenes of slaughter and depredation, with famine and exposure completing the savage work of his troops. William spent the Christmas of 1069 at York and the Anglo-Saxon Chronicle records that he 'laid waste all the shire'. Certainly Yorkshire seems to have suffered most heavily for the rebellion, and even in 1086 Domesday Book could still record dozens of settlements as 'waste'. William continued his marauding north to the Tees, then he crossed the Pennines and subdued Chester and Stafford before returning south.

This ferocious response to the northern rebellion evidently worked. Edgar fled into Scotland and Swein's sons joined Hereward the Wake in the eastern Fens; the inhabitants of those unhappy lands were too busy trying to save themselves to think of rebellion in the future. It is an interesting sidelight that, in the midst of the slaughter, the Conqueror turned his mind to the foundation of the Benedictine abbey of Selby during that black Christmastide in York; was this in propitiation for his sins? That the north was reduced to subjection is clear from the sparseness of Norman castles in the area and the general absence of later troubles. The great Honour of Richmond controlled the heartland of the north and lordships were established at Conisbrough, Skipsea, Clitheroe and Middleham, amongst others. At each of these sites, there were 11th-century castles. At Richmond itself a major stone castle was erected from the first whilst at Scarborough, Middleham and most dramatically of all at Conisbrough we see the later history of castles unfolding.

Whilst the military history of the north after the infamous 'Harrying' was uneventful, the Church made great strides in the region. The foundation of Selby in 1069 has already been mentioned, and a second major Benedictine foundation was made at York after the false start by the community at Lastingham. Thus it was the 'Black Monks' who arrived first in the north, but it was to be the Cistercians, the practical sheep farmers and land improvers, who were to make the greatest contribution. Selby's building programme proceeded well during the first quarter of the 12th century, but after that time it came to a grinding halt. The initiative was seized by the new reformed order of Cîteaux whose asceticism and penchant for labour held more appeal for the layman.

The first Cistercian foundation was at Rievaulx in 1131, and Fountains, actually founded as an offshoot of the Benedictine abbey of St Mary's at York, followed shortly thereafter; both these remarkable sites, which have extensive Norman work in them, will be described in more detail in our forthcoming *Guide to Medieval Sites*. Kirkstall was founded in 1152 and Byland, after the wanderings of its community described on p.149, in 1177. There were, of course, more Cistercian foundations as well as those of other orders, but we have included the sites of Kirkstall and Byland here to illustrate the generality.

Large parts of the northern landscape probably owe their present form to the careful husbandry of the Cistercians or 'White Monks'. We know that the various abbeys had many grange farms from which flocks, herds and arable lands were controlled. Land drainage schemes, road and bridge building as well as coal and iron mining as at Bentley Grange were well within the capacity of the Cistercian planners and their workforce of lay brothers. Many of these aspects will be considered more fully in our later *Guide*, since few surviving examples can be dated with certainty to the Norman period, but we know from documentary evidence that these activities were commonplace.

When we turn to Norman parish churches in the north, we find a picture of change and development. Beginning with the Saxo-Norman overlap, represented by the early and primitive East Yorkshire fonts with their cartoon-like carvings, we proceed to the rigours of North Newbald, which reminds us of nothing so much as a Cistercian abbey in miniature. This early restraint – which was perhaps due both to the effects of William's policy and to the ascetic influences of the Cistercian order – did not last long, however. By the mid-12th century, the 'Yorkshire Revival' had come to pass in which the artistic endeavours for so long absent were triumphantly introduced. At Barton-le-Street, Birkin, Adel and on the west front of Selby Abbey we see sculpture of such quality that it rivals much contemporary work in the south. The early dearth of decoration, which happened elsewhere in Norman England, continued longer here, but when happier times did finally arise the local craftsmen responded magnificently.

114
Prestbury Church, Cheshire

In the churchyard of St Peter's church at Prestbury stand the much altered remains of the small Norman chapel which preceded it. The structure is of interest not least because it was subject to a comparatively early restoration; a stone on the west front records the date as being 1747. The chapel has two cells, a nave and a square-ended chancel; the proportions of the nave roof in particular have obviously been altered during the restoration. Both nave and chancel have small single-splayed windows with monolithic heads, and look more Anglo-Saxon than Norman.

At the west end, however, there are more clearly Norman features. The west doorway has two orders of moulding above rather thick nook-shafts, and in the tympanum is an abraded figure of Christ in Majesty, in a mandorla supported by two angels. Above the doorway are seven small figures which have been reset to form a very un-Norman composition. The central figure is presumably Christ, since the halo bears a cross, and another seems to bear a sceptre and hence is a king, but the others are too abraded for certain identification.

115
Conisbrough Castle, South Yorkshire

The keep of Conisbrough Castle is a celebrated feat of military architecture which prefigures many of the details of later medieval castles. It was apparently built in about 1180 by Hamelin, half-brother to Henry II. In the innovatory design of Conisbrough we can almost sense a rivalry between the two men. Henry had built Orford keep a few years before, and that had incorporated many new ideas, but Conisbrough takes the whole process a stage further. Conisbrough is a truly round buttressed keep. The keep protrudes through the curtain wall, anticipating the later development in which keeps were used as angle towers in the defences rather than standing alone in their baileys. Like Orford, Conisbrough has a fine battered base designed to deflect stones dropped from above into the ranks of the enemy, but unlike Orford Conisbrough has rounded rather than square bastions on its curtain wall.

The keep was entered at first-floor level by a stone staircase on the site of the modern access; the principal entrance has the adv-

The small two-cell chapel at Prestbury which was heavily restored during the 18th century.

Map Reference: SJ 901769 (metric map 118. 1-inch map 101)
Nearest Town: Macclesfield
Location: Prestbury is 2½ miles (4 km) north of Macclesfield on the A538. The chapel is in the churchyard.

Map Reference: SK 515989 (metric map 111. 1-inch map 103)
Location: Conisbrough is off the A1(M), 3 miles (5 km) south-west on the A630. The castle is in guardianship and is open standard hours and on Sunday mornings from 9.30, April–September.

anced feature of a 'joggled' lintel. Inside, the stairways are relatively generous since they are contrived in the thickness of the walls rather than 'corkscrewing' up a turret. The principal chamber has a fine fireplace, again with a lintel, and beside it is the rare luxury of a small washbasin. This was fed from one of the cisterns in the top of the great external buttresses. The use of plumbing here complements the use of lead piping in Henry's great keep at Dover, and indicates the growing sophistication of life in castles. There is a further large chamber above the hall proper which served as a solar, and this is similarly equipped with fireplace and washbasin. At the top of the keep, there were actually two tiers of battlements to increase firepower, and the projecting buttresses would have enabled the defenders to bring a certain amount of flanking fire to bear on an attacker.

The inner bailey in which the keep stands probably follows the outline of the 11th-century earth and timber defences built by William de Warenne. It seems that the outer bailey wall was built slightly later than the keep, and it too has some interesting features. The first of these is the use of solid semicircular bastions on the curtain wall. Normally such bastions were either square or, occasionally, polygonal and hence they are another example of the designer's innovation. Furthermore we see here the emergence of a new type of gateway. Instead of the old idea of a single tower pierced by a gate passage, as at Richmond and Newark, two flanking towers are employed with a consequent increase in firepower at this weak point. A further embellishment was the use of a barbican before the gate which appears to be much the same date as the rest of the inner bailey. This is one of the earliest occurrences of a barbican, and in this as in so much else Conisbrough looks forward to later developments.

The four great buttresses of the keep supplied additional accommodation and their hollow tops contained two water cisterns, an oven and a pigeon loft.

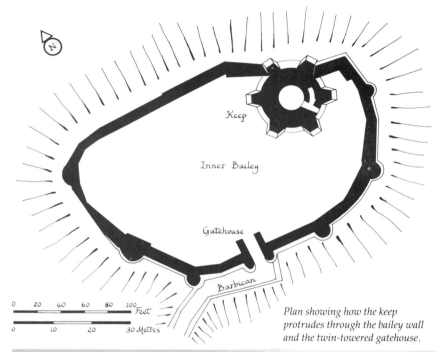

Plan showing how the keep protrudes through the bailey wall and the twin-towered gatehouse.

116
Alkborough Maze, Humberside

The maze at Alkborough is one of a handful of 'turf mazes' in England which are simply cut into the turf, apparently without any permanent marks. There is no way of directly dating such a feature – there is nothing for the archaeologist to excavate, and no early documentary evidence. As a result, we can only proceed on the basis of comparison with other dated mazes elsewhere.

The design of the Alkborough Maze is similar to that of some mazes set into the floors of French cathedrals during the 12th century, for example Chartres, and this has encouraged the belief that it is of the same date. Local tradition has been quick to seize on the rather dubious ecclesiastical link of a small monastic cell which is known to have existed in the area. All this is little enough to go on, but we must either accept the explanation or turn to others,

such as a Romano-British origin for the maze, or else that it was merely a post-medieval game.

What the French mazes do indicate is that the 12th-century church had come to regard mazes as illustrations of Christian beliefs, perhaps symbolizing the complex voyaging of the soul through earthly life. In this idea we can find echoes of the use made by the church of other earlier ideas, like the 'Virtues and Vices' on the font at Southrop. Certainly here at Alkborough the Christian associations of the maze have been revivified. The maze is depicted in the top of the middle window in the east wall of the chancel, and the design was also let into the floor of the porch during the last century. An even more direct link is provided by a service held on the maze each year at Whitsuntide. Perhaps this ceremony continues an association which goes back 800 years to the 12th century; we will almost certainly never know.

Map Reference: SE 880217 (metric map 112. 1-inch map 98)
Nearest Town: Scunthorpe
Location: Alkborough is on the south bank of the Humber at its confluence with the River Trent. From Scunthorpe, take the B1430 to Flixborough (off the A1029 western bypass). At Burton upon Stather, 5 miles (8 km) north of Scunthorpe, take the minor road north to Alkborough a further 3 miles (5 km). The maze, called Julian's Bower, is on the south-west side of the village and has a commanding position overlooking both Trent and Humber.

The maze occupies an open site above the River Humber; it was plainly intended to be seen, but how old is it?

Although this pattern looks superficially simple, the maze walker must traverse almost the whole path before the centre is reached.

117
North Newbald Church, Humberside

At North Newbald is a large and notably complete survival of a cruciform 12th-century church. Built in fine ashlar blocks, the church has a rather severe aspect which is alleviated only by the restrained doorways, carved corbel table and a carving of Christ in Majesty in a vesica over the south door. This last sculpture is somewhat restored, and the face in particular, which has a distinctly 'Old Testament' look about it, has actually been stuck on over the place where the original would have been. An interesting feature of the plan is the occurrence of doorways in the ends of both the north and south transepts. If they were wider, then they could be interpreted as processional entrances, but as it is they are unexplained. There were originally chapels projecting to the east of the transepts; the blocked entrances to them survive within.

Inside, the nave is tall and bare with, at the west end, a fine font of late-12th-century date consisting of a tub decorated with foliage standing on eight engaged shafts. The crossing is particularly elegant and spacious with restrained zigzag on the axial arches. Altogether, Newbald has rather an ascetic air about it and provides a good indication of architectural style in Yorkshire before the later excesses of sites like Birkin and Barton-le-Street. In the 20 or so years between Newbald and Birkin (1140–60), a dramatic change came over Yorkshire building – it has been called by some the 'northern revival'.

Map Reference: SE 912367 (metric map 106. 1-inch map 98)
Nearest Town: Market Weighton
Location: North Newbald is on the east side of the A1034 4 miles (6.4 km) south of Market Weighton.

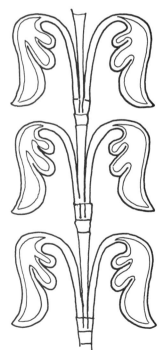

Decorative detail from the late-12th-century font.

Left: The restrained south door with the Christ in Majesty set above it.

118
Skipsea Castle, Humberside

For the year 1069, the Anglo-Saxon Chronicle records:

> . . . there came from Denmark three of King Swein's sons with two hundred and forty ships, into the mouth of the Humber. There they were met by . . . all of the people of the land, riding and marching with an immense force greatly rejoicing – all of one mind they went to York, stormed the castle, threw it down, and won there countless treasures. There they killed many hundreds of Frenchmen . . .

This rebellion against Norman authority was one of the events which precipitated the 'Harrying of the North', but the memory of it must have lingered on and this area called Holderness on the south-east Yorkshire coast was a critical military province. Quite apart from invasion threats, it was open to the depredations of seaborne pirates. A strong man was required for such a sensitive area, and William chose one Drogo de Bevrere to be Lord of Holderness. The castle at Skipsea was built by this Drogo, and the complex defences illustrate the importance of his charge. For although Skipsea Castle is in essence a motte and bailey, such a term seems quite inadequate when it is realized that the bailey was fully 8½ acres (3.4 ha) in extent!

Map Reference: TA 163551 (metric map 107. 1-inch map 99)
Nearest Town: Hornsea
Location: Skipsea is half-way between Bridlington and Hornsea on the North Sea coast. From Hornsea take the B1242 north for 5 miles (8 km). The castle is in guardianship and is open at all reasonable times. It is signposted Skipsea Brough. The approach is through a very muddy track for about three-quarters of a mile (1.2 km), so wellington boots are advisable!

View across the massive 'bailey' of the castle which was in reality Skipsea Mere. The boggy nature of the ground is indicated by the deeply rutted track on the left.

119

Scarborough Castle, North Yorkshire

The commanding coastal site occupied by Scarborough Castle was used by the Romans for a signal station, which provided advance warning of pirates on this exposed coast. Later, there was a Scandinavian settlement here founded by one Skarthi, who gave his name to the place – 'Skarthi's burgh'.

The Norman history of the site apparently began during the Anarchy of Stephen's reign (1135–54) when in 1140 William le Gros, Earl of Albemarle, built a castle on the headland. Parts of the curtain wall on the west and south-west sides remain but no trace of his keep survives. The present great keep at Scarborough was built by Henry II, and although it was efficiently ruined after the Civil War it retains several interesting features. There were four storeys, with the entry at first-floor level from a forebuilding on the south side. An unusual aspect of the arrangements is the relatively large and frequent two-light windows; these lit not only the top storey, as might be expected, but also the more vulnerable first-floor hall. They do not accord with the general strength of the keep and its site.

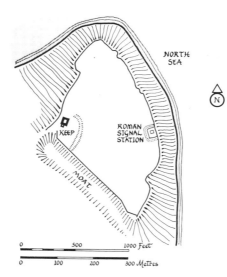

Map Reference: TA 050893 (metric map 101. 1-inch map 93)
Location: The castle is on a headland which divides North Bay from South Bay. It is in guardianship, open standard hours and Sunday mornings from 9.30, April–September.

Plan showing the relatively small area occupied by the Norman castle; the large surrounding enclosure probably defended the earlier Scandinavian borough on the site.

120

The East Yorkshire Fonts

There are four rather crudely carved fonts in the eastern part of Yorkshire which appear to belong together in a group. They are large and cylindrical with bold low-relief carving on their sides. Most art historians have dismissed them as being brutish and nasty, but we felt that they had an undeniable charm and, at North Grimston, there is a 'Last Supper' scene which illustrates aspects of contemporary eating habits. The Apostles, with Christ in a special niche in the centre, are shown tucking into a feast of round bread rolls with crosses on

A rare representation of St Lawrence on his red-hot gridiron on the font at Langtoft – he looks remarkably happy!

Map References (metric/1-inch map numbers follow each entry in brackets):
North Grimston SE 842678 (100/92)
Kirkburn SE 980551 (106/99)
Cowlam SE 966655 (101/93)
Langtoft TA 008670 (101/93)
Nearest Town: Great Driffield
Locations: Langtoft is 5 miles (8 km) north of Driffield on the B1249. Cowlam is off a tiny road south of the B1253, about 2 miles (3.2 km) east of Sledmere which is 7 miles (11.2 km) north-west of Driffield. Kirkburn is 3 miles (5 km) south-west of Driffield on the A163. North Grimston is south-east of Norton, 4 miles (6.4 km) down the B1248.

Fine low-relief scene of the Last Supper at North Grimston. The details of the scene – the serious faces and the feast of bread and fish – all mark this out as a delightful piece of primitive sculpture.

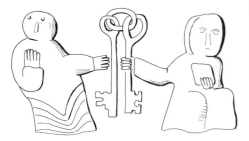
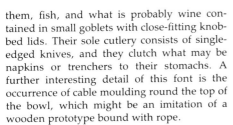

The Charge of St Peter on the font at Kirkburn.

them, fish, and what is probably wine contained in small goblets with close-fitting knobbed lids. Their sole cutlery consists of single-edged knives, and they clutch what may be napkins or trenchers to their stomachs. A further interesting detail of this font is the occurrence of cable moulding round the top of the bowl, which might be an imitation of a wooden prototype bound with rope.

Other examples in the group also repay close examination. At Cowlam are two struggling wrestlers; at Langtoft is a rare representation of St Lawrence on his gridiron; whilst at Kirkburn are the Baptism of Christ and an unusual scene of St Peter in which he is being charged with the Keys of Heaven. Many of the details of these scenes are delightful, and as with all such primitive works the simplicity of the design acts in refreshing contrast to more mannered compositions. The group probably dates to the 11th century, and illustrates the continuation of Anglo-Saxon traditions in this part of rural Yorkshire.

121
Barton-le-Street, North Yorkshire

St Michael's church is a remarkable tribute to the reforming zeal of Hugo Francis Maynell-Ingram, who is suitably commemorated in the church by a monument in the Norman taste. Indeed, the whole essay is so meticulously Norman that the effect is somewhat overwhelming – even the altar rails and pulpit have Romanesque arches and dogtoothing.

Zealous though the restoration was, much of the original church, which dated to around 1160, is left and the sculpture in particular is of the greatest interest. In the north porch, sections of a remarkable corbel table are incongruously set in the side walls; parts of the original north doorway now serve as the outer door and the original south door has been reset to form the inner opening. To add to the confusion, there are fragments of finely decorated panels set into the wall above the north

Map Reference: SE 721742 (metric map 100. 1-inch map 92)
Nearest Town: Malton
Location: Barton-le-Street is north-west of Malton 4 miles (6.4 km) along the B1257 Helmsley road. The village is just off the road on the north side.

door. There are three complete figures and other fragmentary ones from a cycle of the 'Labours of the Months' as on the lead font at Brookland. Two rectangular panels show on the left a scene interpreted as the Virgin Mary in bed with bearded censing angels above, and on the right a spirited scene in which the Three Kings hurry to pay homage. The hooded figures behind presumably represent the Shepherds, and in this transposition, as in other details of the iconography, there is a feeling of muddle, as if the sculptors were not entirely at home with their subjects.

The north door itself is equally remarkable; there are interesting paired heads and figures in the outer order. On the jambs is a fascinating collection of animals and figures including angels, cat heads, birds and a representation of Samson wrestling with the lion. Some of these scenes can be interpreted, but generally they are a product of the extraordinary pictorial imagination of the sculptors of the so-called 'Yorkshire School'. The designs on the outer door show Anglo-Saxon influence in the intertwining animal tails, whilst the arched design of the corbel table in the porch finds its closest parallels in western France.

Internally there is a mixture of 'real' and 'imagined' Norman elements. The scrolled frieze at the level of the window-sills is especially fine, and preserved sections can be seen on the west wall of the nave. The chancel arch is similarly a mixture of new and old, with the shafts and capitals being original, and the arch itself a later recut. A notable survival is the decorated pillar piscina near the altar which was used for washing the sacred vessels.

Impost of the chancel arch showing fine foliate and animal carvings, but note that the human head on the right is a 19th-century restoration!

Samson wrestling with the lion (his long hair and beard are much in evidence before the attentions of Delilah).

Part of the delightful string course in the nave.

122

Lastingham Crypt, North Yorkshire

The church of St Mary at Lastingham is only a fragment of the original design intended for the site. There was an Anglo-Saxon monastery on the site founded by St Cedd in 654, but it fell into disuse as a result of the Danish raids during the 9th century. There was then a break of over 200 years until the monastery was refounded by Stephen of Whitby in 1078. This refoundation was part of the drive towards the 'resurrection' of earlier monastic sites of which Whitby itself had been a beneficiary. For, until monks from Winchcombe in Gloucestershire had come north to visit the ruined shrines of earlier Christianity, Whitby, like Lastingham, had long lain neglected.

Stephen must have been a very capable builder, for we know that by 1086 Lastingham was again abandoned, the community having moved to York where they founded St Mary's Abbey. It appears therefore that all the Norman building at Lastingham must have been accomplished within eight years at most.

As was normal, the monastic builders began at the east end of their church, and the whole of the existing structure would have formed only about the eastern third of the complete plan. The surviving elements consist of an apsidal sanctuary with the four pillars of the crossing to the west of it. The present west wall of the church merely links the two western pillars of the crossing, and the aisles to north and south were added when the church devolved to parochial status during the 13th century. The whole is sombre early Benedictine work with decoration being limited to restrained window moulding and a corbel table round the exterior of the apse. The scale of the work is suitably substantial, however, and the building makes an atmospheric, if rather dark, parish church.

When seen from the outside, the apse is particularly impressive by virtue of its great height; this is because it was sited on a steep slope in order to accommodate a crypt

beneath. This apsidal crypt is undoubtedly the chief glory of Lastingham, and it has been suggested that parts of it may belong to the Anglo-Saxon church which stood on the site. In particular, the lower parts of the stubby columns supporting the vaulted roof have been claimed as Saxon, and this seems likely enough in view of their simple design. If this is the case, they are probably *in situ*, and hence the Norman church was sited so that its altar stood above this holy of holies in which St Cedd himself may have been buried.

Map Reference: SE 728905 (metric map 100. 1-inch map 92)
Nearest Town: Pickering
Location: Lastingham, a very picturesque village, is in the North Yorkshire National Park. From Pickering take the A170 east in the Helmsley direction. In 6 miles (9.6 km) turn north up the minor road to Appleton-le-Moors and Lastingham (4 miles/6.4 km).

The superb crypt at Lastingham. The bases of the pillars could be Saxon and the basic layout of the crypt is perhaps the same as when St Cedd was buried there in the 7th century.

123
Byland Abbey, North Yorkshire

At Byland we can see a remarkably clear and complete monastic plan, with the church, cloister, lay brothers' and monks' accommodation all laid out in the approved Cistercian style. There is still a feeling of quiet efficiency about the site even in its ruined state. It must have seemed a fantastic place when it was in use, a perfect colony set down in the midst of what had been a boggy wasteland. At Byland we see made manifest the Cistercians' vision of God's ordered society existing against a backdrop of 'wild' countryside.

Yet if that was the end product, the story of how the Cistercians came to Byland was anything but neat and orderly. The group of monks which eventually founded the abbey left their mother house at Furness in Cumbria in 1134. They were actually Savignacs, and settled first at Calder in Cumbria. This site was plundered by the Scots in 1138, and the community returned to Furness. Later, they went to Hood near Thirsk, but that site proved too small for their growing numbers, and a further move was made to Byland in Ryedale, not far from the Cistercian abbey of Rievaulx. Unfortunately, the bells of the two abbeys caused confusion and annoyance and the monks of Byland, being the newer arrivals, had to move. In 1147, they set off once more to a place called Stocking which lay to the west. They built a small church and claustral range there, and in that same year the order of Savigny merged with the Cistercians. Finally, in the years after 1147, the monks set about draining a boggy site east of Stocking, and it was to that place that in 1177 the monks finally moved. What a bizarre saga this is – whilst many communities shifted their sites, as at Lastingham, few underwent such vicissitudes as the monks of Byland!

Map References: **Byland Abbey** SE 549789 (metric map 100. 1-inch map 92) **Old Byland Village** SE 549860
Nearest Town: Helmsley
Locations: Byland Abbey is on a minor road between Coxwold and Ampleforth. From Helmsley take the A170 in the Thirsk direction and follow the signs to Byland which is south of the main road 5 miles (8 km) from Helmsley. The abbey is in guardianship and is open standard hours.

The earthwork road and boundary can be seen on the south side of the abbey, beyond the stream. Take the road towards Coxwold, and walk along the first farm track on the left – the earthworks can be seen ahead. The track itself forms a sunken way and platforms can be seen in the valley side.

Old Byland is up on the hills to the west of Rievaulx and can be reached by winding minor roads from the B1257. 2 miles (3.2 km) north-west of Helmsley, turn west along a minor road and follow the signs to Old Byland. Note the open green of this planned village. Taking the road back towards Rievaulx, take the farm road towards Tylas Farm, which is on the left. The original abbey site can be seen on the west bank of the River Rye.

Elaborate steps leading from the cloister into the monks' choir. In the background can be seen some of the round and pointed arches which indicate the Transitional nature of the church.

The original site called Byland near Rievaulx actually had a village on it when the monks were given it by Roger Mowbray. The village was promptly removed to a new site in order to ensure the seclusion of the new monastery. The new village site, confusingly called 'Old Byland', is therefore of interest because it is a regularly planned village with a relatively secure date attached to it – 1143. Such wholesale removal of villages was quite common, and well illustrates the power of monastic communities. We know that the monks also provided the villagers with a new church, and it has been presumed that the existing church at Old Byland was the one mentioned in the documents.

To return to the abbey itself, the plan illustrates the scale and refinement of later Cistercian planning. Building went on here right through the fourth quarter of the 12th century and well into the 13th. The west end of the church is fully Gothic, and in this building we can trace the transition of the styles, with round and pointed arches being used in the successive building campaigns. The rest of the plan is an almost perfect Cistercian composition, with the huge cloister being a particularly notable feature. Interestingly, the geometric tiled pavements inside the church have survived; these belong to the years about 1200, and are the earliest large-scale tiled pavements in the country. In the Abbey Museum are fragments of sculpture which retain their delicate red lining as well as more unusual objects such as the base of a stone lectern and a gaming board.

In addition to the church and claustral buildings, we can also see something of the practical organization of the monastery at Byland. Some of the drainage ditches still exist, and on the side of the valley opposite the main site can be seen the foundations of the precinct wall and the grassy line of a medieval road. The precinct wall shows as a long narrow mound a little over three feet (about a metre) high which runs

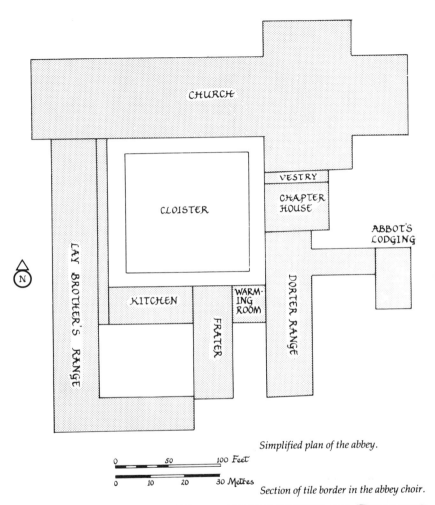

Simplified plan of the abbey.

Section of tile border in the abbey choir.

parallel with a farm track. The road is about 20 yards further down the slope, and appears as a low-crowned linear earthwork, in part contained between high banks where it has worn to form a 'hollow way'. Beside the road is the outline of a rectangular building, and further building platforms can be seen set back into the hill slope.

Once the eye has become attuned to such earthworks, the visitor will be able to see many other pieces of evidence in the landscape around the abbey. There is much ridge and furrow, especially on the road towards Coxwold, and in one case the earthworks of a probable small farm can be seen next to a later farmhouse. All this reminds us that sites like Byland were not merely religious centres – they were the hub of a local road system and had granges, farms, quarries, fisheries and other services around them. It is important to look for such evidence at all monastic sites, and this is normally to be found. Large communities could not exist in economic isolation, and for Byland we not only have the evidence immediately around the site but also the far-flung grange at Bentley Grange which supplied the monastery with iron.

At Byland the crown of the medieval road can be seen in the middle distance and the hump of the ruined precinct wall appears on the right.

This splendid tiled roundel occurs in the chancel of the village church at Old Byland. Its presence here provides a compelling link between the village mentioned in the documents as being built by the monks and the existing settlement.

124
Richmond Castle, North Yorkshire

There appears to have been no substantial settlement at Richmond before Norman times, and Alan 'the Red', the first Norman to hold what later became the mighty 'Honour of Richmond', seems to have begun work on a 'green field site' in 1071 or thereabouts. It is the placename itself which gives the key to his decision. 'Richmond' derives from the French for 'strong hill', and it was clearly the defensive potentialities of the hill above the River Swale which attracted him. From Alan's viewpoint, this made perfect sense. Less than a year had passed since the 'Harrying of the North' (1068–70), and we must imagine that Normans were scarcely popular hereabouts.

His first priority was to 'dig in' and then to control his restive English subjects.

That we can still see so much of Alan's original work is a tribute to the uneventful history of Richmond thereafter. Unlike so many of the other northern fortresses, Richmond never attained any great strategic significance, and hence was never drastically replanned. Here we have a fascinating glimpse of an early Norman castle which was stone-built from the first. In this it resembles Chepstow; this is unsurprising, since there was Fitz Osbern, the Conqueror's regent, and here was Alan, near relative of the powerful Duke of Brittany.

Map Reference: NZ 174006 (metric map 92. 1-inch map 91)
Location: Richmond is in Swaledale 4 miles (6.4 km) south-west of Scotch Corner on the A1. The castle is in guardianship, open standard hours and on Sunday mornings from 9.30, April–September.

Richmond Castle has something of a 'dan-dified' air about it since the evidence suggests that Alan's most imposing building was his comfortable stone hall. This structure, which was entirely unsuited to defence, took advantage of the fine views across the valley, and was ancestral to later first-floor halls at places like Boothby Pagnell and Christchurch. True, there are the remains of a strong gate tower buried in the mass of the later keep, but the hall is an example of comfortable accommodation at a very early date. Perhaps the Harrying had been so effective that the natives were not expected to make trouble.

Earl Alan also built the main walls of the triangular great court, and traces of his her-ringbone work can be seen at various points. The court was entered through a gatehouse at the apex of the triangle to the north, where the principal gate arches can still be seen. Three early square towers survive on the east cur-tain, but only one on the west; there must have been more.

There is a handsome chapel built into the base of the Robin Hood Tower on the east side of the great court.

Interestingly the hall still has the name 'Scol-land' associated with it; the first Scolland was Earl Alan's 'sewer'. This unpleasant-sounding title referred to his job as table steward for his master. His was the responsibility of arranging guests at table, of carrying in the choicest foods and of generally ensuring that a jolly time was had by all. It is fitting that the name of a man and his descendants (for the job was hereditary), who prepared many a fine feast here, should be thus remembered.

About a hundred years after Earl Alan's time Henry II took the place in hand and built the keep which is such a feature of the site today. The keep was built on top of the earlier gate tower, the openings of which were blocked. A

Plan of the castle showing the triangular bailey with Scolland's Hall set in the south-eastern angle. Note how the early gatehouse tower was encased in masonry during the late 12th-century.

Above: Seal of Conan, Earl of Richmond (1146–71), and Duke of Brittany, mounted on his caparisoned destrier.

Left: The gatehouse keep as it exists today is a two-phase structure. The 11th-century gate tower was substantially lower, but the original entrance survives, visible in the centre of the picture.

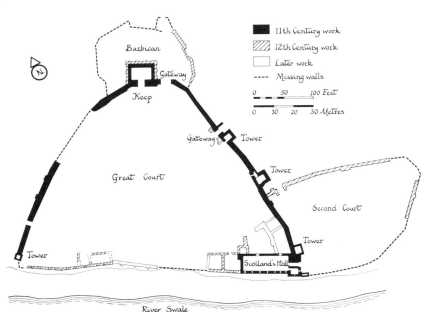

new entry was made on the site of the modern entrance, but all trace of that has gone. Scolland's Hall was extended at this time, and apparently remained the principal domestic quarters of the castle. One of the most notable, if involuntary, inhabitants of the castle was William the Lion, King of Scotland, who was imprisoned in the Robin Hood Tower in 1174.

Finally, the town of Richmond is of interest. There was apparently a French colony established here in what was fairly certainly a new town established by Earl Alan. The town plan is semicircular, and it might well have been contained in a defensive circuit. Although it was not walled until 1312, it is difficult to believe that it was entirely undefended before then. The large market-place and the slight but impressive 12th-century work in the parish church suggest that Earl Alan's town was a success.

125
Middleham Castle, North Yorkshire

Middleham was first granted in 1069 to that same Earl Alan who built Richmond Castle. In 1086, the land which included Middleham was held by his brother Ribald, who was presumably builder of the first castle here. This castle was a small motte and bailey, and was sited on a ridge to the south-west of the later castle and town. This first castle, which had some stone buildings, was in use for about a hundred years until, in 1170, Robert Fitz-Ralph, grandson of Ribald, conceived a grandiose plan for the much larger stone castle which is the principal survival at Middleham today.

The early site is worth visiting not least because it affords an inspiring view of the later work. The town has so impinged upon the surroundings of Fitz-Ralph's great keep that it is difficult to appreciate its magnificence from ground level. Apart from this, the motte and bailey is marked by a good set of earthworks, including a motte with a polygonal curtain wall, now represented by banks, and what must have been the base of a lookout tower.

The inner bailey probably had a wall, now represented by a bank with a stony core, and there is a small half-moon-shaped outer bailey, in the entrance to which is a cobbled surface. East of the main earthworks there are slight traces of a third bailey which include a deeper section of dyke across the crest of the ridge.

The later castle at Middleham was on a very substantial scale, though only the rectangular hall-keep remains. The plan must originally have consisted of two courts with the present buildings occupying the inner, and the outer being on the site of the farmyard to the east. Traces of the great bank around the eastern court can still be seen at the bottom of Canaan Lane.

The keep consisted of two storeys with high-status accommodation on the first floor and domestic offices beneath. Entry was at first-floor level on the east side up a flight of steps of which only traces remain. The ground floor was divided up the middle by a spine wall and had a stone vault. The hall on the first floor seems to have had the archaic feature of an open hearth, since there is no fireplace. The curtain wall and the other buildings surrounding the keep are all later.

Map Reference: SE 128875 (metric map 99. 1-inch map 91)
Nearest Town: Ripon
Location: Middleham is some 17 miles (27.3 km) north-west of Ripon on the A6108. Famous both for followers of a certain Yorkshire vet and for members of the White Boar Society, it is a much-visited spot. The castle is in guardianship and is open standard hours.

The motte and bailey castle, called Willias Hill, is reached by a narrow lane to the left of the guardianship site. After a bungalow on the left is a small gap in the wall with a stile. Go along the field boundary, across the fence, and up to the castle which lies in permanent pasture. It is well worth the walk for the views of Middleham and the castle below.

View of Robert Fitz-Ralph's castle and town from the original early Norman motte and bailey on the ridge above.

126

Hemingborough Misericord, North Yorkshire

Although parts of the church at Hemingborough are Norman, the principal interest attaches to the presence here of what is thought to be the oldest misericord in the country. The name 'misericord' literally means a 'pitying heart' and refers to the design of a wooden seat which could be turned upwards during divine service in order to permit the user to lean against the upper part of the seat. The idea of such hinged seats probably originated in monastic churches, where the offices could be a long endurance for the elderly or infirm. The example here at Hemingborough is well designed and finished, and bears typical decoration on the underside of the seat. Accordingly, though this is the earliest surviving example, and probably dates to around 1200, it is unlikely to be the first.

The misericord is the westernmost of the seats on the south side of the chancel and has finely carved 'stiff leaf' decoration on the underside. It is this style of decoration, which is reminiscent of late-12th-century sculpture, which indicates its likely date.

127

Selby Abbey, North Yorkshire

Selby Abbey was founded by William the Conqueror in 1069, and was the first Benedictine monastery to be founded in northern England after the Conquest. It is remarkable that William apparently decided to take this step whilst at York during the 'Harrying of the North'; was his action motivated by conscience as much as by the desire to establish a colony of loyal monks in an area of resistance to his authority? Whatever the precise reasons for the foundation, Selby opened a new chapter in the fortunes of the north in which monasteries were to become an important feature. At first, the Benedictines were alone in the field and,

The misericord – perhaps the earliest in England – decorated with 'stiff leaf' foliage.

during the reign of Henry I (1100–35), Selby prospered. But in 1131, the first Cistercian abbey was founded at Rievaulx, after which the earlier foundation at Selby went into something of a decline. These changing fortunes are reflected in the surviving buildings at Selby. The Durham-style nave of eight bays dated to the early 12th century indicated the massive scale of the original concept, but the western parts of the church were not completed until the close of the century. It is to this later period that the splendid west doorway belongs with its waterleaf capitals, fully detached nook-shafts and deeply cut mouldings round the head of the arch.

An unusual feature of this doorway is that the wooden door might also be Norman. If this is so, then the lattice construction may have been inspired by the great bronze-covered doors of Italian cathedrals of the 11th and 12th centuries. It is even possible that this door was similarly covered by bronze plates bearing scenes of religious subjects. What a fine composition this would have made – the ornate carving of the arch and the great metal doors catching the sun – a fitting portal for the majestic Norman nave within.

Map Reference: SE 673306 (metric map 106. 1-inch map 97)
Nearest Town: Selby
Location: From Selby take the A19 north for 1 mile (1.6 km), then turn south-east on the A63 for 3 miles (5 km) in the direction of Howden. Hemingborough is just south of the A63 and the church stands by the main road in the village, about ¼ mile from the A road. The misericord is the most westerly one on the south side of the choir.

The late 12th-century west door with its excellent carving parallels the sculpture in other Yorkshire parish churches, but the contemporary wooden doors mark Selby out as being a most unusual survival.

Map Reference: SE 615325 (metric map 105. 1-inch map 97)
Location: The abbey is in the centre of the town.

128

Birkin Church, North Yorkshire

This small though fine Norman church stands in the midst of rather flat countryside. Viewed from the exterior, the tower commands the attention since it has a rather incongruous top stage in contrasting white Tadcaster stone. Apart from this, the basic Norman plan of west tower, nave, chancel and apse is virtually intact, the only addition being the 14th-century south aisle. It is in its details that Birkin pleases, since the south doorway is finely decorated, although its detail is somewhat obscured by the careless application of brown wood preserver to the later porch. The doorway, which is presumably reset in this position owing to the addition of the later south aisle, has fine medallions in the outer order, a zone of chevrons and finely cut beak heads which are notably slim and elegant.

All three compartments of the church have good corbel tables; the windows have nook-shafts and, in the case of the apse, chevron, beak head and medallion decorated heads. The eastern apse window is unusual since a later, presumably 14th-century, traceried light has been fitted into the Norman opening, providing a remarkable juxtaposition of two contrasting architectural styles.

Internally there is a fine tower arch, but the chancel arch is the more remarkable. This has three shafts down each side with zigzag moulding on the arch above. The apse arch matches the other two, and the apse roof is original. The interior then is reasonably intact, but when we visited the site we were disconcerted to see that the chancel floor had heaved upwards by several inches, presumably as a result of the underlying coalmine. We must hope that Birkin church, which has already suffered some indignities, will not be further damaged in future.

Some of the ornate roundels on the south door.

Documentary evidence suggests that the Knights Templar held the advowson of Birkin church after 1152, and this might explain the occurrence here of such a finely decorated church which is obviously influenced by the 'Yorkshire School'. The date of this work is, like Barton-le-Street and Selby west door, *c.* 1160.

Map Reference: SE 530265 (metric map 105. 1-inch map 97)
Nearest Town: Selby
Location: From Selby take the A63 west for 5 miles (8 km), then take minor roads south to Birkin for a further 3 miles (5 km).

View of the church from the north-east showing the fine ashlar work of the walls.

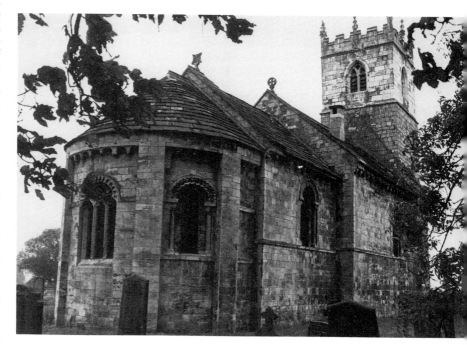

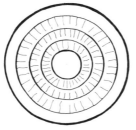

129

Bentley Grange Iron Mines, West Yorkshire

As the name suggests, there was a monastic grange or settlement here. The word 'grange' originally meant a barn, and most such sites were farms established by monasteries to cultivate lands given to them by lay benefactors. The term did not have an exclusively agricultural meaning, however, and here at Bentley Grange the estate was concerned with the winning and processing of iron rather than with farming.

The monks of Byland were granted the right to mine iron ore at Bentley Grange during the second half of the 12th century, and unusually there is some physical evidence of that process for the visitor to see. Although in some ways undramatic, the site is nonetheless worth seeing because it does enable us to remember the great technical and physical difficulties involved in winning iron during our period. When we look at the ironwork on the church doors at Staplehurst or Sempringham we should recall that the raw material was laboriously won at sites like this.

On the ground, the pits appear as circular flat-topped mounds about 6½ feet (two metres) high. These mounds represent the waste piled round the pit openings, and the positions of the collapsed shafts at the centres of the mounds are marked by small depressions containing odd trees and tangles of thorn. The pits beneath, called 'bell-pits' because they were wider at the base than at the top, were about five feet (1.5 metres) wide at the surface. The pits were sunk down through the shale beneath in which the nodules of iron were found. The sides were shored with wooden planks, but the work must still have been difficult and dangerous. After it had been mined, the ore was taken to furnaces built by the stream next to the wood.

Charcoal was probably used to fuel the furnaces, though coal occurs at distances varying between 10 and 25 feet (3–7.3 metres) below the ironstone beds which were being

mined. There is no record of coal winning here at Bentley Grange, however, although the monks of Kirkstall and Fountains both had coal workings not far away to the north-west. The stream was dammed and a water-wheel provided power for finishing the iron after smelting. Part of the river bank is actually constructed of furnace slag, and heaps of waste can still be seen. Pieces of iron ore and fragments of forge and furnace slag litter the site. Forge slag is light coloured and porous like pumice stone whereas the furnace slag is black and glassy.

Annual iron production from Bentley Grange could be as high as 25 tons a year, and this must have represented a considerable income for the monastery. That this industry

Aerial photograph of the iron pits; note the regularity of their layout. (Courtesy of the Curator in Aerial Photography, University of Cambridge. Crown Copyright reserved.)

Map Reference: SE 261138 (metric map 110. 1-inch map 102)
Nearest Town: Huddersfield
Location: From Huddersfield take the A642 in the Wakefield direction. In 6 miles (9.6 km) take the A637 to Flockton (1 mile/1.6 km). In Flockton, go down Church Lane to Emley. At the T-junction, turn east towards West Bretton. 1 mile from Emley the ironstone pits can be seen in the fields either side of the road, the field to the south being especially busy. The furnaces were built along the stream next to the wood.

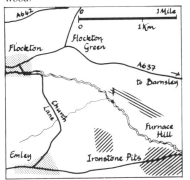

was taken seriously is evidenced by several factors. First, the site is a long way from Byland – over 40 miles (64 km) – which suggests that it was considered worth exploiting the resource irrespective of administrative inconvenience. Secondly, when seen from the air, the bell-pits are seen to be in neat rows, suggesting considerable organization. Finally, and most importantly, we know that Byland was in frequent and acrimonious dispute with other monasteries owning iron mines in the vicinity; a sure sign that these rights were well worth protecting!

130
Kirkstall Abbey, West Yorkshire

Kirkstall Abbey, which was founded in 1152 as a daughter house of Fountains, is the best-preserved early Cistercian house in the country. Here it is possible to obtain a good impression of the monastic environment; and the church in particular, which is virtually unaltered, provides a magnificent impression of the severe architectural style which was their hallmark. Apart from the church, much of the claustral range survives, including the chapter house with its handsome double doorway and freestanding pillars, the night stairs and even the recess in which the service books were kept. Virtually the whole plan, with the exception of the later infirmary hall and abbot's lodging, belongs to the second half of the 12th century.

Little of the outer court remains at Kirkstall, but the gatehouse is incorporated into the building containing the abbey museum. Recent excavations have disclosed some 12th-century remains beneath the 13th-century gatehouse west of the church. These include lead water pipes carefully laid in trenches and packed round with puddled clay. This interesting practical evidence of monastic organization provides a pleasing contrast with the liturgical and architectural nuances which have attracted so much attention in the past.

View of the massive south aisle of the abbey church; this picture clearly demonstrates the excellent state of preservation of this major Cistercian monastery.

Map Reference: SE 260361 (metric map 104. 1-inch map 96)
Nearest Town: Leeds
Location: The abbey is beside the River Aire on the west side of Leeds on the A65. Open daily from dawn to dusk, admission free. The abbey gatehouse is a folk museum, open April–September, weekdays 10–6, Sundays 2–6, and October–March, weekdays 10–5, Sundays 2–5.

131
Adel Church, West Yorkshire

The church at Adel, although a celebrated example of Norman architecture, has a curiously unbalanced look to it; there must surely have been an apsidal sanctuary to balance the relatively large nave and chancel. What survives is impressive enough, however, and the south door is a memorable composition. This entrance is in some ways out of scale with the church which it serves; it is far advanced beyond the wall face simply in order to accommodate the four deeply recessed orders of moulding about its head. The doorway is a superb work with chevrons, roll mouldings and beak heads. It is, of course, a carefully composed work; the height and width are the same, with the capitals neatly occurring exactly half-way up the sides.

Inside, the chancel arch is as fine, with three orders of deeply cut moulding and nook-shafts. On the capitals are lively carvings of the Baptism of Christ on the north side and the Deposition from the Cross on the south. A curious feature of these carvings is the occurrence of a little monster, presumably representing the Evil One, which on the north side drinks the holy water, but on the south slinks away in the face of Christ's victory over Death. The middle capitals have a centaur fighting a dragon and opposite a mounted knight.

One further delight must be mentioned; this takes us back to the south door. On the outside of the door is a fine bronze sanctuary knocker which is part of the original fabric. Apart from foliate decoration, the handle attachment shows a beast head, probably representing Hell's Mouth, from which emerges a small human head. This is probably an illustration of the saving power of the Church, delivering mortals from the perils of Hell. In this small detail, we see the same acute penetration of iconographical significance as in the rest of the decoration at Adel; some of it we understand, but much we do not.

Map Reference: SE 275403 (metric map 104. 1-inch map 96)
Nearest Town: Leeds
Location: Adel is on the north-west side of Leeds. Follow the signs to Otley (A660). As the outskirts are reached watch out for signs to Eccup. Take the minor road north-east. Adel church is 1 mile (1.6 km) up this road on the east side opposite open fields.

The 12th-century bronze sanctuary knocker on the south door which shows a demon disgorging a small human head, symbolizing the saving power of the Church.

The south doorway surmounted by a panel showing Christ in Majesty flanked by the Symbols of the Evangelists; the date is c. 1160.

132
Clitheroe Castle, Lancashire

The smallest Norman keep in England, but it is strongly sited in a commanding position for all that.

Map Reference: SD 740416 (metric map 103. 1-inch map 95)

Location: Clitheroe is north-east of Blackburn. The castle is in the centre of the town. It is always open and is set in municipal gardens adjacent to the museum.

Clitheroe Castle has the distinction of possessing what is perhaps the smallest Norman keep in England. Although the lordship of Clitheroe is heard of soon after the Conquest and a castle is known to have stood here as early as 1102, it seems unlikely that this small structure dates from that period. It seems more probable that the tiny keep was little more than an 'estate office' set up to administer the area after it had been swallowed up by the much greater Honour of Pontefract in the period 1177–94.

The keep is entered at first-floor level, and there is a small square store in the basement. A spiral staircase leads to an upper chamber. A further entrance led onto the wall walk of the surrounding curtain. To the south and west was a triangular bailey, the walls of which have now disappeared. The view into the bailey is interesting, however, since the later buildings along the now-vanished lines of its walls provide a good impression of the structural 'clutter' of such a space.

Although the keep is small, it occupies a commanding position at the west end of the main town street. The regularity of the town plan suggests that it was probably a Norman plantation. It has a broad market street with subsidiary roads going off at right angles and, whilst the present parish church is modern, there is documentary evidence for a church here in 1122.

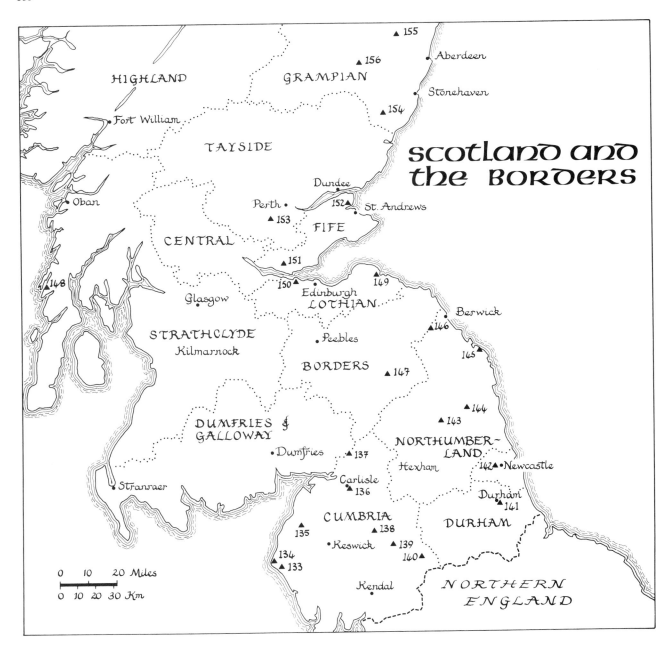

scotland and the borders

HIGHLAND

GRAMPIAN

▲ 155

• Aberdeen

▲ 156

• Stonehaven

• Fort William

▲ 154

TAYSIDE

Dundee

• Oban

Perth •

▲ 153

152 ▲ • St. Andrews

FIFE

CENTRAL

▲ 151

148

150 ▲

▲ 149

Glasgow

Edinburgh

LOTHIAN

Berwick

STRATHCLYDE

Peebles •

▲ 146

Kilmarnock

165

BORDERS

▲ 147

▲ 164

DUMFRIES &

▲ 143

GALLOWAY

NORTHUMBER~

• Dumfries

▲ 137

LAND

Hexham

142 ▲ • Newcastle

Stranraer

Carlisle •

136

Durham

141

CUMBRIA

DURHAM

135

▲ 138

• Keswick

▲ 139

134

140 ▲

133

Kendal

NORTHERN

ENGLAND

0   10   20 Miles

0 10 20 30 Km

Scotland and the Borders

Introduction

Under the Canmore dynasty, founded by Malcolm Canmore (from the Gaelic Ceann Mor, meaning 'bighead') in 1057, Scotland gradually achieved a stable monarchy with an assured succession. In this Scotland was more successful than Wales where the 'divide and rule' policy of the Normans eventually resulted in substantial territorial gains. In Scotland, by contrast, the Norman kings of England faced a formidable adversary which they had to treat more as an equal than an easy conquest. Norman influence in Scotland was exercised both culturally and militarily. Malcolm Canmore had spent his early years in England and had married the English princess Margaret who had fled north after the Norman Conquest; English ways became fashionable in the lowlands at least and feudalism was introduced into southern Scotland during Malcolm's reign.

This process of change was continued by Malcolm's sons, despite some dispute after his death which occurred whilst fighting in Northumberland in 1093. David in particular (1124–53) was a man of broad vision who did more than any other individual to ensure that Scotland took her place on the European stage. For David, quite apart from being King of the Scots, was also Prince of Cumbria and Earl of Northampton and Huntingdon; he was an English nobleman in his own right and had spent his early years at the Norman court. During David's reign, many Normans were given lands in southern Scotland and others married into Scots families; in this way the peaceful 'conquest' of Scotland was accomplished. The feudal system was extended and names like de Comines, de Bailleul and Fitz Alan became as familiar north of the border as they were in the south.

These peaceful contacts have left an interesting legacy of 'Norman' sites in Scotland. At Inverurie and Lumphanan we see castles which would not have been out of place in England and which, like their English counterparts, acted as the caputs of feudal estates. At Inverurie, a borough was founded as well, indicating the extension of urbanization into the northern kingdom. Castle Sween does not belong with these; as far as we can tell, there was no feudalism in the west at the time it was built, and hence it acted as a fortress rather than a castle in its fullest sense. Dalmeny, Tyninghame and Leuchars represent the new Romanesque churches which those same lords built on their new lands.

It was King David himself who was responsible for the major innovations, as became his position in the van of Norman influ-

ence. At Dunfermline we see the great abbey church, founded originally by the saintly Margaret, but extended and beautified by her son. This building, which is a smaller version of the massive work at Durham, is a concrete statement of David's wish to identify with Norman culture. That this desire affected secular as well as religious affairs is evident from the introduction of feudalism and Norman-derived Forest Law. The site of the deer park at Kincardine illustrates just one of the few aspects of early medieval secular life which has left physical evidence in Scotland, but it serves to remind us that there were other preoccupations than the purely military and spiritual. It was, however, in the spiritual field that David made his greatest mark. The Border Abbeys, those four great powerhouses of the faith in the Scottish lowlands, are his memorial. At Dryburgh beside its tranquil river, or Jedburgh where its jagged ruined nave cuts across the sky, we can still summon David to mind and respect his courage. For whilst the Normanizing policies of the Canmore dynasty seem sensible and reasonable today, they were much resented in the Celtic northlands where the king's writ ran less surely.

We do not know how the Anglo-Saxons had held the Scottish border, but the Normans employed their customary thoroughness. By 1090, Norman lords had been settled in Northumberland and had installed themselves in strong castles like Elsdon. William Rufus's successful campaign against Carlisle in 1092 opened Cumbria to Norman settlement, and Liddel Strength, that parlous border stronghold, was held by Turgis Brundis for the English Crown. Other castles followed at Brough and Brougham, while at Norham we see the powerful bishops of Durham asserting their authority in their wide province.

The Scots watched events in England with a careful eye. They seized their opportunity during the chaos of Stephen's reign, and in 1138 King David invaded England, ostensibly in support of the Empress Matilda. He was defeated at the Battle of the Standard in 1138, but Stephen's terms were so generous that Scotland was allowed to control much of the northernmost parts of England, saving only Bamburgh, where a keep was raised at this time, and Newcastle. It was not until the reign of Henry II (1154–89) that the Scots were finally driven back. It was Henry who built the strong keeps at Carlisle and Brougham, but even then the Scots were not quiescent. William the Lion invaded England in 1173, but he was captured and imprisoned at Richmond. The keep at Brough was built after the castle had been razed by him, but his was the last of the major Scottish attacks, and it was left to Edward I, 'Hammer of the Scots', to press English claims a hundred years later.

This area of the country displays a fine range of Norman military architecture, with several of the sites continuing in use right down to the Union of the Crowns in 1603. There is, however, a slender legacy of civilian and in particular ecclesiastical sites. At Bridekirk the remarkable font graphically records the meeting of Norman culture with native Norse elements. At Bolton in the same county, a sculpture of two knights reminds us of the recreational joust rather than full-blooded warfare. The priories at St Bees and Brinkburn, the cathedrals at Carlisle and Durham and the little church at Norham show how the civilizing influence of the church was gradually extended into these inhospitable northern lands. When we stand in the majestic nave at Durham, a cross between a house of God and a fortress, we should ponder on the vast northern estates which the bishops of Durham controlled. After the tragedy of the 'Harrying of the North', the Church helped to restore the ravaged countryside to a productive condition and at Norham we also see just one of the castles with which those same churchmen sought to assure its future safety. Order was gradually wrested from chaos and the savagery of the Norman border was to pale into insignificance compared with that of later periods.

133
Egremont Castle, Cumbria

The castle and town of Egremont and St Bees Priory really went together, since each reflected a different aspect of the Norman presence in Cumbria. Egremont as the military and commercial centre acted as both citadel and market-place for the lordship of Copeland, whereas the priory embodied the religious authority with which the Norman conquerors sought to invest themselves. The Norman history of Egremont begins after the grant by Henry I of the lordship of Copeland to William Meschin in about 1120. Egremont was the caput of the new lordship, and we can well imagine that William lost little time in building a motte and bailey castle there. We also know that William built a chapel nearby, perhaps rather like the one at Seaton Delaval, and that it was served by monks from his foundation at St Bees. Later, the chapel was extended to become the parish church, and Egremont itself became a fully fledged borough. Whilst these changes did not occur until the time of William's grandson, it is likely that both had existed *de facto* long before.

Egremont Castle dominates the town in a remarkable way, and looking down from the motte you can see the broad market street below with tenement plots running off from the shops on the frontages. This basic early medieval plan has obviously been extended on its fringes by houses and schools, but the bare bones of the settlement are clear enough. Here was a small lordly castle strategically located on a hillock beside a crossing of the River Ehen – which gave rise to the name 'Egremont' – with its attendant church and town.

Looking more closely at the castle, we see that the original earth and timber motte and bailey plan was later 'fossilized' in stone. The motte, although lacking its keep, has plenty of

Left: The fine late 12th-century gatehouse, a smaller version of the mighty gates at Richmond and Exeter.

stones jutting from it to attest its former presence. The bailey wall has fine herringbone work on its western side, and at the southwest angle is a simple square gatehouse with an unusual vaulted roof. All this belongs to a period of consolidation during the later 12th century.

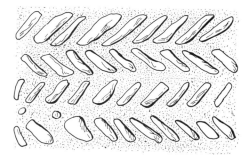

Section of herringbone work in the western wall at Egremont Castle.

134
St Bees Priory, Cumbria

The site of St Bees Priory was already ancient before William de Meschin, Lord of Egremont, founded a Benedictine priory there in 1120. Indeed the name St Bees derives from a St Bega, an Irish nun who lived there during the 7th century. Be that as it may, in founding the priory William was following the general policy of introducing the civilizing influence of the monastic orders into newly won territory. The difference in Cumbria was that the process happened about 50 years later than in the rest of England because Carlisle was not wrested from the Scots until 1092. Even after that there was considerable Scottish pressure for its return; this is probably why major building did not begin at St Bees until about 1150.

Of the original priory church, the great west door is the principal survival. This is deeply recessed and has three heavy orders of chevron moulding about its head. One feature of this doorway is the occurrence of protruding heads amongst the chevrons, a design which

Map Reference: NY 010103 (metric map 89. 1-inch map 82)
Nearest Town: Whitehaven
Location: Egremont is south of Whitehaven, 5 miles (8 km) down the A595. The castle is in municipal gardens and is open daily.

Map Reference: NX 969121 (metric map 89. 1-inch map 82)
Nearest Town: Whitehaven
Location: St Bees is 4 miles (6.4 km) south of Whitehaven on the B5345.

West door of St Bees with three massive orders and protruding grotesque heads in the manner of Dalmeny (Lothian).

was taken up in Scotland at Dalmeny and elsewhere. A Norman window can be seen in the surviving first bay of the chancel, and recent excavations have revealed the eastern part of the chancel under the 'Old College Hall', which now forms part of St Bees School.

135
Bridekirk Font, Cumbria

The church of St Bridget ('St Bride') at Bridekirk is a magnificent essay in the 'Norman Revival' style by Cory and Ferguson, 1868–70. Even the cast-iron grilles covering the underfloor heating pipes have foliate decora-

tion which would not be out of place on a string course at Barton-le-Street. There are materials from the original church reused in the later building, as demonstrated by the tympanum and arch over the south door of the south transept and the arch over the organ. Only the chancel of the early church survives to the east of the later structure. Apart from the splendours of its 19th-century interior, Bridekirk claims our attention because of its notable font. This celebrated object illustrates the meeting of two cultures – the Norman and the Norse.

Map Reference: NY 116338 (metric map 89. 1-inch map 82)
Nearest Town: Cockermouth
Location: From Cockermouth take the A595 Carlisle road. 1 mile (1.6 km) from the town turn north on the minor road to Bridekirk, which is a mile further on.

East face of the font showing opposed griffins above inhabited vinescroll, the ribbon bearing the runic inscription and the figure of the carver – Ricard.

Cut from a single block of stone, the font is rectangular in shape and has remarkable decoration on its tapering sides. On the north and south 'ends' are respectively a Tree of Life above a patera supported by a griffin and a salamander and a two-headed mantichora above a scene of the Baptism of Christ over which hovers a portly dove. On the west side are further scenes featuring a griffin and a centaur, a swordsman and a supplicating figure with, perhaps, a further Tree of Life.

It is on the main east face that we find the principal scene. In the upper part of the panel are two opposed griffins with a foliate sprig between them. Below are two zones of inhabited vinescroll divided by a ribbon. In the upper zone a man eats from the fruit-laden branches and a dog bites the stem, whilst in the bottom left-hand corner a mason works with an outsize hammer and chisel. Some believe that this is a self-portrait of Ricard, the creator of the font. We know his name because the ribbon dividing the vinescrolls bears an inscription in the English tongue but rendered in Scandinavian runes. It reads: 'Ricard made me and . . . brought me to this splendour.' It is possible that the gap in the middle of the inscription originally recorded either the name of the donor of the font or else that of some other craftsman, perhaps a painter, who finished off the work.

The peculiar interest of the Bridekirk font is both that it is a very rare example of a 'signed' work and that the inscription is executed in runes. The font is a 'fossil' of the period when Cumbria was gradually being opened to the influence of Norman ideas during the 12th century. This is made manifest by the iconography which shows a clear knowledge of the Bestiary. But here also is a remnant of that older Anglo-Norse culture to which Cumbria was heir; here we see the use of a type of script which had died out in the rest of England long before.

136
Carlisle Castle, Cathedral and Town, and Warwick-on-Eden Chapel, Cumbria

Carlisle, called the 'Key to England' after its capture by William Rufus in 1092, was the great English bastion on the west end of the border. Nothing now remains of the castle William built here but at the core of the later defences stand the four-square walls of the keep built during the reign of Henry II. In this building, as in so many others on this northern frontier, we see the strong hand of that capable yet tempestuous monarch. Only the outer walls of Henry's great keep remain, since much of the interior and top of the tower have been remodelled to meet the social and military needs of later generations.

Map References: Castle NY 397563 (metric map 85/86. 1-inch map 76)
Cathedral NY 382589
Warwick-on-Eden NY 473565
Locations: The castle is on the north-west side of the old city, separated from it by Castle Way dual carriageway. It is in guardianship and is open standard hours and on Sunday mornings from 9.30, April–September. The cathedral in its precinct is in the centre of the city, off Castle Street. Warwick-on-Eden is east of Carlisle, 5 miles (8 km) on the A69; it is west of the Warwick Bridge, on the south of the main road. The chapel is approached down a narrow lane called Old Chapel Lane on the west side of the village. Carry on past the Nonconformist chapel down the footpath and the Norman chapel is at the far side of a small churchyard.

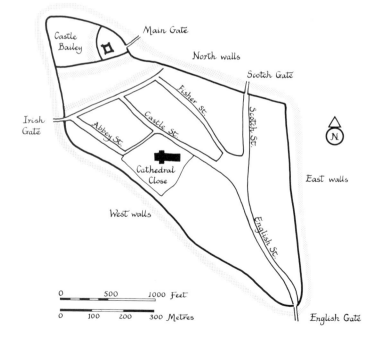

Plan of Carlisle showing how the castle dominated the town, although separated from it by ditches, and how the street names – Irish Gate, English Street and Scotch Street – commemorate the diverse population of William Rufus's new colony.

When William captured Carlisle, the castle was but one element of his plan. The Anglo-Saxon Chronicle tells us that 'he built up the town and raised the castle', he drove out Dolfin, the governor of the place, and after he had returned south he 'sent there many peasant folk with women and livestock to dwell there and till the land'. Plainly William intended more than a mere military strong-point at Carlisle; he also built a town and caused settlers to colonize it. This broader policy was aimed at influencing these wild Border lands, and we know that Flemings as well as southern Englishmen came to dwell here amongst the native 'English and Irish-men' – the area about Carlisle had been a cultural melting-pot for hundreds of years before Rufus subjugated it.

The site of Carlisle had been a major Roman town called Luguvallium, and it was here that Rufus set about establishing his colony. It seems that the new citizens were defended by stone walls from the first, and part of the surviving west wall near Abbey Street is claimed as 11th-century. Both castle and town were planned together, but the castle was separated from the town by wide ditches, presumably in case a revolt broke out amongst its polyglot inhabitants. As in Southampton, the different peoples were given separate areas of the town to live in, with English, Irish and Flemings each being allocated a different 'quarter'.

Almost at the centre of the new settlement was founded the great Cathedral of the Holy and Undivided Trinity. Although the origins of the church are obscure, the intention was plain enough; it symbolized ecclesiastical authority in the same way that the castle dominated the temporal sphere. It was Henry I who introduced the 'Black Canons' of the Augustinian order to the city, and it was doubtless under his patronage that their great church was built. But the new church was still under the authority of Scottish bishops, who had held sway here when Carlisle was part of Scotland. In 1133, Henry took the logical step of causing a new see of Carlisle to be formed,

and installed Adelulf as its first bishop. Carlisle was thereafter both temporally and spiritually a part of England.

Just outside Carlisle to the east is the village of Warwick-on-Eden which has a church of most unusual design. It was presumably built as a lord's chapel, and it is first mentioned in 1131, which seems a likely date for the building. The main interest attaches to the extraordinary east end, which is apsidal and decorated externally with numerous pilasters which are linked at the top by simple round arches. This highly distinctive feature finds parallels in France, and its occurrence here might suggest the influence of some of Rufus's new settlers in Carlisle. The apse is built of red sandstone which still bears masons' marks. Inside, the chapel is suitably dark, though mostly rebuilt in the 1860s. Few Norman features survive, but the handsome baptistry arch at the west end of the nave could well have been the original chancel arch in view of its quality and dignity.

Warwick Chapel possesses this most unusual apse which stems from French designs; it looks like a cross between a church and the bastion of a castle.

The lowering keep of Carlisle Castle, originally built by Henry II but altered later to accommodate cannon on its topmost storey.

137
Liddel Strength Castle, Cumbria

Liddel Strength was literally in the 'front line' of warfare between England and Scotland. It was sited to control the main Roman road north from Carlisle and to protect the important gap between the Solway Moss to the west and the hills to the east. The strategic value of the site had long been appreciated, since there was a Roman fort at Netherby nearby. The barony of Liddel was granted by Ranulph de Meschines, Lord of Carlisle, to a Fleming called Turgis Brundis; Liddel Strength was the caput of the barony. The site was besieged by two Scottish kings, William the Lion in 1174 and David II in 1346.

In order to reach the site you must cross fields which still bear faint traces of ridge and furrow, though this is probably later than the Norman period. At first sight, the defences do not look particularly impressive, since the castle is sited on a forward slope overlooking the Liddel Water into Scotland. On the landward side there are in fact three deep ditches before the motte, and they still contain water despite the elevated position. The innermost ditch has been artificially deepened to about 30 feet (nine metres) by counterscarping, in which the upcast from the ditch has been heaped on the uphill side. On the downhill side there is an immense kidney-shaped bailey which is cut off from the motte by a further deep ditch. The bailey bank has some stone in its core, so it is likely that a stone phase was built some time after the initial earth and timber defences were raised. The bailey is protected by a wide shallow boggy ditch, rather after the fashion of Lumphanan. Beyond the bailey is a piece of rough pasture with established trees, and if you look carefully in the grass before the bailey you can see strange trenches cut diagonally across the approach to the castle. It is possible that these were dug in order to break up a direct frontal assault on the bailey, but their date is unknown.

Turning back towards the castle, you recross

Here we see the earthen motte from the landward side of the defences; there are actually two ditches to be crossed before the motte is reached.

the outer bailey and scramble up the still awkward inner ditch. There is an inner bailey next to the motte which is as large as the full baileys of many castles. Although partly dug away, the motte is still impressive. From its top you can understand why the castle was sited here, for the views into Scotland are tremendous. As you look down on the massive defences, you get strong feelings both of the necessity and of the perils of this bastion of defence hard upon the Border.

Map Reference: NY 402741 (metric map 85. 1-inch map 76)
Nearest Town: Longtown
Location: Liddel Strength lies beside Liddel Water, close to its confluence with the River Esk, on the south side of the Scottish border. From Longtown take the minor road to Carwinley in a north-easterly direction. From there carry on half a mile (0.8 km) until the first minor road left (north); stop by the first farm on the left-hand side and ask permission (there is no right of way).

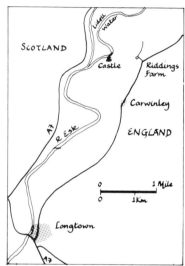

138
Brougham Castle, Cumbria

At Brougham, like Brough, history repeats itself since the strategic potential of the site occupied by the Norman castle had been recognized in Roman times. To the south of the castle the outlines of the Roman fort of Brovacum, some 4½ acres (1.8 ha) in extent, can be descried. Later, during the reign of Henry II, the site again came to prominence by virtue of

Map Reference: NY 537290 (metric map 90. 1-inch map 83)
Nearest Town: Penrith
Location: Brougham is 2 miles (3.2 km) north-east of Penrith on the A686. It is in guardianship, open standard hours and on Sunday mornings from 9.30, April–September. The castle stands beside the River Lowther.

the dispute between England and Scotland over Westmorland. Although William Rufus had captured Carlisle and the area round it, and had built castles like Brough to defend it, Westmorland was held less firmly by the English Crown. But with the death of the doughty King David and the resolute action of Henry II, the north-west was finally brought under English control. Brougham, built almost a hundred years after Brough was started, belongs to this later phase of consolidation of the northern frontier. At Brougham the great square keep formed the core of the defences from the start, whereas at Brough the keep was added afterwards.

As first built the keep had three storeys and was entered at first-floor level via a forebuilding containing a staircase. The interior was arranged in the familiar fashion with a ground-floor store, first-floor hall and a solar or retiring room above. The top storey was added in the 13th century and in this as in its other details it closely resembles the keep at Brough. There are now so many buildings to the north and east of the keep that it is difficult to imagine it as the freestanding solitary structure which it must originally have been. However, its thick walls with their small grudgingly decorated windows still exude an aura of power and menace; no wonder it was called 'The Pagan Tower'.

139
Bolton Sculpture, Cumbria

The little church of All Saints at Bolton is basically a Norman structure with decorated doorways and round-headed windows. There is a curious stone here, however, which has been the source of some debate. It is now built into the exterior of the north wall, but it seems to be reused in that position. The stone depicts a conflict between two mounted knights armed with long lances. One knight has apparently broken the other's guard, and his lance has hit his opponent, knocking him

The massive keep of Brougham Castle built by Henry II after he had wrested Cumbria from Scottish control. Only the bottom three storeys were built by Henry; the topmost storey – distinguishable by the tall thin arrow slits – was a 13th-century addition.

backwards in his saddle. Although abraded, the knights are probably wearing chain mail and have pointed helmets and kite-shaped shields. The defeated knight has a fine pennon on his lance with deeply slashed edges.

Unfortunately, there is no recorded event which could account for this unusual stone, but it has been suggested that it commemorates a tournament held here. On stylistic grounds the work belongs to the early 12th century, so perhaps some Norman knight was thankful for his delivery from death or injury. It is possible, in view of the fact that it is the defeated knight who holds the pennon, that the 'underdog' won, and that he ascribed his good fortune to divine intervention. Nearby is a further small stone which bears the inscrip-

Map Reference: NY 636233 (metric map 91. 1-inch map 83)
Nearest Town: Appleby
Location: Bolton is just to the west of the A66, 2 miles (3.2 km) north-west of Appleby.

We do not know who these two knights were, but this stone might commemorate a tournament here.

tion, 'Sir Lawrence de Vere gives to the men of Bolton . . .' Was this the name of the victorious knight? We will probably never know.

140

Brough Castle and Town, Cumbria

The site of Brough was already old before the Normans used it. On the rounded hill beside the Swindale Beck the Roman fort of Veterae had been established in order to control the important road which led westwards from York to Carlisle and ultimately into Scotland. When William Rufus accomplished his conquest of Cumbria in 1092, a castle was built within the circuit of the Roman defences, and a little town grew up below it. Although quite large, the Norman castle takes up only about a third of the rectangular plan of the Roman fort, and the shape of the Roman ditches which protected the rest of the fort can still be seen quite clearly to the south.

Although the first castle here seems to have been built of stone, not much of it escaped the attentions of William the Lion in 1174. A few sections of the curtain wall, principally on the north side, survived, but that is all. Little time was lost in making good the damage, however, and the fine rectangular keep, so familiar from other northern sites like Norham and Newcastle, made its appearance.

The keep is now entered at second-storey level by a wooden staircase; parts of the original stone stair in the same position still survive. The lowest storey was used as a store, the next as a hall and above that was a solar; a further storey was added later. Below the keep is a fine cobbled courtyard which, although later, gives a good impression of such a space. Later, in the 13th and 14th centuries, a new hall block was built in this courtyard, the gatehouse was strengthened and the mighty Clifford's Tower was added to the south-east angle of the defences, reflecting Brough's continuing role as a major Border fortress.

The villages at Brough are also interesting since they illustrate the ways in which military and commercial priorities differed. In the first instance, a village with an open market green grew up below the castle in time-honoured fashion. Castle and village were served by the church of St Michael, which still retains some Norman fabric, and the place was called 'Church Brough'. However, even by 1196, there appears to have been a settlement at 'Market Brough', which is a little higher up the valley where the all-important road crossed the Beck. By the later 13th century, this second settlement appears to have become more dominant, and its market was actually granted a charter in 1330. But whatever the commercial attractions of Market Brough might have been, we must imagine that its traders must have been grateful for the sanctuary of the castle so close by.

Map Reference: NY 791141 (metric map 91. 1-inch map 84)
Nearest Town: Appleby
Location: Brough is 8 miles (12.8 km) south-east of Appleby on the A66(T). The castle is in Church (or Old) Brough on the south side of the town; it is in guardianship, open standard hours.

Cat's head from the church.

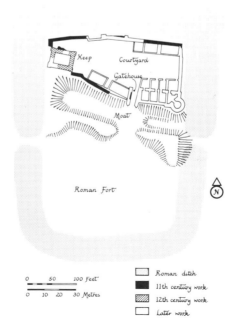

Plan of the castle.

141
Durham Castle and Cathedral

The Norman history of Durham had an inauspicious beginning since the townspeople refused to accept the Conqueror, but he marched northwards and the rebels capitulated. In 1069, William created Robert Comin Earl of Northumberland, and he came to Durham. The then bishop came out to warn Robert that he would be attacked, but he ignored him, saying that no man would dare. He entered the town with 700 men, and the following morning all were slain. William was furious, and this event was instrumental in his policy of 'Harrying the North'. That this was a horrendous episode is unquestioned; chroniclers record corpses littering the provinces, and refugees appeared as far south as Evesham in Worcestershire. The Anglo-Saxon Chronicle entry for 1069 says of Yorkshire that William had 'laid waste all the shire'. By the time of Domesday Book in 1086, the North was still littered with waste settlements. We can only guess at the scale of the carnage; today it would be called genocide. One reminder of that terrible time is the curfew bell which is still tolled in Durham at nine o'clock each evening except Saturdays, as originally ordained by the Conqueror himself.

Today our thoughts of Durham dwell on happier results of its Norman history. The cathedral and castle serve to remind us that it later became the major centre of Norman influence in the North. The cathedral in particular has been rightly claimed as the noblest example of the Romanesque style in England. Begun in 1093, the choir and transepts were rib-vaulted from the first – an astonishing feat; and although the choir vault cracked during the 13th century, the great vault over the nave shows that the masons improved their techniques as they went along. Incredibly, the whole church apart from the western towers was completed within 40 years. This great building, with its innovatory vaults, flying buttresses and great decorated drum pillars, influ-

enced designers all over the country. At nearby Pittington is a smaller version of the style, but at Dunfermline David, King of Scots, indulged in the sincere flattery of imitation, and even as far away as Orford in Suffolk we can see Durham-type drum pillars. This great church was to be the ecclesiastical 'caput' of the mighty bishops of Durham, and it was their initiative and enterprise which finally redeemed the promise of the northern lands which William had wasted.

Across the green from the cathedral is Durham Castle, which denoted the temporal power of the bishops. Although much altered, the basic plan of a shell keep on a motte with a bailey below probably goes back to 1072 when Waltheof, last of the Anglo-Saxon lords of Northumbria, built a castle here. The principal survival of the early castle is the superb chapel which was for many years used as a storeplace. This neglect probably saved it from later attentions, and its interior is a remarkably complete and unaltered example of early Norman work. The capitals of its six free-standing pillars are the finest collection of early carving in the country, and display a wide variety of decorative techniques at an early date. They are still effective now, but with their original paint they must have been magnificent.

Map Reference: NZ 273420 (metric map 88. 1-inch map 85)
Location: Durham Castle belongs to the University of Durham and is open to the public on Monday, Wednesday and Saturday, 2–4.30. It stands beside the cathedral.

Two of the splendid capitals from the 11th-century castle chapel. The top one has two opposed patterned cats whilst the lower one might represent the legend of St Eustace, patron of Huntsmen, and doubtless a favourite of the aristocratic users of the chapel.

The famous sanctuary knocker on the main north door of the cathedral, now replaced by a modern copy. The eyes would originally have been made of semi-precious stones or enamel.

Later, during the second half of the 12th century, Bishop Hugh Puiset (or Pudsey), whose work can also be seen in the great keep at Norham, built a splendid hall in the bailey below the motte. There have been later subdivisions and accretions onto Puiset's original grand first-floor hall, but its quality is manifest in the 'Norman Gallery' in the present castle. There is a superb entrance into the hall with double billet, lozenge and other ornament which is deeply cut in the finest style, and the south and west walls are enriched with chevron wall arcading between the decorated windows. The whole dates from about 1170, and must have provided a fitting presence chamber for the prince-bishops.

142
Newcastle Castle, Tyne and Wear

The 'new castle' from which this great city derived its name was the first castle built on the site of the present keep by Robert Curthose, the Conqueror's son. Robert had come north in 1080 after Walcher, Bishop of Durham and Earl of Northumberland, had been killed at Gateshead which lies just across the river from Newcastle. This outrage had been but the latest in a series of disturbances since the Conquest, of which the most famous had been the revolt of 1069 which resulted in the savage 'Harrying of the North'.

William responded to this dangerous situation by sending his son Robert, who founded a motte and bailey castle on a site opposite that of the massacre. (No trace of this structure remains, but it was presumably on the site now occupied by Henry II's keep tower). This tower, designed by Maurice 'the Engineer', prefigures many of the details of the great keep at Dover which Maurice also had charge of. Both have elaborate forebuildings, and each has a multiplicity of chambers contrived in the thickness of the upper walls.

The keep, which cost £911 10s to build, was originally three storeys high; the vaulted roof

and battlements are modern. It is rectangular in plan with three square and one multangular angle turrets. The complicated forebuilding takes up the whole of the eastern side of the keep, and contains a fine chapel at ground-floor level. The entrance to the castle was by the steps above the chapel roof, through a guardroom and then up a further flight of stairs to the main room of the keep. Off this room to the south is the king's chamber, built in the thickness of the wall. The hall itself is of very noble proportions, being fully 40 feet (12.2 metres) high with a gallery arranged in the thickness of the wall 30 feet (9 metres) above the ground. It is the scale of this room together with the quality of the chapel in the forebuilding which advertise royal patronage.

Map Reference: NZ 249640 (metric map 88, 1-inch map 78)
Location: The castle stands by the River Tyne on the north bank close to the railway station. It is open at the following times:
Apr–Sept Mon 2–5
          Tues–Sat 10–5
Oct–Mar Mon 2–4
          Tues–Sat 10–4

The keep from the river wall; the complicated forebuilding on the right contains a fine chapel. Although restored, it is remarkable that it survives at all in the centre of the bustling modern city.

Outside the keep, scanty traces of the triangular bailey survive, some of which are 12th-century. The 13th-century Black Gate entrance tower dominates the scene, but there is a 12th-century postern gate in the south wall above the river. This river wall has now been consolidated and it is possible to walk along it to a square angle tower which is probably also Norman. The keep occupies an exciting position in the heart of Newcastle where road and railway rush past. The proximity of these modern lines of communication reminds us that the castle was a jumping-off point for the subjugation of Northumbria.

143
Elsdon Motte, Northumberland

Elsdon, like Liddel Strength, was in the forefront of the fighting between England and Scotland. It was held by the Umfravilles who obtained it early in the 12th century on condition that they closed the Rede Valley, in which it lay, to robbers; this they effectively did. Elsdon commanded the Dere Street route cross the Border, and it provided a safe haven for travellers from the depredations of the lawless inhabitants of these disputed lands. It is likely that the broad village green at Elsdon was also laid out at this early period, since its dual function of providing a market-place for cattle traders and a safe refuge for those same herds in time of trouble would have been valuable from the first.

The plan of Elsdon Castle is of the simplest, consisting of a large flat-topped motte with slight traces of a bank round its edges and a large sub-rectangular bailey. There is a ditch between the motte and the bailey, and the bailey bank appears to return along the edge nearest the motte opposite the narrow entr-

View past the motte, which is on the right, showing ridge and furrow cultivation on the hillside beyond picked out by driven snow; a wild and empty landscape indeed!

ance. Although simple in conception, the scale of the earthworks dwarfs the little farmhouse beside it, and the bailey bank hangs menacingly above the road which led to the royal castle at Rothbury.

Elsdon is a classical frontier village, with the great castle providing an armed guard for the people gathered there. Elsdon church has been described as the 'tomb of Border life', and the mighty earthworks of its castle mark it out as the 'Capital of Redesdale'. But what a territory it was: in the words of an 18th-century vicar of Elsdon, 'There is not a single tree or hedgerow

Map Reference: NY 937935 (metric map 80. 1-inch map 77)
Nearest Town: Alnwick
Location: Elsdon is in the Cheviot Hills on the B6341 some 24 miles (38.6 km) south-west of Alnwick. The motte is on the north-east side of the village. Park beside the village hall and take the lane up from the hall; the castle is reached on the left.

The scale of the motte and bailey dwarfs the church on the wide village green.

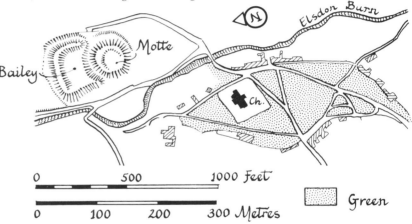

within twelve miles to break the force of the wind; it sweeps down like a deluge from hills capped with everlasting snow, and blasts almost the whole country into one continued barren desert.'

144
Brinkburn Priory, Northumberland

The principal interest of Brinkburn Priory resides in the Transitional nature of its architecture. Here we see throughout the structure the gradual change from the Romanesque features so familiar elsewhere in this book to the pointed arches and more fully rounded details of Gothic work. Nowhere is this change more apparent than in the doorway into the north aisle, which formed the principal entrance to the lay as opposed to the monastic church. Here a straightforward Romanesque doorway with four orders of moulding about its head, including beak heads, is surmounted by three trefoil-headed arches with freestanding shafts. Elsewhere in the building round and pointed arches are used with equal facility. Brinkburn, spanning as it does the closing years of the 12th century and the opening of the 13th, stands at the threshold of a new style and a new age.

Map Reference: NZ 116984 (metric map 81. 1-inch map 71)
Nearest Town: Morpeth
Location: Brinkburn is north-west of Morpeth. 2 miles (3.2 km) north of Morpeth on the A1, take the A697 Rothbury and Wooler road. In 8 miles (12.8 km) take the B6344 east to Rothbury. After 1½ miles (2.4 km) Brinkburn Priory is signposted down a narrow lane to the south. Park in the car-park and walk down the track to the priory (wellington boots are recommended!). The site is in guardianship and is open standard hours and Sunday mornings from 9.30, April–September.

The celebrated Transitional doorway at Brinkburn combines familiar Romanesque elements like the orders round the head of the door and the angle shafts with such Gothic details as the trefoil-headed arches and the free-standing columns in the arcade above.

12th-century seal of the priory depicting St Peter and St Paul.

145
Bamburgh Castle, Northumberland

Bamburgh must occupy one of the most impressive sites anywhere in England. The great keep, probably built during the reign of King Stephen (1135–54), stands above the harsh storm-swept coast looking out towards the Farne Islands. This place had been central to the history of Northumbria for many years before the Normans came. The presence of this great keep was a symbol of more than local domination; it set the seal on the overthrow of the Northumbrian royal house.

Map Reference: NO 185350 (metric map 75. 1-inch map 78)
Nearest Town: Wooler
Location: Bamburgh is on the coast and has a wonderful commanding position. From the A1 at Belford, half-way between Morpeth and Berwick, take the B1342 east for 5 miles (8 km) to Bamburgh. It is open to visitors daily as follows:
25 Mar–31 Oct
April, May, June, 1–5; July, Aug, 1–6 Sept, 1–5; Oct, 1–4.30
There are conducted tours when conditions permit. The car-park opens at 12 noon and there is a small charge payable. The tea-room opens at 1 p.m.

The keep as first built consisted of three storeys, although a fourth was added later in the roof space. Unusually, it is entered at the ground floor, but the strong natural defences of the site, doubtless enhanced by a substantial bailey wall, were probably proof against all save the most determined aggressor. The principal domestic accommodation was on the first floor, and consisted of a hall, chapel and solar. Only the first two floors are now open to the public, since the rest is still used as a private residence.

The citadel of Bamburgh on the storm-swept coast of Northumberland; already ancient when the Normans built a large square keep here during the troubled reign of Stephen.

146
Norham Castle, Northumberland

The first castle at Norham was built by Ranulf Flambard, Bishop of Durham, in 1121. This was almost certainly an earth and timber structure, probably with a 'ringwork' plan rather than a motte and bailey. Norham controlled an important ford over the River Tweed, and its exposed position resulted in its being destroyed by the Scots twice during the first half of the 12th century. During the reign of Henry II Hugh Puiset, the then Bishop of Durham, rebuilt the castle in stone, thus falling into line with the royal policy of stabilizing the Scottish Border. The date of this work is not certainly known, but it must have been before 1174 when Hugh fell from royal favour.

Norham's strategic importance meant that its castle remained in use up to 1550, and this has naturally resulted in many changes to Puiset's original structure. The lower storeys of the keep are Norman, and the roof scar survives in the later top storey. The forebuilding which provided access at first-floor level was removed during remodelling in the 15th century. Apart from the great keep, which must always have been the kernel of the

One of the windows in the south side of the chancel of Norham church; the elaborate chevrons round the head can be paralleled at Durham Cathedral.

Map Reference: NT 907476 (metric map 75. 1-inch map 64)
Nearest Town: Berwick upon Tweed
Location: Norham is right on the Scottish border on the River Tweed. Take the A698 south-west for 6 miles (9.6 km) and turn west into Norham on the B6470. The castle is in guardianship and is open standard hours.

Right: The shattered remains of the great keep seen across the inner moat. This powerful castle was the northern outpost of the bishops of Durham and the advanced design of its hall-keep reflects their patronage.

defences, both the inner and outer wards were defended by curtain walls and square gate towers. Whilst the remaining elements of the early castle are, with the exception of the keep, unimpressive, the scale of the original defences is reflected by the area of the enclosures.

The village of Norham is also interesting since it has a broad triangular green which was presumably a market-place. The castle dominates the town in the same way as at Egremont, and off another angle of the green is the church of St Cuthbert. The church shows extensive traces of its Norman origins, and it was probably built as part of the same campaign as the castle in the third quarter of the 12th century. The main survivals of the early church are the chancel excluding the easternmost bay, the south nave arcade, three bases of the north arcade and the lower parts of the side walls. The church was evidently a substantial structure, as became the episcopal owners of the castle and town.

147
The Border Abbeys

The four abbeys of Melrose, Dryburgh, Kelso and Jedburgh were all founded either directly by or under the aegis of David I. The influence exerted by these centres of culture and learning in these remote places was considerable, despite their troubled history of sackings by invading armies. The abbeys were colonized by monks from Rievaulx, Alnwick, Tiron and Beauvais in France. They were Cistercians, Premonstratensians, Tironesians and Augustinian canons. These titles must have seemed even more bizarre and incomprehensible to the average Scottish layman of the 12th century than they do to us today. They came from a distant European milieu, from a foreign culture in which the differences between these orders were vital matters for debate. Here in Scotland they indicated the broadening vision of her rulers, their desire to take part in the wider world. Though alive to the benefits of such innovations, David also sought to safeguard the Scottish Church, for whilst he accepted the authority of Rome in matters spiritual, he always resisted the supremacy of Canterbury.

Map References (metric/1-inch map numbers follow each entry in parentheses):
Kelso NT 728337 (74/70)
Jedburgh NT 650204 (74/70)
Dryburgh NT 591317 (74/70)
Melrose NT 549342 (73/70)
Locations: All four monuments are in guardianship and are open standard hours; all are well signposted.

Looking upwards across the cloister at the gaunt nave of Jedburgh. The church was built from 1140 onwards and was not completed until the mid-13th century; this accounts for the Transitional nature of the building in which round and pointed arches are used side by side.

What remains of these great abbeys? At Melrose, all the Norman buildings have gone barring a few foundations of the claustral ranges. Dryburgh has the west front of the church and much of the claustral range including a vaulted chapter house. At Kelso the mighty west end is a shattered remnant of an unusually grand Transitional structure which featured transepts at the west end of the nave as well as at the crossing. It is only at Jedburgh, where the gaunt nave of the abbey church dominates the Jed River, that we get any real impression of the magnificence of those great abbeys. As we look more closely at the stonework of the west door, scarred by fires of invading armies as well as by time, we are moved to wonder not at the madness of destruction but at the faith which remained undaunted in the face of seven recorded attacks.

148
Castle Sween, Strathclyde

Castle Sween, which was probably built around 1200, illustrates the gradual filtering of Norman ideas into western and northern Scotland. The castle was apparently built by a certain Suibhne, 'Sween' being a corruption of his Gaelic name, who had no direct connection with the Normans at all. However, the idea of the castle had obviously commended itself even in these remote quarters and hence we must take some account of it. The difficulty with Castle Sween is that whereas it does show certain features of design and construction which are of Norman inspiration, we cannot really call the building a 'castle'. This is because its builder was not a feudal lord in the sense that Scots lords in the Lowlands became,

The simple angular plan reminds us of early Norman castles in England, an impression heightened by the shallow pilaster buttresses on the external faces of the walls.

The delicate doorway from the cloister into the church at Dryburgh.

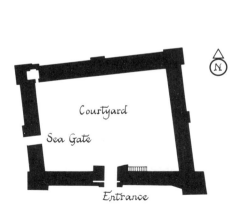

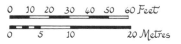

The elaborate north door into the western crossing of Kelso abbey church; although fully Romanesque it actually dates to c. 1180–1200.

Map Reference: NR 713789 (metric map 62. 1-inch map 58)
Nearest Town: Lochgilphead
Location: The castle stands on the coast overlooking Loch Sween. From Lochgilphead, take the A817 north-east in the Oban direction; 2 miles (3.2 km) later turn west on the B841. In 3 miles (5 km) take the B8025 west and in a further 2 miles (3.2 km) turn south down the minor road which runs down the east side of Loch Sween. The castle is a further 8 miles (12.8 km) down this road. It is a guardianship site and is open at any reasonable time.

but he was a chieftain within the clan system. In this difference, we touch on the difficulty of the definition of the castle, for Sween should probably be called a fort since it probably acted only as a stronghold rather than as the caput of a feudal estate.

Apart from these reservations, Sween appears as a small quadrangular shell keep with massive walls which originally contained wooden buildings. Such architectural features as there are comprise a round-headed entrance arch and flattish pilasters in Norman style. The entrance was protected by a draw-bar and the inner courtyard contained a well. A horizontal chase in the inner faces of the walls was designed to accept a now-vanished timber floor. Sween is a small and lonely outpost of Norman architectural influence; only the Romanesque splendours of Kirkwall Cathedral in the Orkneys exceed it for unexpectedness.

149
Tyninghame Church, Lothian

Even in its ruined state, the church at Tyninghame is still a most interesting structure. The plan of western tower, nave, chancel and apse is straightforward enough and in this it closely resembles Dalmeny. However, there are certain details here which are if anything finer. Still miraculously standing, the chancel and apse arches have the customary chevron moulding, but the capitals of the chancel arch are enriched with fish-scale decoration on the south side and volutes on the north. In the apse, the vaulting shafts have collars half-way up rather in the fashion of St Peter's Northampton. This is an unusual detail, and provides strong evidence of the high quality of the Tyninghame work; perhaps the link with the English Midlands reflects one of King David's personal titles which was Earl of Northampton. Whilst the south door at Dalmeny is instructive, it is still barbarous; here we see a lighter touch in which the logic of the structure is more clearly dominant.

The church from the west; the base of the tower can be seen in the right foreground and the fine chancel and apse arches still miraculously stand.

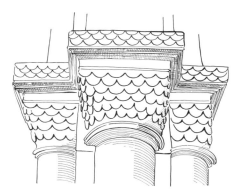

Southern impost of the chancel arch with fish-scale decoration.

Map Reference: NT 620798 (metric map 67. 1-inch map 63)
Nearest Town: Dunbar
Location: The ruined church is in the grounds of Tyninghame House. This is on the east side of the A198, on the opposite side of the main road from the village. If the grounds are closed, it is usually possible to obtain permission to view the church from the Estate Office.

150
Dalmeny Church, Lothian

The small church at Dalmeny is justly celebrated as a gem of Romanesque architecture. Apart from the later western tower, which is built on Norman foundations, the nave, chancel and apse are intact. The founder of the church was almost certainly Gospatric who, like his monarch King David, was the descendant of dispossessed Anglo-Saxon nobility, in this case the Earl of Northumberland. He was nephew to the Earl of Dunbar who fell at the Battle of the Standard in 1138, and must have stood high in royal favour. It is likely that the fine sarcophagus near the south door of the church contained his body, and its ornate decoration suggests that it was displayed within his church.

The external walls are enriched with chevron moulded window heads, a scrolled string course and on the chancel and apse a fine though weathered corbel table. It is the south doorway which merits the closest attention, however, since it is a remarkable essay in sustained decoration.

Although weathered, it is possible to suggest interpretations for most of the figural panels in the second and third orders. They appear in the main to be derived from the Bestiary, which was a medieval treatise in which Christian morals were illustrated by real and mythological creatures. Bestiaries had existed since early Christian times, but they enjoyed a particular vogue during the later 12th century. The use of the imagery here at Dalmeny suggests that the church's patron was 'up with the times'.

Some scenes are taken from real life, however, and their inclusion with the Bestiary figures suggests that they were intended to be regarded in the same light, as moral verities. Significantly, the first of these figures on the bottom left probably shows a lord swearing fealty to his king, thus underlining the divine sanction of the feudal hierarchy. Similarly, again in the outer order, we see the king who

rules by Divine Right, the feudal lord who held his land by the king's (royal) authority and finally the knight who defended the king's peace. We may be sure that the significance of these scenes was not lost on the 12th-century users of this doorway.

Inside, the church is surprisingly light because the windows are relatively large. There are fine arches into the chancel and apse which are roofed with stone vaults springing from grotesque corbels. There are sockets for a light beam in the capitals of the apse arch which either carried a cloth to veil the altar in Lent or else a carving of the Crucifixion. Finally, there is an excellent collection of masons' marks inside the building, some of which recur at Leuchars and Dunfermline.

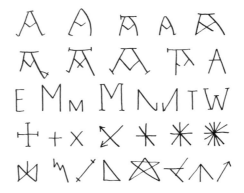

Masons' marks inside the church.

Map Reference: NT 144775 (metric map 65. 1-inch map 62)
Nearest Town: Queensferry
Location: Dalmeny village can be quite tricky to find as it is right beside the major A90 dual carriageway leading to the Forth Bridge, but it is not directly accessible from it. Take the B924 to Dalmeny/ Queensferry, then the first left for half a mile (0.8 km), then right into Dalmeny main street and the church is on the left, set back from the road.

The remarkable south doorway. The pale innermost order is a 19th-century restoration, but the rest appears to be original. Note the scar of a later porch roof to each side of the head of the arch.

The two decorated outer orders of the southern doorway. The numbered panels, some of which are too weathered for positive identification, probably represent the following themes:

1. Lord (of Dalmeny?) doing homage to his king.
2. Centaur perhaps shooting at a dragon symbolizing the Harrowing of Hell.
3. Tree of Life.
4. Wodewose or Wild Man(?), often battles with a lion symbolizing Man's mastery of fleshly desires.
5. Whale with two mariners who have landed on his back, believing it to be dry land – 'Look before you leap'!
6. King or Christ in Majesty.
7. Mantichora with the head of a man, body of an ox and the tail of a scorpion.
8. Mounted knight – perhaps the founder of the church.
9. Serpent (?) or merely a panel of interlace.
10. Phoenix, the knotted tail representing the flames from which it was reborn.
11. Terrobuli, male and female stones which burst into flames when brought together, probably symbolizing lust.
12. Basilisk, hatched from the egg of a cock incubated by a toad – the serpent on the right might represent the beast's tail.

13. Griffin with the forepart of an eagle and the hindpart of a lion, said to guard treasure and to destroy the covetous.
14. Superficially resembles a dragon, but probably a wyvern since it only has two feet.
15. Peacock or perhaps an eagle rising from the water after having burned off its old plumage by mounting to the sun.
16. Probably a deer or hart which was said to pant for cooling streams after its conflict with fiery serpents, shown below.
17. Pelican in her peity shown feeding her young with blood from her own breast, symbolizing the self-sacrifice of Christ.
18. Probably a pair of dragons, symbolizing evil.
19. Lion, either a symbol of St Mark or of good when it fights the dragon of evil.
20. Griffin with forepart of an eagle and hindpart of a lion.
21. A serpent which crawls through a tight crack in the rocks to slough its skin, representing Man putting off sin.
22. Agnus Dei – the Lamb of God bearing the Cross.

151
Dunfermline Abbey, Fife

The nave of Dunfermline Abbey stands as a grand tribute to the Canmore dynasty and in particular to the reforming zeal of King David I. Under his able leadership many Anglo-Norman institutions, which he had imbibed during his boyhood in England, were introduced into Scotland. Here at Dunfermline we see his regal vision made manifest. For whilst David founded many monasteries, more than any other king of his age, Dunfermline was undoubtedly intended as the spiritual focus of his kingdom.

The site had already been favoured by the attentions of David's mother, Queen Margaret, who had founded a small Benedictine priory here in 1072. But it was only after 1129, when David made the site into an abbey, that Dunfermline began to take on its present appearance. Work was sufficiently advanced to allow at least part of the structure to be dedicated in 1150. This ceremony was doubtless attended by much pomp, and the setting of one of the consecration crosses, which was set with gold and precious stone, survives in the north aisle. Dunfermline became one of the wealthiest abbeys in Scotland, and no fewer than eight Scottish kings were buried here including David himself in 1153.

Today, the nave is all that remains of David's great church but it is impressive enough. The massive cylindrical piers with chevron and spiral ornament, the scalloped octagonal capitals and the severe crenellated moulding round the heads of the nave arches provide the same feeling of gravitas as the nave of Durham from which they are so obviously derived. But kingly restraint is evident in the treatment of the triforium and clerestory, since both are plain. On the eastern processional doorway in the south aisle we can see the high quality of the detailing of the building. Here, owing to the fortuitous siting of a royal burial vault in 1602 or thereabouts, the carving of the capitals, abaci and extrados

are as fresh as the day they were made.

Dunfermline preserves another link with the Canmore dynasty. 'King Malcolm's Tower' stands on a rocky crag near the abbey, and although in part barbarously 'restored', its popular association with Malcolm Canmore commands our interest. We are reminded of the opening lines of the famous ballad of 'Sir Patrick Spens':

> The King sits in Dunfermline toon,
> Drinking the bluid-red wine . . .

The ballad, of course, belongs to a later age, but the west window in the nave of the abbey church sums up the deep significance of this place for the Scottish nation. There are depicted Malcolm Canmore, his wife St Margaret of Scotland and those two later heroes Bruce and Wallace. Dunfermline Abbey became the shrine of Scotland, just as its founder King David had intended.

Map Reference: NO 087874 (metric map 65. 1-inch map 55)
Location: The abbey is in the old town which is on the south-west side of the city. There are car-parks close by. The old nave is in guardianship and is open standard hours.

Masons' marks.

Above: The imposts of the 'hidden doorway' into the cloister are as fresh as the day they were made, thanks to their later protection inside a tomb.

Left: The mighty Durham-style drum pillars of the nave illustrate King David's desire to emulate Norman taste.

152

Leuchars Church, Fife

Leuchars church stands at the centre of the old village on a mound beside the road. It presents a strange and arresting spectacle with its two tiers of bold external arcading and bizarre post-medieval eastern tower. Only the chancel and apse of the Norman church remain, but they speak eloquently of the aspirations of the family who built them. 'Ness son of William' is first heard of in 1145; he became Lord of Leuchars, where he evidently lived in some state in the castle near the church, and was Sheriff of Perth by 1160. His daughter Orable was the mother of Saher de Quincy, a great magnate in both Scotland and England, who was made Earl of Winchester. Ness was the founder of Leuchars church, and the scale of his ambition is evidenced both by the quality of the building itself and by the illustrious career of his grandson.

Externally, the apse has two tiers of blank arcades springing from coupled column shafts. The chancel walls have similar decoration in the upper tier, but the lower bears delicately fluted intersecting arcades. Both chancel and apse are surmounted by a fine corbel table which on the better preserved north side boasts muzzled bears like Dalmeny, Janus heads and grotesques. The string courses and window heads are alive with well-cut guilloche, chevron and billet moulding – the whole a remarkable display of the Norman decorative repertoire.

Upon entering the Norman chancel it is the tall and noble proportions which impress, and the details do not disappoint. The chancel arch has well-modelled decoration about its head including an outer order of faceted chequerwork designed to catch the light. The apse arch has competent chevron work, with an outer order of alternating billets. The underside of this arch bears a most unusual motif of crosses set between the chevron moulding on each side. Inside the apse the fluted ribs of the vault spring from vaulting shafts which rest upon corbels bearing cat-heads and Dalmeny-type muzzled bears. Notice in the apex of the apse vault there is a chevron-decorated stone with an iron ring set in it. This was probably the fixing for the Norman sanctuary lamp.

On the north wall of the chancel there is a large collection of masons' marks, and almost every stone has one. On the south side they are less well preserved, perhaps due either to recutting or cleaning of the surface. It occasions no surprise that several of these marks are repeated at Dalmeny and, perhaps, at Dunfermline Abbey. King David set the pace of innovation by his espousal of things Norman, and at Leuchars and Dalmeny we see his 'new men' following in their master's footsteps.

Map Reference: NO 465215 (metric map 59. 1-inch map 56)
Nearest Town: St Andrews
Location: From St Andrews take the road north-west to Dundee. Leuchars is 6 miles (9.6 km) along this road. Pass by the RAF base and turn into the old town where the church can be clearly seen.

Masons' marks.

The apse is surmounted by a curious post-medieval tower, but there is no mistaking the superb Romanesque blank arcading on the lower walls.

Two of the beast-heads from the interior of the apse, one of which is a muzzled bear of a type also found at Dalmeny.

153

The Central Scottish Towers, Tayside and Fife

There are five of these lofty towers in the 'group', at Muthill, Dunblane, Markinch, Dunning and St Andrews. They belong to a general type of tower which was relatively common in late Anglo-Saxon England, but which seems to have continued here in Scotland well into the 12th century. The towers at Dunblane Cathedral and St Rule's church at St Andrews are perhaps of the later 11th century, the latter being associated with Queen Margaret (1070–93). The chronology of the other towers is uncertain; Dunning at least is probably of the 12th century since there is a piece of scallop-moulded stone above the south door which, if not inserted, could hardly be earlier.

The functions of these towers are, like those of their Anglo-Saxon forebears, disputed. That they were used as belfries is clear enough since there are large paired openings in their topmost stages. But the occurrence of doorways at the top of the St Andrews tower in conjunction with apparently structural square holes at the angles suggests some sort of vanished timber superstructure. This feature is familar to students of Anglo-Saxon towers, and might be concerned with the display of relics or banners on feast days. There is a similar doorway on the south side of the tower at Dunning, but there the smaller holes appear throughout the structure, and might be best seen as scaffolding supports. In view of these and other differences such as the presence or absence of external stages and string courses, as well as the likely chronological span, it might be that the 'group' is more a reflection of patterns of survival rather than common architectural inspiration.

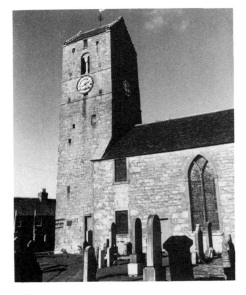

Map References (metric/1-inch map numbers follow each entry in parentheses):
St Andrews NO 514167 (59/56)
Dunning NO 019145 (58/55)
Muthill NN 868173 (58/55)
Dunblane NN 782014 (58/54)
Markinch NO 298019 (59/56)
Locations: St Rule's Tower at St Andrews is part of the cathedral site and is in guardianship, open standard hours. Dunning church stands in the centre of the town and has been taken into the care of the National Trust for Scotland. Muthill Tower is part of the ruined church on the north side of the town. It is in the care of a local trust.

Left: St Rule's Church, St Andrews.

Below left: The tower of Dunning Church.

Below: Muthill Tower.

Detail of the decorated string course on the tower at Muthill.

154

Kincardine Deer Park, Grampian

Hunting, especially for deer, had been a favourite pursuit of the Scots nobility for hundreds of years before the Normans came. But the organization of hunting – by limiting who could kill deer, what the fine would be if that law were transgressed, who could hunt over particular lands and the direct involvement of the king in the granting of such hunting rights – was a Norman innovation. During the 12th century, there is evidence that the concept of 'Forest Law' was introduced into south and central Scotland, and that it followed the broad outlines of the Normans' hunting laws in England.

In this process we see once again the influence of King David's Norman childhood, and of the demands of his new Norman subjects. For whilst the general thrust of the Forest Laws was the same as those in England, it appears that they were less rigorous and also allowed landowners other than the king himself to hold hunting rights. The concept of the Forest Laws is explained more fully in the entry for the New Forest, but they were basically concerned with the restriction of hunting rights either to the king himself or, by grant, to others whom he appointed.

In the nature of things, hunting 'forests' leave few traces on the ground, since they were legal rather than physical entities. Indeed the very word 'forest' gives a misleading impression, for many hunting forests were not wooded at all. 'Forest' is a term of art in this connection, and refers to a hunting reserve, irrespective of vegetation cover.

There are, however, two features associated with organized hunting which might be expected to leave physical evidence behind them; these are the hunting lodge and the deer park. During the early Middle Ages in Scotland, hunting 'lodges' were apparently not purpose-built as they were later, but were merely a further function served by the ubiquitous castle. At Kincardine, it was to the castle of that name that the hunters repaired after a day's sport. Little can now be seen of the early castle at Kincardine, but the reason for its inclusion in this book is that part of the deer park 'pale' near the castle can still be seen.

Deer parks were intended as hunting 'reserves' in which deer were held captive, either to ensure a successful hunt for the owner when he chose or else to assure a supply of venison for his table. The park 'pale' was a deer-proof boundary consisting of a ditch with an earthen bank which was probably topped by a palisade. Park pales differ from defensive works in that the ditch was inside the bank, in order to make it more difficult for the deer to escape.

At Clatterin' Brig near Kincardine we can see the best remains of a deer park to survive from early medieval Scotland; it was probably built by William the Lion late in the 12th century. The pale comprises a bank varying from about

Map References: NO 632772–NO 662777 (metric map 45. 1-inch map 43)
Nearest Town: Laurencekirk
Locations: From Laurencekirk, which is on the A94 between Stonehaven and Forfar, take the B9120 north-west to Fettercairn (4 miles/6.4 km). Take the B974 north to Clatterin' Brig (4 miles/6.4 km); about a quarter to half a mile (0.4–0.8 km) before the village you see a piece of forestry on the left and a trackway with a sign saying Arnbarrow. Follow the road right round to some cottages, park nearby and follow the track through the forestry plantation onto the top of the moor. The moor is used for grouse shooting and is private property, so permission should be sought in advance.

For the less adventurous, you can also see the pale from the road on the Banchory side of Clatterin' Brig. There is a ruined house on the west side of the road, and looking across the valley to the east the park pale can be seen climbing up the valley on the other side.

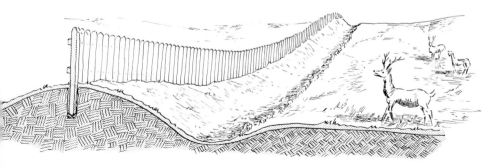

An impression of the pale as first built; the bank is heightened by a timber palisade and the ditch occurs inside the bank to increase the distance a deer would have to jump in order to escape.

The deer park pale striking across the moor. The heather-grown bank appears as a hump in the middle ground and the ditch is marked by a lighter line to the right of the bank in the distance.

10 to 15 feet (3 to 4.5 metres) in thickness and standing to a height of 5 feet (1.5 metres) above the bottom of an internal ditch 6 to 10 feet (2 to 3 metres) broad. The line of the main pale can be traced with only minor breaks from the edge of Garrol Wood to the west to a point south of Clatterin' Brig in the east. A small northerly extension of the main pale crosses the Black Burn of Arnbarrow and finishes south of Redstone Hill.

The best view of the park can be had where the track from Arnbarrow crosses the line of the pale, and towards the east you can see it going up the hillside beyond and breaking against the skyline on the hill top. On the skyline you can see very clearly the nick of the inner ditch on the right and the bank on the left. The track is still well used by deer, as the many spoors indicate. If you proceed carefully you might be lucky enough to see a deer which might even be a descendant of those hunted by the kings of Scotland 800 years ago.

155
The Bass of Inverurie, Grampian

Although considerably tidied-up during the last century, when landscaping works were put in hand for the neighbouring municipal cemetery, the Bass must rank as one of Scotland's most imposing motte and bailey castles. The Bass itself, which is partly natural and partly artificial, is a large regular mound rising to a height of 50 feet (164 metres). The 'Little Bass', or 'Castle Yards' as it was formerly known, formed an unusual raised bailey, and was apparently cut off from the motte as late as 1883. Both mounds are now flat-topped, and no trace of the bailey bank can be discerned.

This castle should be seen as representing a late stage in the process of feudalization initiated by King David I. The Celtic district of Garioch in which Inverurie lay was granted by William the Lion to his brother David, Earl of Huntingdon, in 1179–82. This David then set about establishing a feudal fief on the Anglo-Norman model with the Castle of the Bass, which may already have existed, as its caput and the new burgh or town of Inverurie as his revenue base. Both town and castle were well sited near the confluence of the Waters of the

Map Reference: NJ 781206 (metric map 38. 1-inch map 40)
Location: Inverurie is on the A96 north-west of Aberdeen. The Bass is situated in the town cemetery on the south-east side of Inverurie beside the River Urie. It is reached by taking the B993 to Newmill/Whiterashes and is a quarter of a mile (0.4 km) up this road on the east side, just below the railway bridge.

The motte at Inverurie beside the reedy river.

Ury and Don, and they effectively controlled the traffic and trade of the new fief. The Bass must have provided an excellent symbol of the dominance of the new feudal lord, though it is suggested that its cramped site forced a move away to Caskieben before too long.

156
The Peel Ring of Lumphanan, Grampian

The unusual name of this site, which means the 'palisaded enclosure' of Lumphanan, immediately suggests that it was out of the general run of Scottish castles. Lumphanan is one of only a handful of 'curtain wall' castles known in Scotland. This type of castle, which was common enough in England and Wales, departed from the motte and bailey type seen at Inverurie by having a single large enclosure for buildings rather than a motte with a tower and a bailey for ancillary structures.

The castle consists of a large, roughly circular mound which is probably a heightened natural knoll, surrounded by a wide ditch. Although flat now, the edges of the mound would have been strengthened by a crenellated wooden palisade with a fighting platform behind. There would have been a timber gate tower and probably a wooden causeway in place of the existing cobbled approach. The width of the ditch, about 50 feet (164 metres), would have compensated for the lack of height, and it would have made a safe refuge. The idea of using water defences in this way was generally a later medieval one, but here we see an early adaptation of military architecture to local conditions. The castle was probably founded late in the 12th century, and the larger defended area would have been useful in its function as an administrative centre. One of the main disadvantages of the motte and bailey plan was the lack of open space, a problem which the curtain wall castle neatly overcame.

Map Reference: NJ 577037 (metric map 37. 1-inch map 39)
Nearest Town: Banchory
Location: From Banchory take the A980 north to Lumphanan (10 miles/16 km). The Peel Ring is about half a mile (0.8 km) south-west of the village. The main road kinks sharply northwards where a minor road to Dess carries straight on. Take this minor road and the Peel Ring is found just the other side of a disused railway bridge. It is in guardianship and is open at any reasonable time.

The Peel Ring of Lumphanan seen across its wide and boggy moat; the cobbled pathway in the centre still marks the entrance to the site.

List of Norman Kings

1066–1087 William the Conqueror

1087–1100 William II (Rufus)

1100–1135 Henry I (Beauclerc)

1135–1154 Stephen

1154–1189 Henry II

1189–1199 Richard I (Coeur de Lion)

1199–1216 John (Lackland)

Glossary

ABACUS (plural abaci)   The flat slab on the top of a capital.

ACANTHUS   A plant with thick, fleshy, scalloped leaves used in the ornamentation of capitals; inspired by classical decoration.

ADVOWSON   The right of the patron of a church to nominate a new parson.

ADZE   Tool used in masonry which resembled an axe with an arched blade at right angles to the handle.

AISLE, AISLED HALL   In a church, an aisle is a space parallel to and divided from the main nave, choir or transept. In secular architecture, it describes a building in which the main rectangular space is flanked by parallel aisles.

AMBULATORY   An aisle enclosing an apse or straight-ended sanctuary, often used for processional purposes.

APSE   A semi-circular termination of a chapel or chancel.

ARCADE, BLANK ARCADE   An arcade is a row of arches on pillars or columns; a 'blank' arcade is one in which the arches are left solid, and normally refers to surface decoration on walls.

ASHLAR   Masonry constructed of square hewn stones.

AUGUSTINIAN ORDER   Popularly known as 'Black Canons' from the colour of their habits, they were an order of priests organized on monastic lines.

BAPTISTERY   Part of a church used for baptism.

BARBICAN   An outward extension of a gateway.

BAROQUE   17th- and 18th-century architecture characterized by exuberant decoration and expansive curvaceous forms.

BASTION   Projecting part of a fortification.

BATTER   The inclined face of a wall, normally at the base.

BATTLEMENT   Indented parapet of defensive wall made up of merlons (raised parts) and embrasures (the gaps between).

BAY   Division of wall between columns or buttresses.

BEAK HEAD   A norman decorative motif consisting of a row of bird, animal or human heads biting a roll moulding.

BELFRY   Bell tower, attached or separate; bell space in church tower.

BENEDICTINE ORDER   The 'Black Monks' of the order founded in 529 by St Benedict of Subiaco. The Rule of St Benedict formed the basis of practically the whole of later monasticism in medieval Europe.

BESTIARY   Medieval moralizing treaty on beasts, often illustrated and which provided the inspiration for much 12th-century decoration.

BILLET   A Norman moulding consisting of several bands of raised short cylinders or squares placed at regular intervals.

BOSS   An ornamental knob or projection covering the intersection of ribs in a vault, often carved.

BUTTRESS   A mass of masonry projecting from or built against a wall to give additional strength.

CABLE MOULDING   Carving imitating thick twisted rope.

CAMERA   A private withdrawing room.

CAPITAL   The head or crowning feature of a column. Cushion capitals were popular in early Norman times, and other common types were scalloped, foliate, waterleaf and historiated – the last so-called because it depicted scenes from a narrative tale of 'history'.

CENTAUR   Mythical creature with the body of a horse and the upper parts of a man.

CHANCEL   The east end of a church where the main altar is placed; reserved for clergy and choir.

CHAPTER HOUSE   Room in a monastery where the business of the community was transacted and where a chapter of the Monastic Rule was read each day.

CHEVRON   Bent bar of inverted V shape.

CISTERCIAN ORDER   A 'reformed' order founded in 1098 at Citeaux in Burgundy, a stricter offshoot of the Benedictines.

CLAUSTRAL   Of the cloister, monastic buildings.

CLERESTORY   The upper stage of the main walls of a church above the aisle roofs, pierced by windows.

CLUNIAC ORDER   Founded at Cluny in Burgundy early in the 10th century, this order became famous for its elaborate liturgy and ceremonial and for its patronage of the arts.

CORBEL TABLE   A range of corbels, which are projecting blocks of stone supporting a beam or other horizontal member, and which are often elaborately carved.

CORINTHIAN   One of the three Greek architectural orders, having a bell-shaped capital with rows of acanthus leaves.

CROSSING   The space at the intersection of the nave, chancel and transepts of a church; often surmounted by a crossing tower.

CRUCIFORM   Cross-shaped.

CRYPT   Underground room beneath a church, often used for burials and the display of relics.

CURTAIN WALL   A wall which connects two towers of a fortification; so-called because it 'hangs' between the (taller) towers.

DAIS   Raised platform at the end of a hall for a high table, throne, etc.

DIAPER   Ornamental design of diamonds.

DRIP MOULD   Projection above a window or door which keeps rain from the parts below; also called a 'hood mould'.

DRUM PILLAR   Large cylindrical columns, e.g. in the nave at Durham Cathedral.

EARLY ENGLISH   The architectural style which succeeded Romanesque and which featured pointed arches, lancet windows and simple tracery.

EXTRADOS   The external face of an arch.

FINIAL   Ornament finishing off the apex of a roof pediment or gable.

FOREBUILDING   An additional building against a keep, in which is the stair to the doorway and sometimes a chapel.

FREESTONE   Any stone that cuts well in all directions and especially fine-grained limestone or sandstone.

FRESCO   Method of painting a picture in watercolour on a wall or ceiling before the plaster is dry.

GABLETTE   A decorative motif or feature in the form of a small gable.

GILBERTINE ORDER   A double order of monks and nuns founded during the 12th century by St Gilbert of Sempringham.

GOTHIC   The pointed-arch style prevalent in western Europe from the 12th to the 16th century.

GROTESQUE   A bizarre distorted figure or design.

GUILLOCHE   A pattern of interlacing bands forming a plait and used as an enrichment on a moulding.

HATCHING   A pattern of parallel lines on a surface.

HERRINGBONE WORK   Type of walling in which the stones are laid diagonally rather than horizontally. Alternate courses lie in opposite directions, forming zigzag or herringbone pattern on the wall face.

ICONOGRAPHY   Illustration of a subject by drawings or figures.

IMPOST.   Bracket set into a wall upon which the end of an arch rests.

INTERLACE   A pattern created by intertwining one or more ribbons.

JOGGLE   A term used to describe a joint in masonry which is designed to prevent the two stones from slipping or sliding, by means of a notch in one and a corresponding projection in the other.

KEEP   Great Tower or donjon, the main element of a castle.

KNIGHTS TEMPLAR   A military order originally formed to protect pilgrims to the Holy Land, suppressed in 1312.

LABEL STOP   An ornamental or figural boss at the beginning and end of a drip mould.

LAVATORIUM   A place for washing hands before meals in a monastery.

LAY BROTHER   A man who has taken the habit and vows of a religious order but is employed in manual labour and is excused other duties.

LOZENGE   A diamond shape.

LYNCHETS   Long parallel terraces commonly found on hill slopes and formed by the extension of ploughing onto marginal land.

MANDORLA   An almond shape.

MEDALLION   Decorative panel in the shape of a medal.

MINSTER   The mother church (not necessarily a cathedral or monastery) serving an area eventually divided up into parishes.

MISERICORD   Shelving projection on underside of hinged seat in choir stall, serving when seat was turned up to support person standing.

MONOLITH   A single stone.

MOTTE AND BAILEY   Castle comprising a mound of earth or turf (motte) and a defended open courtyard (bailey).

NAILHEAD DECORATION   Consisting of small pyramids set in a band.

NARTHEX   A porch or vestibule at the entrance of a church.

NAVE   The western arm of a church, which normally forms the main body of the structure.

NIMBUS   Bright cloud or halo over the head of a saint.

NOOK-SHAFT   Shaft set in in the angle of a pier or respond or wall, or the angle of the jamb of a window or doorway.

ORDER   In Norman architecture, a pair of shafts or columns on either side of an arch together with the arch itself. Openings can be framed by one or more orders which recede in a series of concentric steps.

PALMETTE   A fan-shaped ornament composed of narrow divisions like a palm leaf.

PASSING BRACE   A long stiffening piece in a roof.

PENNON   A long narrow flag, triangular or swallow-tailed, often attached to a lance.

PIANO NOBILE   Principal storey of a house with the reception rooms; usually on the first floor.

PILASTER   Shallow rectangular column projecting only slightly from a wall.

PISCINA   Basin for washing the Communion or Mass vessels, provided with a drain; normally in or against the south wall of the chancel near the altar.

PRECINCT   Space around a church or monastery enclosed by a wall.

PRESBYTERY   The part of the church lying east of the choir; it is the part where the altar is placed.

PRIORY   Monastic house whose head is a prior or prioress, not an abbot or abbess.

PSYCHOMACHIA   Poem describing the symbolic conflict between the Virtues and the Vices.

QUATREFOIL   Symmetrical four-lobed shape.

RAMPART   Stone wall or wall of earth surrounding a castle or other fortress.

RELIC   Revered object associated with a saint. This could either be a piece of clothing or some similar item, or else a fragment of the saint's body.

REVETMENT   Retaining wall or facing.

RINGWORK   A type of enclosure castle with earth and timber defences and normally without a keep or motte; they could be any shape, but many were circular or nearly so.

ROGATIONTIDE   Days of prayer and fasting in the early summer associated especially with prayers for the harvest.

ROMANESQUE   That style in architecture which was current in the 11th and 12th centuries and preceded the Gothic style; the 'round-arch' style.

RUNES   Letters of the Germanic alphabet which was developed by modifying Greek and Roman characters to suit carving in wood and stone.

SANCTUARY   Area around the main altar of a church.

SARCOPHAGUS   Stone coffin, often decorated with sculpture.

SEDILIA   Seats for the priests, usually three in number, on the south side of the chancel of a church.

SHELL KEEP   Type of keep in which the buildings were ranged round the inner face of a concentric wall on top of a motte, leaving an open space at the centre.

SOLAR   Upper living room of a medieval house.

SPRINGING   Level at which an arch rises from its supports.

STIFF-LEAF   Type of foliage decoration with many-lobed shapes.

STRING COURSE   Projecting horizontal band or moulding set in the surface of a wall.

TENEMENT   A piece of land held by one owner; often such legal entities have survived almost unaltered from Norman times, thus providing a distinct plan element in an otherwise modern arrangement, e.g. long, narrow tenements survive in the centres of many old market towns.

TIE BEAM   Beam connecting the two slopes of a roof at the height of the wall tops to prevent the roof from spreading.

TRANSEPT   The transverse arms of a cross-shaped church, normally between nave and chancel.

TRANSITIONAL   Term used to describe the buildings showing the change between the round-arched Romanesque style and the thinner-walled pointed-arch style of Early English Gothic, *c.* 1180–1200.

TREFOIL   Symmetrical three-lobed shape.

TYMPANUM   Space between the lintel of a door and the arch above it; often decorated.

VAULT   An arched ceiling or roof in stone; can be barrel, groined or ribbed.

VERNACULAR   Native or indigenous architecture using local styles and materials to hand.

VOLUTE   A spiral scroll.

VOUSSOIR   A wedge-shaped stone used in the head of an arch.

Suggested Further Reading

Allen Brown, R., *English Castles*, London, 1976.

Beresford, M., *New Towns of the Middle Ages*, London, 1966.

Clapham, A. W., *English Romanesque Architecture After the Conquest*, Oxford, 1934.

Douglas, D. C., *William the Conqueror: The Norman Impact Upon England*, London, 1964.

Loyn, H. R., *The Norman Conquest*, London, 1982.

Renn, D., *Norman Castles in Britain*, London, 1968.

Rowley, T., *The Norman Heritage 1066–1200*, London, 1983.

Stenton, F. (*ed.*), *The Bayeux Tapestry: A Comprehensive Survey*, London, 1957.

Zarnecki, G., *English Romanesque Sculpture, 1066–1140*, London, 1951.

Index

NB: Numbers in bold type indicate the principal entry on the subject.